INTERNATIONAL PORT OF CALL

"PARTNERS IN PROGRESS" BY J.J. LAMB
PICTORIAL RESEARCH BY JUSTINE HUME

PRODUCED IN ASSOCIATION WITH THE
MARINE EXCHANGE OF THE SAN FRANCISCO BAY REGION

WINDSOR PUBLICATIONS, INC.
WOODLAND HILLS, CALIFORNIA

INTERNATIONAL PORT OF CALL

An Illustrated Maritime History Of

THE GOLDEN GATE

BY ROBERT J. SCHWENDINGER

I DEDICATE THIS BOOK TO MY
WONDERFUL FAMILY:
BETTY, RACHEL, AND LAURA
WHO UNDERSTAND MY
LOVE OF THE SEA
AND SHARE IT IN MANY WAYS

Windsor Publications, Inc.
History Books Division
Publisher: John M. Phillips
Design Director: Alexander D'Anca
Marketing Director: Ellen Kettenbeil
Editorial Director, Corporate Biographies: Karen Story
Assistant Director, Corporate Biographies: Phyllis Gray
Editor, Corporate Biographies: Judith Hunter

Windsor Publications' Staff for
International Port of Call
Editor: Annette Igra
Picture Editor: Julie Jaskol
Layout Artist: Ellen Ifrah
Editorial Assistants: Kathy M. Brown, Patricia (Nye) Buzard, Lonnie Pham, Patricia
  Pittman

Library of Congress Cataloging in Publication Data

Schwendinger, Robert J., 1930-
  International port of call.

  Partners in progress / by J.J. Lamb
  Bibliography: p. 170
  Includes index.
  1. Navigation—California—San Francisco Bay Area—
History. 2. Fisheries—California—San Francisco Bay
Area—History. 3. San Francisco Bay Area (Calif.)—
History. I. Marine Exchange Inc. II. Title.
VK24.C2S39 1984   387.5'097946 84-25733
ISBN 0-89781-122-4

Frontispiece: *The Panama Pacific Exposition was held in the Marina district in San Francisco in 1915 to celebrate the completion of the Panama Canal. The central Tower of Jewels dominates the exposition grounds. Architecturally the general style was an eclectic, fantasy Mediterranean. All that remains of these temporary buildings is the Palace of Fine Arts by Bernard Maybeck. Courtesy, The Bancroft Library (TBL)*

Endpapers: *This map of San Francisco in 1853 features the government buildings, churches, and theatres of the young city. Shaded areas indicate development. (TBL)*

Following page: *This view of the Cliff House, a leisurely beachcomber, and some timid bathers is circa 1870. (TBL)*

Contents

Acknowledgements

The scope of subject matter required for this text represents many years of study, teaching, and writing. Also of significant value was the rare opportunity to direct events for the Maritime Humanities Center, in which outstanding investigators shared their special knowledge of maritime studies. No less can be said of those people who gave aid and encouragement so the Center could flourish, sharing with all the people their heritage of the sea. I wish to acknowledge the following with deepest appreciation: Sally Yerkovich and the National Endowment for the Humanities; Richard H. Dillon; Charles Wollenberg; Charlie Seemann; Karana Hattersley-Drayton; Jack Davis, Brian O'Neill, Lowell Johnson, Bill Thomas, Lynn Thompson, Jim Delgado, Shirwin Smith, Glennie Wall, Steve Hastings, Steve Haller, Harry Dring, Carol Kiser, Ellis Wallace, Harry Johnson,

Dave Nettell, Herbert Beckwith, Irene Stachura, Steve Canright, and the Golden Gate National Recreation Area; Kevin Starr; Roger Abrahams; Peter Darnell; Oscar Toback; Stan Hugill; Ron Walpole; Hi and Julia Schwendinger; John Holmgren; Phil Choy, Thomas Chinn, Him Mark Lai, Judy Yung, and the Chinese Historical Society; Dianna Gumina; Alessandro Bacarri; Jerome Lucido; Sandy Lydon; Dave Nelson, Barbara Gatov, Bill Whalen, and the National Maritime Museum Association; Paul Dempster, Tommy Zee, and the Sailor's Union of the Pacific; Herb Mills, George Benet, and the International Longshoreman and Warehouseman's Union; Kenneth Martin; Marc Kasky, and the Fort Mason Foundation; Members of the Square Rigger's Club; Archie Green; Arthur Haskell; Robert Langner; Ted Hinckley; Russell Frank; Pamela Ow; Jim Holliday, and the California

Historical Society; Michael Herz, and the Oceanic Society; Ed Turner, and the Seafarer's International Union; The Honorable Milton Marks; The Honorable Louise Renne; Mayor Dianne Feinstein; Robert Middleton; advisors to and members of the Maritime Humanities Center, including all the investigators, demonstrators, performers, readers and volunteers who have taken part in Center events these past four years.

A special appreciation goes out to the publisher of this volume, who, by making this history available, reveals a genuine interest in and sensitivity to our heritage at the Golden Gate. A final note of appreciation is appropriate for the sponsors who helped to make this project a reality.

ROBERT J. SCHWENDINGER,
BERKELEY, CALIFORNIA

Preface

Imagine a public forum in the history, folklore, and literature of the sea taking place within view of the Golden Gate on the shore of San Francisco Bay. The forum is one of many that have been given by the Maritime Humanities Center in the past four years covering a wide spectrum of subject matter—Russian America, Italian Fishing, Lighthouses, Rosie the Riveter of WW II Shipyards, Chinese Fishing, Joseph Conrad and Jack London, Dog-Hole Schooners of the Redwood Coast, Native American Fishing, Folklore of the Waterfront, and much more. If the reader had attended any one of the forums, he or she would have noted that the audience represented a cross-section of the Bay Area community—people who have a fascination for our maritime heritage on the West Coast. They are enthusiasts, students, specialists, and a general public that confirm the fact that populations in the Bay Area, directly or indirectly, are profoundly influenced by the sea. There are strong ties to the sea, whether through immigration, sea-related occupations, the military, embarking or disembarking in time of war, conservation or science, travel, education, or recreation. The region itself, with the vast ocean, a world renowned bay, and significant tributary rivers, are daily reminders and prominent symbols of our maritime heritage.

The visitor to the forum would have also found that the speaker or panel participant was sharing new knowledge or new insight, or information that represented years of research or occupational experience. The forums have shown that Russian hunters were not wholly responsible for the decimation of sea otters, that Italian immigrants chose Pittsburg to settle in because the land at the Carquinez Strait resembled the fishing village they left behind in Sicily, that ghosts haunt some of the lighthouses on the coast, that Chinese sailors served Admiral Dewey at Manila Bay with courage and valor, that women made the difference in adequate support in the shipyards of World War II, that many Native Americans in California continue to depend on their ancient industry of fishing for survival, that the last steam schooner of the redwood coast is currently undergoing a critical period of restoration, and a good deal more.

In a large sense this text is an extension of the activities initiated by the Center. Founded in 1980 as a result of a generous award from the National Endowment for the Humanities, the Center set out on a new, unchartered course. The National Maritime Museum complex did not have an educational and public programming unit and the Center was designed to fulfill that role. Part of its mission was to show significant relationships of various populations to our maritime heritage in California, particularly the Bay Region. Through the kind aid of dozens of investigators working in the history, folklore, and literature of the sea, the Center has shared cultural and historical treasures with the greater society. The contributions of men and women of sea and shore, demonstrators of the sailor arts, and performers of sea music from many lands, have been recognized and validated through Center programs of exchange and cultural preservation. Erroneous views or stereotypic images have been challenged through exposure to the eloquence of the men and women themselves.

When this writer was asked to undertake the writing of this history, he thought of all those people who attended Center events—the Public Forums, Festivals of the Sea, conferences—some 68,000 people over the years, and he believed they would welcome such a volume. He also considered existing publications and concluded there were important reasons why the effort would be a worthwhile one. There is no general survey beginning with the Native American. There is a need for a survey written for the general reader to return information about our fascinating maritime heritage back to the populations that made it possible. No volume exists that includes an unbiased assessment of the contributions of all people regardless of race and national origins.

The San Francisco Bay Region is a child of the sea, having been shaped, touched, and influenced by all the significant geological changes and historical movements. Early in time the ocean intruded, causing an enormous inland sea, covering the region as far east as the Sierra foothills. The sea has been essential to all populations of the region: a provider of food, clothing, medicine, minerals, fuel, lubricants, petroleum, luminants, and harnessed energy; an inspiration for poets, novelists, playwrights, and composers; a territorial boundary, a battleground, a graveyard; a unique playground for recreation, and a marvelous laboratory for scientific investigations. The sea, unlike the fixed roads of the land, has afforded ocean highways that radiate to every part of the world, creating bridges for communications and trade, and freeing the human mind to infinite horizons of imaginative power.

This survey is a treatment of some of those elements as they relate especially to the maritime development of the San Francisco Bay Region, and the human equation responsible for that history.

I
Expanding Empires of the Great Pacific

In the beginning all was water.
—Achomawai peoples

*In the very beginning of all things, all
the world was under water.*
—Mono peoples

*All the earth was covered with water, and
everything was dark in the beginning.*
—Maidu peoples

*In the beginning there was no land. There
was nothing but saltwater, the great primeval ocean.*
—Diegueño peoples

THE GOLDEN GATE OF TIME

Earth's evolutionary process blessed California with a magnificently varied topography and a wealth of natural resources. The coastal regions owe their great diversity to changes that span 28 million years, known on the geological time scale as the Miocene, Pliocene, and Pleistocene epochs. They are the last three out of seven epochs assigned to the Tertiary and Quaternary periods. Both periods make up the Cenozoic era. That era of 70 million years includes our present day, indicating that our land is still changing, however gradually. Considering that our earth is well over two and a half billion years old, the era we are a part of appears as a short interlude in the overall life of the planet. Higher forms of plants and animals evolved during the Cenozoic era, and the San Francisco Bay Region can trace its outstanding landscape to the last three epochs.

During the Miocene epoch our ancient coast was the scene of an enormous intrusion by the Pacific Ocean, which flooded approximately one-third of California from Eureka to San Diego. The Miocene sea moved as far inland as the western slopes of the Sierra Nevada range. Several islands occupied this sea, one of which was long and narrow, extending some 100 miles from the present cities of San Raphael to Salinas. The coast range constituted early versions of the Santa Lucia mountains, the northern extremity at what is now Carmel Valley. Active volcanoes were numerous, and the landscape was continually changing, being shaped by the tremendous forces on the earth's crust: uplifting, folding, and cataclysmic eruptions spewing forth ash and rock, while the inland sea shifted in a series of advances and retreats. Milleniums of wind, rain, and erosion also worked changes upon the imposing Sierra Nevada range, and its deposits of sediment and runoff of water in turn effected changes in the land and sea below. The most prominent activity during the Pliocene epoch was that of volcanoes throughout the Bay Region laying down lava, ash,

cinder, and rock fragments over an area of 350 square miles.

Our current epoch, the Pleistocene, was visited by the Great Ice Age in the last million years. The descending glaciers carved out the majestic valley of the Yosemite and were responsible for further inundation of the coastal regions and the creation of additional inland seas. Uplifting and the tilting of land masses formed the coast ranges. Volcanic activity was responsible for such scenic wonders as Clear Lake. Earthquakes and crushing zones ended up generating long, attractive valleys, and the collapse of immense stretches of land resulted in habitable lowlands, such as those throughout the Bay Area itself. Water, as always, remained a constant catalyst for change: oceanic wave action and the laying down of sediment formed beaches, sand spits, dunes, and bars. Riverbeds of the Sacramento, San Joaquin, and Carquinez Strait deepened and widened despite general land upheavals.

The Golden Gate is the result of a combination of those forces: an ancient river canyon at the Gate maintained its unrelenting course, aided by runoff from the Sierras and powerful surges from the glaciers. Depth of the main channel between the peninsulas of Marin and San Francisco is 367 feet. If one could pull a fantastic plug to drain the waters of the famous bay, while at the same time holding back the ocean, we would witness a 60-mile-long, relatively shallow valley rimmed by hills and a deep gorge at the Golden Gate.

NATIVE AMERICANS

The first peoples to inhabit the Western Hemisphere were truly pioneers. The human family that initially took the momentous step from one continent to another possessed a boldness and vision that has rarely been matched in the history of the world. The Aleutian land bridge, once a reality, was the probable route taken by those Asian peoples some 11,000 to 12,000 years ago. They traveled by foot onto the northern coast and plains, some stopping to settle along the way, some

Facing page: *Georg Heinrich von Langsdorff was the physician on a Russian scientific expedition which visited San Francisco Bay in 1806. Here Langsdorff shows San Francisco as the Russians found it. Small as it seems, it was a busy establishment with presidio, mission, cattle ranching, a brisk trade in sea otter skins, and the base for Spanish surveying expeditions to the interior of the territory. The tule rush bundle canoe was a common means of transportation for the Native Americans of the Bay Area. (TBL)*

Right: *This study shows
five representatives of
the Indian tribes living
at the Mission of San
Francisco in 1816.
Ludovik Choris, the
illustrator on a Russian
voyage of discovery,
comments on the Indian
languages and customs.
Although this painting
shows his careful and
sympathetic observation,
the accompanying text
betrays the ethnocentric
attitudes of the European
settlers. (TBL)*

Right: *The dance
headdresses of the
Indians of the San
Francisco Mission were
made of feathers. Sashes
decorated with feathers
and small pieces of shell
were also worn. The male
dancers painted their
bodies with red and
black lines crossed by
strokes of white pigment.
Men and women danced
in separate groups. (TBL)*

waiting in one place or another for a difficult season or seasons to pass, and others exploring out of curiosity about the terrain and resources therein. When the right time came, those not satisfied with their lot moved on, no doubt joined by additional generations of the newborn and other immigrants recently drawn across the transcontinental bridge. In increasing numbers they dispersed across the virgin lands. By the time 1,000 years had passed, descendants of those early peoples had penetrated or settled every corner of the North and South American continents, developing distinct societies and cultures.

Those who established settlements in what was later named California increased in population to about 310,000 by the time the Spanish arrived. This was the largest concentration of Native Americans on the north continent. Researchers have been able to identify 60 major tribes and six main language families throughout California. The six main Indian language families are Athabascan, Yukian, Hokan, Uto-Aztekan, Penutian, and Algonkian (no relation to the Algonquian languages of the Eastern tribes and the people who spoke them). The Penutian language family, which was spoken by Indians in a large area of the West, including much of the San Francisco Bay Region, consisted of Costanoan, Miwok, Yokuts, Maidu, and Wintun language stocks. There were also multilinguists among the Indians, especially where adjacent borders of different tribes encouraged economic and cultural intercourse. At least 100 tribes existed in the territory that we designate California, and they spoke many more languages and dialects than are known in the modern period. Unfortunately more than one-third of their tribal names and the languages they spoke are lost forever.

The aboriginal peoples who made California their home, especially the San Francisco Bay Region, chose a land more kind and generous than any of their distant ancestors had ever known. The coastal area, the large landlocked bay, the marshlands, the numerous creeks, rivers, and delta network, the gentle hills and

valleys, the temperate climate—all provided a rich variety of foods and materials. Ample sealife, plantlife, and wildlife helped to sustain human communities that lasted more than 5,000 years.

An amazing 425 shell mounds have been found in Berkeley, Emeryville, Richmond, Corte Madera, San Francisco, Tiburon, Half Moon Bay, and other cities of the Bay Region. Those rare time capsules, literally ancient garbage heaps, contained remnants of a fishing, hunting, and gathering people who maintained a remarkably stable civilization. Among the fascinating secrets those mounds revealed is that the Indians of the Bay Region lived through dramatic changes in sea level. This unusual discovery suggests the landscape was undergoing significant changes throughout the Indian occupation, and the inhabitants could have been here for many more years than previously believed, possibly back to 9,000 or 10,000 B.C. Various myths of different tribes explaining the origin of the world recount the belief that there was "only water in the beginning," that "all the world was under water." Perhaps this was the California inundated by an ancient, inland sea.

Most California Indians established villages beside bodies of water, especially where lakes, rivers, streams, springs, the open bay, and ocean merged. Sea hunters and fishers or tidelands gatherers lived in the coastal regions. Further inland were riverine fishermen or lakeshore fishermen, hunters, and gatherers. Those who did not depend on a water economy inhabited the interior valleys, foothills, and desert country.

The Chumash of the Santa Barbara Channel Islands and mainland had an extensive maritime economy. Those skilled mariners managed the ocean in plank canoes for thousands of years. As far south as San Diego they fished offshore resources of great variety and abundance. With the use of nets, hooks, harpoons, and basketry traps, they caught salmon, tuna, herring, shark, swordfish, sturgeon, flounder, cod, and halibut. They also hunted seals, sea lions, and sea otters with spears, and took stranded whales. Their sturdy crafts, as long

as 25 feet, were swift and light and transported as many as 20 passengers each. The canoes were constructed from rough-hewn boards of pine or cedar, lashed together with plant fibers or other materials, and caulked with asphalt or natural petroleum tar. A Spanish observer of the 18th century commented on the ingenious design, how the canoes were painted in bright colors, and the use of double-bladed oars for propulsion. He also marveled at how the Chumash handled their canoes with skill and rowed "with indescribable agility and swiftness, holding intercourse and commerce with the natives of the islands."

Oceangoing and river dugout canoes were used by the Yurok, Tolowa, and Wiyot peoples of the north coast, beginning at Humboldt Bay, and of the Luiseño peoples in Southern California. Constructed from the trunks of soft, straight-grained redwood trees, the selected

Above: *Members of the Tcholovoni tribe hunting with bows and arrows on the edge of San Francisco Bay are shown here. The quivers are cases made from the entire skins of sea otters. The region hosted an astonishing array of wildlife, both in the skies and on the ground. The diet of the Native Americans included a great variety of game. (TBL)*

Right: *This lithograph from a painting by Choris shows a tule rush bundle canoe on San Francisco Bay in 1816. These vessels, Choris reports, were made on the spot whenever the Indians wanted to travel by water. The Indians' readiness with this complex technology is remarkable, considering that a modern reconstruction took over a year to complete. (TBL)*

logs were carefully burned out, then dug out and shaped with stone-handled adzes of mussel shell. They extended 20 to 40 feet in length and 5 to 10 feet in beam. These graceful canoes were strong and dependable, having rounded prows and round, gently curved bellies, the gunwales wide and overhanging, the bows and sterns extending about a foot above them. They were eminently suitable for transporting heavy cargo and many passengers on the characteristic rushing and rocky rivers of the north and between island and mainland of the coastal waters.

Throughout California Indians used the tule rush bundle canoe, or balsa. Its basic material was the tule reed that grows in marsh beds along the shores of lakes and bays. The reed, which grows from 10 to as much as 25 feet high, was harvested, left to dry, then carefully laid out on the ground, smoothed down, and joined together to fashion a cigar-shaped bundle, wide in the center and tapering at both ends. Willow poles placed in the center of the bundles provided strength and stability. Three bundles lashed together with plant fibers constituted the tule raft. The joining of two more bundles to each side, thus forming gunwales, transformed what was essentially a raft into a canoe. Propelled by double-bladed paddles, these elegant and luxuriously riding craft, capable of negotiating the narrows of remote shallows, sloughs, and estuaries, were used for fishing and light transportation. They have graced the waters of Clear Lake and the bays of Drake, Bodega, San Francisco, Monterey, Santa Barbara, and others as far south as Baja California and the Gulf.

No authentic plank or balsa canoes have survived over time, yet reproductions have been made in the modern period. An aged descendant of a southern tribe, either Chumash or Gabrielino, constructed a plank canoe for the Panama-California

Below: *A tule rush bundle canoe, built by members of the East Bay Regional Parks staff in 1979 under the supervision of Jan Southworth, is paddled on San Francisco Bay. Tules are sedges that grow in salt or freshwater marshes and on the shores of rivers and lakes from British Columbia to California. Botanist Willis Jepson estimated that at one time there were 250,000 acres of tules in California. The loss of tidal lands and the development of waterfronts has considerably reduced this figure, but in the early 19th century the Indians of San Francisco Bay had an ample supply. Courtesy, East Bay Regional Parks*

Exposition in 1915, drawing from his personal recollection. The tule balsas, literally generated from natural materials, inevitably deteriorated and returned to the earth from which they came. A renaissance in recreating those ancient balsas was begun by a naturalist and her avid supporters in the Bay Area at the East Bay Regional Park of Coyote Hills. The regional parklands were also used by the Costanoans or Ohlones, native inhabitants who lived, fished, and gathered in and around the bay, conveyed in their tule balsas. Under the supervision of Park Ranger Jan Southworth-Kidder, three balsas have been constructed thus far and sailed on the bay. Out of her exciting discoveries of the seaworthiness and graceful movement of the craft came the "sense of primeval luxury, untouched by the sea, yet part of it." She described the sensation as riding in a "floating sofa."

The major rivers north of Monterey that flow into the Pacific Ocean were visited by great numbers of salmon during the seasonal runs. Those rivers were essential lifelines to the tribes that fished them. The salmon, an anadromous fish, hatches in the freshwater stream, finds its way to the ocean where it lives, then migrates to the fresh water to spawn and die. Before the gold mining of the 1850s laid down damaging silt in the crucial rivers and streams, California was teeming with king salmon in May, silver salmon in September, and steelhead salmon in November. The Indians used traps, weirs, and spears to catch as many as possible so that a large supply could be dried and stored for winter use.

The peoples of the north coast included in their diets the many types of shellfish and surfish available, and along with the riverine and lake populations, had access to a large variety of game. Acorns and various plants were also staples in the diet. Water, land, and sky of pre-European California provided adequately for Native Americans. In fact, the California Indians perceived themselves as integral parts of the natural world and, like all living things, partook in the food chain of life. They both respected their world and became highly attuned to it, knowing the habits and nature of all creatures and plants, and utilizing far more in variety for sustenance than Europeans ever knew about or have cared to consider.

There is much that these native peoples have left for us in the modern world, a legacy and history that is being slowly revealed through the labors of capable investigators. An obvious legacy are the common names that have remained. How many Californians and travelers have taken for granted a multitude of names across the landscape, or have forgotten their origins, names that have been a part of the California fabric, it seems, since the beginning of time: Acalanes, Ahwahnee, Carquinez, Chowchilla, Coloma, Colusa, Cotati, Cucamonga, Gualala, Hetch Hetchy, Hoopa, Inyo, Klamath, Malibu, Mattole, Modoc, Mokelumne, Mono, Napa, Natoma, Olema, Petaluma, Pismo, Shasta, Sonoma, Soquel, Suisun, Tahoe, Tamalpais, Tehachapi, Tehama, Tejunga, Tomales, Tuolumne, Ukiah, Yolo, Yosemite, Yreka, Yuba, Yuma, and a great deal more.

The Native Americans of pre-European California were true ecological men and women who practiced conservation and had a reverence for living things that approached a sacred bond. They lived, canoed, and fished the waters and hunted upon the earth for thousands of years, and then the Europeans came.

THE SPANISH SAIL IN CALIFORNIA

From the Portuguese voyages down the coast of Africa to the first crossing of the Atlantic, vessels limited in size and maneuverability had for two centuries braved unpredictable seas, powerful winds, and treacherous shoals. Vessel development was slow, and changes were gradual from one century to another. A major problem early sailing vessels had was beating to the wind, and they invariably found it necessary either to detour many miles from the direct route or to return to the place of origin. The development of the caravel from the 15th century on marked a turning point for the age of exploration and allowed the determined Portuguese to sail on distant coasting voyages. The strong hull constructions and lateen-rigged masts of the caravel solved the crucial problem. Lateens are large, triangular sails that enable vessels to sail closer to the wind. They thus improved the ability of the Portuguese to follow the coast of Africa around to the Indian Ocean and finally to reach the Moluccas, or Spice Islands, of the Indies. For those voyages that required running before the wind across great oceans, the combination of square sails and lateens evolved. Such arrangements were used on the *caravela redonda,* with square sails on the foremast and lateens on the mainmast (midship) and mizzenmast (aft). The *Santa Maria* of Columbus' famous voyage had square sails on the foremast and mainmast, lateen on the mizzenmast; the *Pinta* was a *caravela redonda;* and the *Nina* was a *caravel* with lateen sails on all three masts. These arrangements were the forerunners of the barquentines, brigantines, and schooners that later were part of the important commerce of the West Coast. Lateen sails were already in the Pacific during Columbus' day, and Italian *feluccas* sported the handsome sails centuries later on San Francisco Bay.

The galleon, when compared to later vessels in size, weight, and capacity, was surprisingly small. Columbus' *Santa Maria* was 85 feet overall, 100 tons, and carried a total of 40 men and boys. *Pinta* was 60 tons, and *Nina* was 50 tons, carrying 27 and 21 men respectively. Cramped and uncomfortable conditions prevailed. By comparison, the full-rigged sailing ship of the 19th century averaged 192 feet overall, was 1,190 tons, and held a ship's population of 300 to 600. By the turn of the 20th century, the transpacific steamship *Oceanic,* for example, was 3,707 tons, 420 feet overall, and carried a ship's population of 1,270.

The desire for larger vessels to gain more cargo, comfort, safety, and passengers, plus improved maneuverability, occupied ship designers for centuries. It is no wonder that people nowadays marvel at the exploits of those European explorers. They sailed in slow, overcrowded vessels, on long, arduous journeys through unknown waters, and were plagued by scurvy, hunger, disease, and shipwreck. Yet they established ocean tracks around the world under the most adverse conditions.

All the explorers who sailed the Pacific Coast—Cabrillo, Drake, Cermeño, Vizcaíno—missed the impressive gate just below Drakes's Bay. So did all the Manila galleons. Those slow, treasure-laden vessels had carried away the wealth of the Asian trade for two centuries as they made the passage from Manila to Mexico, by way of Cape Mendocino. The arduous voyages were restricted to two each year. A traveler on one of the galleons wrote of the passage in 1697:

The longest and most dreadful of any in the world; as well as because of the vast ocean to be crossed—the wind always ahead—the terrible tempests that happen—the desperate diseases that seize people—and in seven or eight months lying at sea, sometimes cold, sometimes temperate, sometimes hot—all enough to destroy a man of iron.

Conditions on the imperial galleons are partially explained by the contractual arrangement for the men who labored before the mast. The contract has its origins in the Customs of the Sea, or Consulado del Mare, the basis of maritime law in the Mediterranean and the New World. In the main articles between owners and sailors, both parties agreed to a particular voyage; the route traveled and the length of voyage was at the discretion of the owner; and once the terms were agreed upon, the sailor could go nowhere without the consent of the managing owner (whose powers were vested in the master of the vessel). Upon signing the ship's register or entering into the contract by a handshake, the sailor was bound to do all the work necessary about the ship. In those days this meant, as the sailor's *Black Book,* or *El libro negro,* informs:

The mariner is bound to all things which

Drake believed he was welcomed by the coastal Miwoks and central valley Yokuts as a god. Anthropological evidence suggests he and his men were actually greeted as dead ancestors returning from the sea. The Indians believed their dead went to an island across the ocean, and that their return was possible. The gaudily dressed Europeans, whose aversion to baths and to shedding their clothes probably contributed to a pallor close to death, appeared to the Indians to have risen from the dead. (TBL)

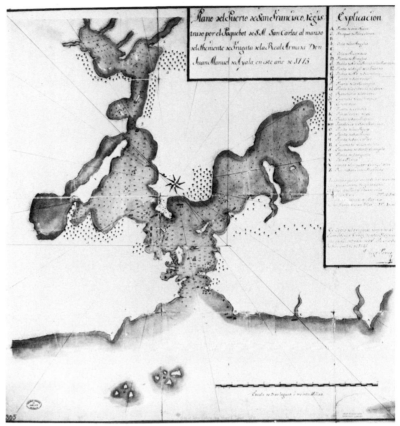

using a double-bladed paddle, with which they get along so nimbly that, as I found out, they went faster than the longboat."

The following year, some two months after the 13 colonies declared their independence in Philadelphia, the presidio was formally dedicated, and Mission de los Dolores was founded shortly thereafter. Fort San Joaquin was built on the *cantil blanco,* or white bluff, which was excavated the following century to accommodate Fort Point. It was constructed in a horseshoe shape about 120 feet long by 100 feet wide with a parapet 10 feet thick and pierced with six embrasures made of adobe brick. Six cannons faced the entrance to San Francisco Bay, four of iron and two of bronze, all cast in Manila. The small community of mission and post included sixteen soldiers, most of whom had large families, two priests, seven colonists, servants, muleteers, herdsmen for cattle, provisions, and equipment. This small Spanish outpost served as a nucleus for a port city on the "harbor of harbors."

Jose Cañizares was the surveyor on board Ayala's vessel San Carlos. His map of 1775 of San Francisco Bay shows soundings and recognizable features. Angel Island and what is now Yerba Buena are seen inside the Golden Gate. On the ocean shore to the left is Point Reyes; on the extreme right is Point Año Nuevo. (TBL)

II

A New Nation Claims the Pacific

The Port of San Francisco is a marvel of nature and may well be called the harbor of harbors and I think that if it could be well settled like Europe, there would not be anything more beautiful in all the world—for it has the best advantages for founding in it a most beautiful city with all the conveniences desired by land as well as by sea—with that harbor so remarkable and so spacious in which may be established shipyards, docks and anything that may be wished.
—From the diary of Pedro Font, O.F.M., 1776

In the later decades of the 18th century, Spanish California settled down to the development of its missions, establishing an agrarian society sustained by the labor of Native Americans. New Spain could not have known that the stirrings of a fledgling republic on the eastern slopes of the same continent would eventually change the course of Alta California. With the signing of the Declaration of Independence, the new nation was eager to trade with the world. British Acts of Trade had fostered a system of privilege and monopoly that had strangled maritime activity in the colonies. They had been virtually forbidden to enter such lucrative markets as the West Indies, China, and India.

Freed from a century of restraint, American shipping from Maine to Pennsylvania burst forth with astonishing energy. The Stars and Stripes was carried aloft by mariners of high ambition, who successfully entered the China Trade, the sea otter trade and hide traffic along the West Coast, and the whale fishery throughout the great expanse of the Pacific Ocean. The Yankees of the new republic converged on the West Coast, along with Russians who went island hopping across the Aleutian chain. Those Americans would gradually surpass all other explorers, eventually making way for a prevailing belief that expansion from shore to shore was their logical destiny.

Sloops and brigs with the optimistic names of *Empress of China, Experiment,* and *Hope* cleared for China in the 1780s and 1790s loaded down with beches-de-mer (sea slugs used as a delicacy in soup), ginseng (New England root believed to restore virility in males but eventually debunked), silver, furs, and all manner of knicknacks produced in the early factories. Proud, roundly envied officers and crews set out from Boston, Salem, New York, Philadelphia, and other ports to trade for the desired teas, nankeen cotton, porcelain, and silks. Although the trade never grew to substantial proportions, those who completed round-trip voyages were assured ample profits. It was not unusual for

officers to retire from the trade after 15 to 20 years as the wealthy men of their communities. The mariners of the early China Trade were adventurers who fired the imagination of merchants and consumers, for the remote land of Cathay suggested incalculable wealth.

THE SEA OTTER TRADE

The main difficulty in trading with China was that it was self-sufficient, in no particular need of Western products. Although China did welcome specie, the new republic was in short supply of silver. As colonials in the British Empire, the Americans had been kept in a continual state of bankruptcy. Ginseng, also limited in quantity, could not be depended on as an item of lasting exchange. There was an unusual need to identify a product attractive to China, and a solution to the dilemma was found in the sea otter trade of the West Coast from Cape San Lucas to British Columbia.

One year after the *Empress of China* became the first American merchantman to enter the China Trade, the Boston ship *Columbia,* skippered by Robert Gray, rounded Cape Horn, headed up the West Coast of the Americas, and traded at the fur center on Vancouver Island. With his full cargo of pelts, Gray won the distinction of being the first American to exchange furs for the tea of China. He was also the first to return from an around-the-world voyage by way of the Cape of Good Hope. The Cape Horn-West Coast-China route was a particularly advantageous one for mariners, since it kept the holds of vessels full with useful cargo and spurred activity in the sea otter trade of the Pacific Northwest and California.

Discovery of the great potential was an accident, attributed to the experience of sailors who served James Cook on his voyage of exploration to the Pacific Northwest. The sale of sea otter pelts at Canton for a high return became common knowledge with the published account of Cook's voyage in 1784. Prior to Cook, otter skins from the waters of the Aleutian

Facing page: *William Meyer, the acting gunner of the sloop of war* Cyane, *painted this portrait of his vessel as the title page of his journal. The journal covers the year 1840 and is profusely illustrated with lighthearted watercolor sketches. The* Cyane was, at that time, *in the Pacific Squadron and a few years after the journal was completed took part in the war with Mexico. Its role was to carry General Frémont and his troops from San Francisco to San Diego. (TBL)*

This young fur merchant is carrying pelts brought to China by foreign traders around the end of the 18th century. An arctic fox skin is over one shoulder. The Russian American Company with their trading posts in Alaska would have had access to these furs as well as to seal and otter furs. The gouache drawing is by an unknown Chinese artist. Courtesy, Peabody Museum

Islands and Alaska were taken to China by Russian traders, or *promishlennik.* The Manila galleons also carried the pelts to China, although they were those of sea otters taken off the coast of California. This early trade was conducted on a small scale.

By the end of the 18th century, Spain acknowledged the real value of the sea otter in deciding the trade was crucial to its silver mines in Mexico. China had vast quantities of quicksilver (mercury), and Spain needed the element to separate the precious metal from the ore. Sea otter pelts could be traded for an unlimited supply. The main difficulty was a formidable

competition from foreign probes, and attempts to maintain a monopoly on the trade were often demanding, at times overwhelming. Ready to launch their own serious engagement with the sea otter were the Americans and the Russians, inevitable interlopers and eminently suitable antagonists. The Russians had gradually moved across the Aleutian Island chain, trading with the inhabitants and cornering the market on the sea otter of the north. They established a permanent base on Kodiak Island in 1783 just below the Alaskan Peninsula, intending to carry their activities south.

Prior to European contact, sea otters

lived in abundance along an extended five-mile arc from Lower California up and around the Aleutian chain to Northern Japan past the Kuril Islands. There was an interruption in that line where otters were less numerous, approximately the coasts of Oregon and Washington. Explorers noted that the bays and coves of California were populated with hundreds of thousands of the long, sinuous sea mammals. The most valuable pelts were a brownish black, known in the trade as "black." A fully

Americans were well aware that as a result of the Spanish policy of trade restriction, any bartered furs were contraband. The trade required all the characteristics of illegal traffic—cunning and subterfuge above all. British rule, however, had familiarized colonial mariners with restrictions, and they had participated in illegal trade for decades, becoming well-versed in the necessary tactics. American captains devised several pretenses for anchoring in a California port,

The sea otter is usually about four and a half feet long, but its skin can stretch to upwards of six feet. Its fur is dark brown or black on the surface and lighter underneath. With web flippers for hind feet and cat-like forepaws, it is well adapted to its life in the coastal kelp beds of western North America. It was hunted to the brink of extinction in the 19th century. Recent laws in the United States and Mexico have given the sea otter almost complete protection from hunters. (TBL)

grown male measures about 4½ feet long, averaging 85 pounds in weight. The skin is quite loose, and has an unusual stretch upwards of 90 inches long and 36 inches wide, the common being about six feet by 30 inches.

The royalty of China considered the furs to be of great warmth and beauty. Mandarins valued them fashioned into long luxurious robes, while the women coveted them for capes and belts, which they often adorned with pearls. The otter tail was turned into mittens and various trimmings. By 1790 sea otter skins commanded as much as $120 each in the Canton market.

attempting to get close to padres, Indians, and troops willing to trade. Supply vessels from San Blas were infrequent and did not always meet the needs of the Californians. Shoes, blankets, and clothes were especially attractive to the clergy, primarily to pass on to their "neophytes," while trinkets, beads, copper, and abalone shells were traded with the coastal Indians.

A host of New England vessels with such names as *Otter, Eliza, Betsy, Alexander, Lelia Bird,* and *Hazard* entered the ports of Bodega Bay, San Francisco, Monterey, Carmel, Santa Barbara, the Channel Islands, San Diego, and Baja California. The stories they told Spanish

Above: *This circa 1870 photo is of the Spanish battery emplacement of 1797. The site was called Point Medanos. Earlier it had been Point San Jose. The Americans changed its name to Black Point. Black Point and the land behind it became a government reservation in the early 1850s. In 1853 a few well-to-do San Franciscans built houses on the hillside overlooking the guns. Mount Tamalpais is in the upper background, with the Tiburon Peninsula in front. (TBL)*

Facing page, top: *The Aleuts employed by the Russian American Company in the 19th century frequently used the baidarka or kayak to hunt sea otters on the California coast. (TBL)*

Facing page, bottom: *In 1812 the Russian American Company established Fort Ross on the coast north of San Francisco. The company's most important outpost in California, the site was supposed to supply food for the fur traders' settlements in Alaska. (TBL)*

officials concentrated on the theme of need, although they varied considerably, many with imaginative flourishes. Yankee justification for requesting aid had its origins in international law, which bound nations to extend refuge and aid to mariners in distress. There were assuredly many more New England vessels engaging in the illegal trade than were cited in Spanish records and known in the modern period. Records only list those that were exposed accidentally, and those bold enough to enter the ports.

New England seafarers developed a contempt for the New World Spanish as partial justification for their illegal acts. Four seacoast batteries and four presidios defended the Spanish settlements of Alta California against intruders. But the poorly manned garrisons gave the communities little protection. Each of the presidios was occupied by a lieutenant, an ensign, a sergeant, and two corporals, in a company of some 70 to 80 men. This small contingent of no more than 340 troops was supposed to protect a coastline more than 450 miles long. Occasionally armed Spanish vessels patrolled the coast, but they were inadequate in size and appeared too infrequently.

Spain's problems multiplied as a result of its alliance with France during the Napoleanic wars. Its trade in sea otter pelts to China was eventually brought to a virtual end. England's Far Eastern

Squadron blockaded the Canton market from approximately 1805 to 1812.

When Americans combined forces with the Russian American Fur Company in 1803, activity along the coast increased with amazing energy. Native Americans, because of their ancient hunting methods, never caught as many sea otters as the foreign intruders would have liked them to catch. By the turn of the 18th century, the padres' support of the hunt decreased, tending to slow down the overall catch. This created a dilemma, which an enterprising American captain by the name of Joseph O'Cain solved. He proposed a joint venture with the Russians. Under his scheme the traders of the north utilized Aleuts to do the actual hunting. With a spear and kayak, or *baidarka,* these natives of the remote northwestern islands had the ability to slaughter many more sea otters than with the old Californian methods. Captain O'Cain and the Russian Governor Alexander Baranov ostensibly declared the most serious trade war on New Spain.

Throughout this trade war, the kayaks and their owners were stowed on board both Russian and American vessels and taken to the coast of California. The sight of those skin-covered canoes moving swiftly through bays and estuaries for almost ten years was surely a remarkable sight, especially to the Spanish and Native Americans. One dramatic incident took place in San Francisco Bay in 1811. Ivan

Kuskov, master of the ship *Albatross,* had 60 kayaks on board, while O'Cain's *Isabella* had 48. O'Cain's hunters were discovered by the Spanish, and after a bribe was offered to the post's commandant, and refused, the Aleuts were ordered by O'Cain to continue the hunt, nevertheless. They paddled beyond the range of rifle fire from the presidio and scattered in the bay, spearing and retrieving numerous sea otters. A resident of the presidio at the time, Antonio Maria Osio, described the developing conflict in "Historia de California":

When it was known that the canoes were always constructed of sea-lion skins and that they had to be taken from the water to be dried and smeared with oil, a soldier was put on guard. At the end of a few days he came with the communication that at twilight, in one of the most sheltered coves below the hill of San Bruno, the hunters had landed with some canoes. Upon the continuation of the communication, Alferez Don Jose Sanchez later left with 20 men who, after having approximated where the Kodiaks [Aleuts] were, landed and, without being heard and in spite of the watchfulness of the Indians, went hunting for them above the wall of the cove. When they were within gunshot, and although the night was dark, all fired at the most visible objects. This resulted in killing two Kodiaks, and it was not known how many fled wounded, because immediately they embarked and left the shore.

Americans were also killed on San Francisco Bay that day. Baranov wrote about those fatalities in a letter to his friend and merchant-trapper, John Jacob Astor. Still, he praised the success of the expedition that year, having come away from the California coast with 8,118 otter skins.

The same Russian captain, Ivan Kuskov, extended Imperial interests to California in 1812. The development Spain had feared occurred. The Russians established a self-contained community just 18 miles north of Bodega Bay on a bluff overlooking the Pacific Ocean. There they built an unusual rectangular fort and stockade, which became known as Fort Ross, a derivative of "Russia." Warehouses were constructed at Bodega Bay where a good anchorage accommodated a small fleet for repairs and wintering. The Russians intended the fort to supply the Alaskan communities with sea otter skins, cattle hides, and food; but Russian California found little to sustain itself. The settlement experienced large financial losses, as farming along the rugged coastline proved difficult, and the sea otter, almost decimated, ceased to be a viable trade. Finally, a growing population of American settlers infringed on areas all around the settlement. The Russian post disbanded and left California in 1842, never to return.

Throughout the Spanish period, those who engaged in the illegal trade found the going rough. Although presidios lacked the men to enforce the laws, stubborn troops substantially kept the *contrabandistas* in check. Numerous lawless Yankees found themselves incarcerated in Spanish jails and pleading before Spanish courts up to 1820, when Mexican independence brought an end to the hated trade barrier. The sea otter stock, however, had diminished rapidly in the Northwest, placing enormous pressures on the remaining otters off California. Changes in the traditional trades also took place with the establishment of merchants in Hawaii who became middlemen exchanging Chinese goods for sea otter skins. The hide-and-tallow trade also emerged with an increase in whaling and sealing. These new endeavors and different trade routes created a renewed and even greater convergence on California. The Cape Horn route became a well-traveled ocean highway, a major route up to the 1840s, and paved the way for the Gold Rush period.

By the time author Richard Henry Dana appeared on the California coast the sea otter trade had become a minor enterprise. For more than 55 years weapons from club to spear to rifle had been used in the relentless hunt. The American overland trapper introduced buckshot, a devastating technology that killed young and old otters often indiscriminately. In addition to the Aleuts and their kayaks, Americans used what were probably whaleboats, some 28 feet long, broad and klinker-built, sharp at bow and stern, and rigged with two lug sails. They employed Kanakas, expert Hawaiian swimmers, to retrieve the otter in the ocean and, if not dead, to finish it off in the water. Native Americans would eventually take over this task. By the 1830s riflemen were commonly seen along the coast and in the bays standing in canoes or in the bows of boats, firing musket balls at a clump of otters 75 to 100 yards off, then swiftly advancing and picking off the scattered and desperate mammals one by one. The furs eventually fell out of favor

Songs of Labor at Sea

Richard Henry Dana in his *Two Years Before the Mast* wrote about those songs that were used on board sailing vessels to help establish the pace of men at labor and often to make tedious work bearable: "A song is necessary to sailors as the drum and fife to a soldier. They must pull together as soldiers must step in time; but they can't pull in time or pull with a will without it. Many a time when a thing goes heavy, one fellow yo-ho-ing a lively song like 'Heave to the Girls,' 'Nancy, O,' 'Jack Crosstree,' 'Cheerily Men,' has put life and strength into every arm."

Herman Melville added a few years later: "I soon got used to this singing for the sailors never touched a rope without it. . . .It is a great thing for a sailor to know how to sing well, for he gets a great name by it from the officers and a good deal of popularity among his shipmates. Some sea-captains, before shipping a man, always ask him if he could sing out at a rope."

Sometime after Dana's experience in the early 1830s, those songs of labor were being referred to as "sea shanties." The period most noted for the song occurred approximately from 1820 to 1860 during the most active trading and immigration period of the world under sail. Although most of the songs were written then, the latter half of the 19th century and early 20th century were renaissance years for singing of the songs.

Sea shanties were divided into four major categories: the short drag or short haul; the long drag or halyard; the capstan or windlass; and the forecastle song. Others have been called walkaways, hand-over-hand, and pumping shanties. As the work songs of the sea, each type was used for a particular shipboard activity, whether of short or long duration.

This merchant seaman band of the ship Sirra, *out of San Francisco, is typical of "fufu" bands. These ingenious ensembles consisted of whatever was available on the ship, and what seamen brought along. This band consists of button accordians, cymbals (pot covers), mandolin, spoons, penny whistle (homemade), and drums (barrel and kegs). Courtesy, National Maritime Museum, San Francisco (NMMSF)*

Short-haul shanties were sung when a few short pulls on a line were needed. The men on deck literally shaped the massive sails aloft, performing such operations as hauling on the bowline (drawing in corners of sails), hauling out the bowline (letting out corners of sails), boarding tacks and sheets (holding down corners of sails), or sweating up the halyards at the end of a long pull (taking in a very tight line inch by inch). It usually had one solo and one chorus, and no pulling was done until the last word was sung, when all hands gave a mighty pull and "brought her home." Well-known short-haul shanties were "Johnny Boker," "Round the Corner," "Boney," and "Haul Away, Joe."

The halyard shanty was generally used for the longer and heavier tasks aboard ship, such as hoisting sails or raising a yard aloft. It was work requiring a long pull, a strong pull, and a pull all together. The song has two choruses, generally short and of the same length as the solo. Some of these shanties were "Shallow Brown," "Tom's Gone to Hilo," and "Reuben Ranzo."

Capstan shanties were sung during such continuous activities as weighing anchor (heaving up the anchor to get under way), warping (moving a vessel into a desired place or position by hauling on a line or chain that had been fastened to a buoy, anchor, or pier), or loading or unloading cargo. These songs are more harmonious than others and generally have a long chorus and special rhythmical swing to them. They were most likely to be heard on shore by landsmen as the ship offshore weighed anchor, making ready to warp into the dock. At the turn of the century, it was not unusual for men, while heaving on the capstan bars, to take as much as three or four hours to raise the anchor. Favorites among these songs were "Rio Grande," "Sacramento," "Amsterdam Maid," and "Shenandoah."

Each vessel usually had its own head shantyman, who had a spirited voice and the ability to spur on the men in their work. A good shantyman was often paid more than an average sailor. Since shanties, like folk songs, reflected the personalities of the men who sang them, they were rarely sung exactly alike, with the exception, perhaps, of the lead-off verse and chorus.

The forecastle song, pronounced *fo'c'sle,* was the seaman's ballad, and it told of his exploits on land or sea, in peace or war. The tropics, with their long periods of calm, made heaving and hauling occasional activities, affording seamen time for rest, reflection, and the exchange of such forecastle songs as "The Flying Cloud," "The Dreadnought," and "Off to Sea

Once More."

Most of the time the songs were sung a capella, although sometimes a sailor would have a penny whistle, a button accordian, a banjo, spoons, pig bladder drums, or a fiddle to play along. Sometimes the men of a merchant ship would have all those things, including pot covers and whatever else could be used in the "fufu band," the name for such a glorious orchestra.

Today the songs of the sea are preserved by scholars of our maritime heritage as well as by events such as the "Festival of the Sea," presented by the Maritime Humanities Center and the Golden Gate National Recreation Area at the National Maritime Museum.

Stan Hugil, a shantyman and leading scholar of sea music, has performed at the Festival of the Sea at the National Maritime Museum since its beginning. Courtesy, Kristi Humphrey, Maritime Humanities Center

In Two Years Before the Mast, Richard Henry Dana describes hide houses and hide curing. A Yankee trading vessel would leave a few of its crew on such a beach as this to cure hides. It was a process of scraping, salting, soaking in the ocean, pickling in brine, drying, degreasing, and finally beating. The whole procedure took seven or eight days, after which the hides would be stored in the houses until the vessel returned to pick them up. The houses were fitted out at one end as living quarters for the men. (TBL)

in China's royal circles. By that time, the otter had been almost eliminated.

The Mexican government, aware of the disastrous fate of the otter, imposed conservation methods for the first time by prohibiting the killing of pups. Although a wise direction, the act was a long time coming and enforcement was insufficient.

The hide and tallow traffic and the whale fishery took the place of the sea otter trade. Dana's classic, *Two Years Before the Mast,* presents an accurate portrayal of the Boston "hide-droghers"

that traded from Cape Mendocino to the tip of Baja California. They peddled factory knickknacks as well as imported novelties. Hides, when turned into shoes, would eventually return to the Californians as high-priced products. Until 1822 the hide traffic was also contraband, therefore a lively activity was conducted in concealment. The number of vessels increased with open trade. During Dana's voyage of 1834 to 1836, all cargoes entered at the Monterey customhouse where duties ranged from 80 to 100 percent. The duty

The Hide Trade of Old
California, *a 1917
pen-and-ink drawing by
Charles Marion Russell,
depicts the transfer of
hides to a waiting vessel.
Courtesy, Amon Carter
Museum, Ft. Worth,
Texas*

was rarely maintained at the maximum;
even so, evaders continued to avoid paying
any tariffs. The slender ships from roughly
15,000 miles away collected as many as
40,000 pelts of hide per ship, as did Dana's
famous *Alert*. Demands for the attractive
Mexican products—hides, tallow, soap,
horns, and dried beef—rose steadily.
Sealskins also became an important
commodity along the coast.

The low price in California hides was a
strong inducement to send vessels on
voyages of two or more years around the
Horn. Sailors from those vessels waded
waist-high in the California surf—skins
piled high on their heads and shoulders
—from beach to boats. The port that did
the greatest business, wrote Dana, was in
San Francisco Bay, where "large boats, or
launches, manned by Indians, and capable
of carrying from 500 to 600 hides apiece,"
and attached to Mission Dolores, secured
the hides at San Jose, Santa Clara, and
other places on large creeks and rivers that
ran into the bay. At San Diego each of the
main trading firms maintained salt vats
where the hides were cured, then stored
until shiploads were accumulated.

Richard Henry Dana represented a
particular New England perception in his
view of the Californio. Of Boston Brahmin
stock, and with an ethnocentric complex,
he left a world of readers with the image
of unindustrious Mexicans. His claim that
California would be transformed in the
hands of "an enterprising" people, revealed
little of the true character of Mexicans, but
rather it explained the Yankee syndrome
of impatient traders, believing their society
was superior.

EARLY WHALE FISHERY

The American colonies entered the
whaling trade in the 18th century. Whales
were initially caught in the bays and coves
along the coast as whalemen used lookouts
atop bluffs, and when the familiar cry was
given, Cape Cod men set out in boats after
their prey a short distance offshore. As the
pursuit intensified, the boats were replaced
with outfitted sloops and schooners to
increase and hasten the catch. "At length,"
observed an early historian who was
quoted in *Etchings of a Whaling Cruise*,
by J. Ross Browne, "the whales began to be
scarce near shore, and soon larger vessels

Right: *On sailing whalers the lookout posted on the top-gallant crosstrees would scan the ocean for whales. His cry, "There she blows," or "There she breaches," would ring out when he sighted the whale in the distance. From his vantage point as much as 100 feet and more above the water he reported on the position of the quarry. San Francisco came into its own as a whaling center after the Gold Rush. (TBL)*

Facing page, bottom: *This 19th century whaling painting captures some of the intense activity of killing a whale. Three whale boats have attacked a sperm whale; one has been capsized, its crew left to fend for themselves. The harpooners in the other boats attack the whale from the bows of their vessels. With lowered masts and sails furled, the oarsmen maintain a steady position in the turbulent waters next to the struggling leviathan. Courtesy, Massachusetts Institute of Technology*

were needed to send men southward and eastward of the Grand Bank."

Years of slaughter left great stretches of water depleted of the mighty leviathan of the deep. The voyages after whales became longer; the vessels were built larger to accommodate enough men, supplies, and cargo to sustain the long hunt; and the time needed to complete voyages that eventually took men halfway around the world increased upwards of four years. The vessels were essentially factory ships in which the entire process of cutting-in and trying-out took place, the end product stored in barrels on board. Men in open boats chased the right and sperm whales, the former eventually hunted to extinction in the Atlantic, and the latter, noted for its fine oil and massive size—as large as 80 feet long—would become an endangered species in the 20th century.

By 1837 the Sandwich Islands, or Hawaiian Islands, had become the great entrepôt of the Pacific Ocean. Strategically situated equidistant from the southern and northern whaling grounds, and on the famed west-east route to China and Japan, the islands were a familiar refuge to whalers all over the world. Thoroughly exploited and Europeanized, Maui, then the capital, fulfilled the manifold needs of thousands of vessels each year. San Francisco was also in a favorable geographic position, as well as embodying the greatest potential as a major port on the Pacific Rim. The harbor of San Francisco slowly emerged as an important way station. Since 1825 the bay had become increasingly well known to American and English whalers. Sausalito Cove had firm holding ground, and the area offered good water and wood. When right whales were discovered in the Northwest in 1841, San Francisco's importance increased. It was a time when American whaling ruled supreme.

The distinction, however, was not achieved without great sacrifice. Risks of investments in the whale industry gradually proved disastrous ten percent of the time. Ships had been known to return from an eight-month voyage "clean," having failed to sight one whale the whole time out. It was not uncommon for conditions to go from extreme boredom for months at a time to frenetic activity for a few short days. The whaler's job was a difficult one, and the occupation was plagued with dangers. Boldness, strength, and endurance walked the decks of whaleships; hunter and hunted were formidable adversaries. If one would have inquired aboard each of 30 vessels afloat in the 1840s, it would have been found that at least one man in every crew met his death by a whale. Whalers experienced the "Nantucket sleigh ride" where men and boat were attached to a furious and desperate whale who suddenly sounded and changed direction, and the harpooner's line could catch a man in a fatal stranglehold. The soldier who had been to war would have recoiled at the apparition of the sperm whale's tail,

fanning into eddies the air over his head as it descended to stove in the whaleboat, sending men and flotsam adrift or to their deaths numerous fathoms below. The terrifying flukes of a whale could throw a man bodily into the air, and, making a long arc in his descent, fall 50 yards away, annihilated as he sank into the ocean, while not a chip of whaleboat or lock of hair of the remaining men were harmed. Men cut into a whale precariously with their razor-sharp spades as ravenous sharks a few feet away took chunks of blubber out of the dead carcass; if a man slipped off the oily scaffolding, he could be sliced

Left: The classic sailing whaler of the first half of the 19th century was broadly and sturdily built, with full bows to allow for storage on long voyages. It had to be strong enough to withstand the buffeting of moving ice. A wedge-shaped bottom was an advantage. Ice pressing in on such a hull caused the vessel to be lifted up rather than stove in. (NMMSF)

Foul weather created great hazards for the men who went aloft to furl and unfurl sail. Should a man fall into a tempestuous sea, there would be little chance of saving him. Courtesy, Robert J. Schwendinger

seriously or fall overboard, easy prey for the sharks.

Entire ships were known to encounter storms or disease that took the life out of every man on board; the ships became floating tombs, ghost ships on seemingly endless journeys. Ice floes at both poles held special terror, for a moving floe could crush the hull of a vessel as a hand obliterates a paper cup. Men who climbed aloft during blinding snowstorms or freezing rain sometimes found that the yard, on which they clung to for dear life, was completely encased in ice, and they have swayed fifty feet or more above deck while trying to reef sail as a howling wind pounded in their ears and the raging sea drove the vessel into what must have seemed the ultimate maelstrom. Men fell from aloft into the sea or onto the deck below. Others fell into the arctic seas and were sometime found months afterwards, described by Herman Melville as "perpendicularly frozen in the hearts of fields of ice, as a fly is glued in amber." Rupture of the stomach was not an uncommon affliction for men who furled and unfurled sail. Finally, crews sometimes stood on deck and watched helplessly as a 70-foot-long, 80-ton sperm used the solid buttress of his colossal forehead to "smote the ship's starboard bow, till men and timbers reeled" and all were aware that the

voyage was up. There were no other people in the world "more fond of tinkering with their last wills and testaments," says Melville.

The forecastle, or foc'sle, where a man lived on board, was a small, damp hole, never with enough room or air. Melville, in *Omoo*, described his foc'sle on a South Sea whaler thusly:

Myriads of cockroaches, and regiments of rats, disputed the place with us...You may seal up every hatchway, and fumigate the hull till the smoke forces itself out of the seams, and enough {rats and roaches} will survive to repeople the ship in an incredibly short period...the vermin seem to take actual possession.

Whaling vessels were the oldest ships anywhere, some as much as a hundred years old: "She was a ship of the old school...long seasoned and weather-stained, her venerable bows looked bearded...her ancient decks were worn and wrinkled."

After boiling down the blubber and storing the oil in barrels on board the factory ship, the odor from the process remained with the vessel for as much as two weeks. No corner, whether behind closed doors or in the remotest parts of the ship, escaped the overwhelming stench. An ex-whaler, J. Ross Browne, wrote about the six days of trying-out in *Etchings of a Whaling Cruise*:

Working incessantly in oil, which penetrated to the skin, and kept us in a most uncomfortable condition, besides being continually saturated with salt water, produced a very disagreeable effect...by chafing the skin, and causing painful tumors to break out over the whole body. Before I had finished my share of labor, I heartily wished myself in the meanest dog kennel on shore.

Another whaleman-turned-writer, Herman Melville, added an additional view in *Moby Dick*:

The whale supplies his own fuel and burns

his own body. Would that he consumed his own smoke! for his smoke is horrible to inhale, and inhale it you must, and not only that, but you must live in it for a time. It has an unspeakable, wild Hindoo odor about it, such as may lurk in the vicinity of funeral pyres. It smells like the left wing of the day of judgment; it is an argument for the pit.

The character of whaling captains was also in serious question, and their reputations were notorious throughout the industry. Samuel Eliot Morison, foremost maritime historian, informs us in *The Maritime History of Massachusetts* that "they were heartless, cold-blooded fiends of the quarterdeck. Men were hazed until they deserted, became cringing beasts or

mutinied. The ingenuity of whaling skippers in devising devilish punishments surpasses belief." At the end of a 24- or 48-month voyage, the common sailor may have wound up with as much as $300 in wages, but he more likely found himself in debt to captain and owners as a result of the "slop chest." The slop chest was to the ship what the "company store" became to the mining town.

There is no doubt that the whaleman labored against tremendous odds in his quest to control nature, yet, in spite of them, he did succeed. Melville, an advocate for the whalemen, informed the public that "for all the tapers, lamps, and candles that burn around the globe, burn, as before so many shrines" to the industry's glory. Charles M. Scammon, in his history of marine mammals noted:

The sloop of war Cyane, *bristling with guns, is putting on more sail, and appears in hot pursuit of some vessel we cannot see. It is interesting to observe in this picture how many men are engaged in the job of unfurling the Cyane's sails. In the mid 19th century handling a square rigger required great labor. Courtesy, Peabody Museum*

The American force engaged was 678 ships and barks, 35 brigs, and 22 schooners, aggregating 233,189 tons, valued at $21,075,000. At the same time, all the investments connected with the business are said to have been at $70,000,000 and 70,000 persons derived their chief support from the whaling interests.

Congressman Grinnel of New Bedford identified the industry with national purpose when he said:

The whalemen are hardy, honest, and patriotic, and will, as they did in the last war, stand by their country in danger...will man our ships and fight our battles...will be the right arm of our defense.

Unfortunately by the time such men supported and defended the industry in the eyes of the nation, the whale fishery was heading for deep trouble. The high risks and low wages of the industry discouraged new blood from entering the profession. Pleas by such men as Browne were lost in changing events: "There are thousands of enterprising young men in this country who would be glad to find employment in the whale fishery if they could do so without becoming slaves."

By mid-century shipping in general was heading for a steady decline. Americans of ambition and ability gradually turned from the sea to the land with its growing opportunities in mining, manufacturing, construction, banking, and insurance firms. Captains of industry began to overshadow those of the quarterdeck, and the romance of the sea was losing its hold on the national imagination. The American seafarer was standing at the close of a former frontier, a dreamer and dream of unlimited horizons.

CONQUEST OF CALIFORNIA
While the United States moved inexorably

Far left: *Endowed with ruthlessness and energy, John Charles Frémont was the embodiment of the doctrine of manifest destiny. He explored the West for the U.S., and anticipated the war with Mexico by his leadership in the Bear Flag Revolt. He campaigned successfully in the subsequent war, came into conflict with General Kearny over the governorship of California, made a fortune and lost it, and ran for president. He also twice crossed the Sierra Nevada Mountains in the winter. The portrait is probably from the early 1850s when Frémont would have been in his mid to late thirties. (TBL)*

Left: *As a young man Charles Wilkes was chosen to command the United States' exploring expedition of 1838 through 1842 to the Antarctic, Pacific, and the northwest coast of North America. That this voyage took place was due to Wilkes' own perseverance in the face of official apathy. His arrogance and insubordination delayed his rise in the Navy, but these traits were countered by his great ability and tenacity. Distantly related to Herman Melville, he may have served as the model for Captain Ahab. Melville was also influenced by Wilkes' description of the Pacific. Courtesy, Cirker, Dictionary of American Portraits, Dover, 1967*

west, purchasing land, as in the Louisiana Purchase, or taking land, as in the war over Texas, California was a mixture of old world practices and new world influences. Sparsely populated, and with ample land, cattle ranching became its major industry. Its population, several generations removed from those early soldiers, relatives, and colonizers, were gradually joined by traders, seamen, trappers, and merchants from South America, the United States, and Europe. Those men who chose to make California their home, most becoming citizens and marrying Native California women, were genuinely welcomed and lived prosperous lives.

Events in the conquest of California were swift, and interest in wresting the territory from Mexico can be traced back to the presidency of Thomas Jefferson and intensified during the terms of James Monroe and Andrew Jackson. It was Jackson who attempted to buy San Francisco Bay from Mexico in 1835.

After the United States declared war on Mexico, and after the Bear Flag revolt in Sonoma in June 1846, when 24 American settlers rebelled against Mexico and proclaimed an independent republic, clashes broke out between Mexican and United States forces.

During the ensuing conquest, the coast was frequented by naval vessels, especially in the bays of San Francisco and Monterey. Those involved in the takeover were the U.S. frigates *Savannah* and *Congress*, the sloops-of-war *Portsmouth* and *Cyane*, the storeships *Warren* and *Erie*, the schooner *Julia*, and a whaler that aided in courier activity, the *Stonington*. In time six large warships occupied the coastal waters. There was no action at sea; Mexico's negligible navy was elsewhere. The greatest asset the American fleet afforded during hostilities was the capability of transporting large numbers of sailor musketeers, marines, carbineers, and volunteers to strategic encounters with the California force.

On January 13, 1847, the Treaty of Cahuenga was signed just north of the old mission and on the edge of the city of Los Angeles, population 1,500. The agreement was approved by John C. Frémont, a central military figure in the conflict, and was the basis for eventually granting Californians rights accorded citizens of the United States. The matter of land, however, was to become a bitter issue. Many rightful owners eventually lost their

This is a profile from a navigational chart by Cadwalader Ringgold. It shows the Golden Gate from the ocean. It is guarded on the north by the jutting rocks of Point Bonita and on the south by the old Spanish fort, the Presidio. From outside the bay, Yerba Buena seems to be unsettled hills. Hovering above Point Bonita on the horizon is Mount Diablo. The Marin peninsula, East Bay hills, and the San Francisco peninsula appeared as one solid landmass to early explorers, and in the summer fog the bay's entrance was impossible to see. (NMMSF)

lands, and along with them, their livelihoods, status, and political power.

John C. Frémont, an officer in the Topographical Corps of the United States Army, was part visionary as well as catalyst for the California conquest. He had led an expedition along the Oregon Trail in 1842, aided by the legendary pathfinder, Kit Carson. His surveys out West spanned several years and added to the efforts of Commander Charles Wilkes, whose exploring expedition visited the South Sea Islands, Antarctica, the Northwest Coast, Astoria, the Willamette and Sacramento rivers, and San Francisco Bay from 1831 to 1841. Frémont was to name the entrance to the bay in his memoir of 1846, subsequently published in 1848. He sighted the promise of the region with its outstanding harbor, supremely suited for world trade, including the attractive Asiatic potential. He compared the bay to the ancient harbor of Byzantium, called Chrysoceras, or "Golden Horn." In a romantic flourish, he named the famous entrance Chrysopylae—"Golden Gate."

With the conquest there burst forth an optimism that the "harbor of harbors"—connected by unique tributaries, complemented by rich valleys and majestic mountain ranges, all on the Pacific Rim of the world—was a fitting place for a Western metropolis and leading financial center. During 1847, merchants and politicians were interested in devising ways to attract settlers. Substantial populations would ensure both the needs and skills of

modern civilization. One of the first acts toward achieving these goals was renaming the settlement of Yerba Buena. Two of the area's foremost businessmen, Thomas Larkin and Charles Semple, purchased land from Governor Mariano Vallejo on the north shore of the Carquinez Strait. They established a town they called Francisca, in honor of Vallejo's wife. They believed the name, a variant of San Francisco Bay, which was becoming increasingly known around the world, and the excellent anchoring grounds on that side of the strait, would elevate the town of Francisca to the most prominent position in the region. Residents of Yerba Buena took up the challenge, and Alcalde Washington Bartlett issued a decree that changed its name to San Francisco. It was an apparently logical and fortunate choice. Larkin and Semple, outmaneuvered, renamed Francisca, "Benicia," a second baptismal name of Vallejo's wife.

In the same year more than 460 people were residents of San Francisco. General Stephen Kearney of the military government granted the town all the beach and water lots between Clarke's Point (at Broadway) and Rincon Point (near Harrison Street). The old Spanish anchorage just inside the bay's entrance had fallen into disuse when hurricane-force winds caused great damage to vessels anchored there. The customary grounds then shifted about five miles southeast to a safer and more convenient harbor, around North Point, past Telegraph Hill, and south to Clarke's Point, the northern tip of a natural cove. The cove approximated the shape of a crescent moon, going west as far as the current city's Montgomery Street and sweeping down and past where California and Sansome meet, Bush and Market meet, along First and curving out at Beale, Front, and Rincon Point. This shoreline constituted the boundary of Yerba Buena Cove.

Clarke's Point, a small, rocky promontory, was found to be an easy and natural wharfage during the Mexican period. When the missions of Dolores, San Jose, Santa Clara, San Raphael, Solano, and the surrounding ranches were active in trading hides, tallow, and provisions, foreign vessels anchored south of the promontory and sent their boats to pull alongside the rocks. In 1822 William Richardson, an Englishman who was a mate on a whaler, chose the Bay Area as his home. He was baptized a Catholic and married the daughter of the presidio commandante, taking his wife's given name, Maria Antonia, for his middle name. Governor Mariano Vallejo, who was the first to suggest that a settlement be established at Yerba Buena, appointed Richardson captain of the port from 1835 to 1844. The skilled mariner operated two schooners that belonged to the missions and he used them to transport cargoes from the missions and the ranches to Clarke's Point. These were the first California freight boats to operate on the

bay since those of the Native Americans. It was also at Yerba Buena Cove that the trade generated by tributary rivers either got its start or gained momentum. This new metropolis of San Francisco had the potential of becoming the foremost port of the region.

Heightened by the military takeover and inevitable admittance to the United States, there appeared to be an uncanny sense of expectation that the area's destiny would soon be realized. It was found everywhere in San Francisco in mid-1847—in the brisk sales of land and water lots, and in an official report by the town's census-taker: "San Francisco is destined to become the great commercial emporium of the North Pacific Coast." As though a general wave of clairvoyance had taken hold, the discovery of gold made all things possible. Gold was the powerful magnet needed to excite the world and fulfill the dreams of merchants, land speculators, the military, and the politically inclined of the Bay Region. Like the Spanish before them, adventurers from around the world descended en masse on the Western Hemisphere's second El Dorado.

From the 1850s onward, San Francisco takes over as one of the most important ports of call on the continent. In its own unique way, the port would have evoked a haunting, inevitable demise for deep-water seafaring, if not for the great renaissance in shipping brought about by the incredible Gold Rush.

The commercial community of Yerba Buena was established by a franchise granted to the English sailor, William Richardson, by his father-in-law the Spanish commandante. Richardson's tent is visible on the hillside. Nearby is the first house built a year later by Jacob Leese, an Ohioan. The area is what is now Grant Avenue between Clay and Washington streets. Leese's schooner, left foreground, served in the first water delivery system. On the right, American, British, and South American vessels wait to purchase hides and tallow. (TBL)

III

Gold Rush Port

Thus the city San Francisco was truly a fit entrepôt for the gold region. Yet, with the distinctive features of different nationalities, it had in the aggregate a stamp of its own, and this California type is still recognizable.
—H.H. Bancroft, History of California

From the gold found January 1848 at Coloma on the American River, to national confirmation about the find by President Polk at the end of the year, an awakening world gradually responded. With an explosion of genuine belief, fantastic demands were placed on early transportation systems ill-prepared to meet the challenge. An international fever dictated passage to the placers at any price. Where California conjured up distorted images of decadent landowners, untamed wilderness, and savage Indians, the prospect of instant wealth was added. The Far West became in the imaginations of most a place where one travels to, as though equipped for war, labors in, then leaves a wealthy man—although getting there and leaving were actually no small matters.

Distant and remote from all major population centers, those who were closest to John Sutter's Nueva Helvetia, or New Switzerland, arrived at first in small numbers. The ever-increasing circle would include gold-seekers from Northern and Southern California, the Oregon Territories, Mexico, the Sandwich or Hawaiian Islands, Canada, Peru, Chile, Australia, China, the United States, and from across the Atlantic Ocean. The overall process of improving existing routes and developing the required technology for transportation was a long one. The most effective project, in addition to improved ship design and the much later transcontinental railroad, was the 21-mile railroad at the Panama Isthmus. The project was conceived as early as 1835, although it received its crucial impetus with the discovery of gold and was the subject of a memorial to Congress in December 1848. Inauguration of the line did not take place until 1855.

In the early years of the Gold Rush the fastest and most common way for passengers to get to California was by sea. San Francisco's deep-water harbor and significant placement near the entrance of the Golden Gate helped to make it the central city of the region. Sausalito's natural springs had provided San Francisco and arriving vessels with fresh water for

more than 50 years, yet its harbor was too shallow for the larger oceangoing vessels. Benicia, although endowed with an excellent harbor, is 45 miles distant from the bay's entrance, and is situated at the eastern end of the Carquinez Strait for the last ten of those miles. Few steamships operated in deep water at the time, and the vast majority of ocean transports were vessels under sail. Large, deepwater vessels carrying yards of canvas required a great deal of room in which to maneuver, a particular problem at the strait. Also, the additional passage into San Pablo Bay, with its changing currents and highly active, converging winds, especially through the narrow strait, offered pilotage problems. The Peralta Rancho, now the site of Oakland, was acres of *encinas*, or live oaks, with an underbrush of wild blackberry bushes and herds of cattle roaming the *contra costa*. Without a viable harbor and no plans for a settlement until 1850, Oakland emerged as a village in 1852. And since there was neither railroad nor adequate overland roads to allow for portage of large, heavy equipment, all such cargo arrived by sea. By virtue of historical precedent and development, San Francisco was the only city able to meet the unique challenge of the age. Just five miles inside the wide expanse of San Francisco Bay, the anchoring grounds off Yerba Buena Cove were substantial and accommodated all vessels regardless of size.

By the end of 1848 it was estimated that more than 6,000 people were at work in the mines, and the customhouse statistics showed that the gold exported amounted to $2 million, valued at $12 an ounce, later climbing to $16. Early 1849 opened to a flood of men and vessels, and by August, wrote port historian Edward Morphy in *The Port of San Francisco*:

The Gold Rush was in full swing. A new era had opened for California, portending, among other things, that San Francisco was destined to become one of the great entrepôts of the world's commerce—the Queen of the Pacific. As immigrants came crowding in from all over the world,

Facing page: *This 1850 street scene is a caricature of San Francisco during the Gold Rush. The two store ships are wedged between buildings in a way that is not quite accurate. It is the kind of travel picture that is intended to amuse the sophisticated, interesting more as a record of the general opinion about San Francisco than as a documentation of the placement of buildings. (TBL)*

The village of Hock on the Feather River circa 1850 shows how close to their traditional way of life the Indians of California remained at this time. The great influx of newcomers seeking gold in their territory would eventually crowd out the Indians and their way of life would be destroyed. (TBL)

wharves were hastily constructed to accommodate the shipping. An immense fleet of vessels from all parts of the globe, numbering eight to nine hundred, were anchored in the bay, presenting a striking picture—like an immense forest stripped of its foliage.

Historian J.S. Hittell, in *A History of the City of San Francisco*, quotes an argonaut who left New York for California in 1849: "Never since the crusades was such a movement known; not a family but had one or more representatives gone or preparing to go." He explained how every man "was a walking arsenal," equipped for every emergency, certain he would return "loaded with gold."

In the exhilaration of promise there appeared in cities and towns, from nation to nation, warnings of caution and danger. The more stable of society's members viewed the news with alarm, fearing that capable and intelligent young men, on whom the future of the regions depended, would emigrate and leave vacuums impossible to fill. These sober-minded critics suggested pitfalls to no avail, as did a Chilean editor as early as 1848, who implored the young men to consider the consequences:

A true fever of emigration is afflicting part of our population. . . . We do not doubt for the moment all that is said about California, but in a rapidly increasing population the splendor of a great fortune obscures the poverty of others. When America was discovered, the search for gold caused thousands of people to leave homes and families in search of a fortune. The same thing will be repeated in California. History tells much about gold discoveries, but it omits the bitterness of failure, especially the bitterness of self-inflicted failure.

SACRAMENTO: GOLD COUNTRY CROSSROADS

The goal of all who converged on San Francisco in search for gold was to reach the Sierra foothills, and the earliest, most accessible routes were the Sacramento and the San Joaquin rivers. The mining country was to grow at an incredible rate as men with supplies and equipment of all sizes and shapes fanned out across the land from river to stream to foothill and into higher elevations and mountain passes. Within ten years armies of gold-seekers traversed an area as far as Red Bluff, 200 miles northeast of San Francisco by way of Sacramento City, or 320 miles by way of a coastwise voyage via Humboldt Bay; then west from Red Bluff some 90 miles into the mountains as much as 4,000 feet above sea level at towns like Sierra City; and finally along the rugged sierran terrain 140 miles southwest to Mariposa. Where there was once virgin wilderness populated by Native Americans living along streams and rivers, in remote valleys, and on gently sloping

hillsides, outsiders appeared as though overnight to change the face of the land forever.

"We set sail about eight o'clock on Sunday," wrote argonaut Dr. J.D. Stillman of his early experiences when setting out for Sacramento City from Yerba Buena Cove. "Passing through the crowd of shipping anchored off the shore, we stood out for the Island of Los Angeles, just discernible through the haze; then we took the flood-tide, and swept on into San Pablo Bay...When we hauled up on the wind, the rollers were so heavy that our deeply loaded boat shipped an uncomfortable amount of water. It was about 3 p.m. when we entered Suisun Bay. This we were told was dangerous to small boats."

From 1848 to mid-1849 boats were the most common vessels to set out for Sacramento City, usually launches and whaleboats operated by enterprising

entrepreneurs or attached to the ever-arriving vessels anchoring in the cove. Many of the ships' boats were rigged into schooners and carried freight and passengers up the rivers leading to the mines. As more gold-seekers landed in San Francisco, operators of the crowded launches charged from $5 to $25 fare per passenger, and $3 or more per hundred pounds of freight or $60 a ton. It was not unusual for owners of the vessels to sell launches, which had originally sold for $100 each, for $500. Boats once costing $2,000 now sold for $10,000. Barges that hauled every kind of freight conceivable commanded a minimum of $4,000, and ships began at $30,000. Wages for crews, when they could be found, steadily rose to $300 and more a month. River business and traffic during those first two years were chaotic activities that afforded operators unprecedented earnings. Fleets of launches and every kind of boat burst

Nelson's gold-washer was a further development in extracting gold. By moving the screens as the water was flowing through them, more ore could be extracted in a shorter time. All this digging and disturbing of river beds was disastrous for the streams and channels. San Francisco Bay, for example, was choked by silt in many places as the result of mining operations. (TBL)

41

upon the pristine delta country, increasing river traffic a thousand-fold. Long processions, unlike any other in history, set out from Yerba Buena Cove—whaleboats, launches, scows, schooners, tule rush bundle canoes, Chinese junks, and any other floating craft that could carry cargoes, and passengers.

The boats left San Francisco on the last of the ebb tide to take advantage of the flood tide at Angel Island. The tide of the bay ran approximately four miles an hour and ebbed and flowed almost a foot as high up as the Sacramento, a hundred miles above Suisun Bay. "We passed the Islands of Yerba Buena and Alcatraz," wrote Bayard Taylor, a reporter for the *New York Tribune,* who left Clarke's Point in the schooner *James L. Day,* "looked out through the Golden Gate on the Pacific, and dashed into the strait connecting the Bay of San Francisco with Pablo Bay, before a ten knot breeze...In the middle of it stands an island of red volcanic rock

{Red Rock}, near which are two smaller ones, white with guano, called The Brothers. At the entrance of Pablo Bay are two others, The Sisters, similar in size and form." The *Day* sailed easily into Carquinez Strait where Benicia came into view, with the even smaller settlement of Martinez situated in a glen on the opposite shore. It was at Benicia that large vessels could lie close enough to the shore to land goods and passengers without lightering. General Persifor Smith and Commodore Thomas A.P. Catesby Jones established their headquarters there, and in 1851 it became an army ordnance depot, accommodating an arsenal and post.

Suisun Bay was a particular problem for small boats, for there erratic gales blow, making navigation so difficult that at times boats had to wait for favorable weather to continue their way. Many small craft were caught aground on the muddy shores, and the occupants either waited for dubious aid or continued their journey on foot.

Taylor wrote about the short-lived settlement name of New-York-of-the-Pacific, renamed Pittsburg, at which he arrived 50 miles and four hours after leaving San Francisco: "New-York-of-the Pacific with its inspiring but most awkward name, is located on a level plain, on the southern shore of Suisun Bay, backed by a range of barren mountains. It consists of three houses, one of which is a three-story one, and several vessels at anchor near the shore. The anchorage is good, and were it not for the mosquitoes, the crews might live pleasantly enough, in their seclusion. There never will be a large town there, for the simple reason that there is no possible cause why there *should* be one. Stockton and Sacramento City supply the mines, San Francisco takes the commerce, Benicia the agricultural produce, with a fair share of inland trade, and this Gotham-of-the-West, I fear, must continue to belie its title."

Taylor was wrong, of course, for the settlement, which was actually the Los Medanos Rancho, (which was to be called by other names—New York Landing, Black Diamond)—became Pittsburg, a vital community of Italian fisherfolk, and later a major manufacturing center producing steel.

The early days in open boats were frustrating to many who had no experience with the delta, and who, bold and obsessed by the desire to reach the goldfields at all costs, found the sloughs and other tributaries of the Sacramento a puzzling network that could consume the lost voyager for many hours and days. Small boat operators found themselves 10 to 30 miles up the wrong channel, having to backtrack and search out the right slough or river entrance to Sacramento City or Stockton.

The trip to Sacramento had taken as long as five weeks in those early months, a journey that was rigorous and a challenge for many boats. Punctured by numerous sloughs and lined with profusions of thickets, great oaks, sycamore trees, and

A moralist's view of the outcome of the Gold Rush of 1849 shows hordes of argonauts burdened with riches trying to escape California. In fact, few of the gold-seekers struck it rich. (TBL)

43

Typical of iron vessels on the Pacific Coast in the early 1850s, the riverboat Erastus Corning was built in New York and shipped knocked-down around Cape Horn. It was launched in San Francisco, near Steamboat Point, in October 1850. The Corning first saw service running between San Francisco and Stockton, carrying men and supplies to the goldfields. (NMMSF)

crawling grapevines, the picturesque river was abundant with water fowl, giant salmon, and sturgeon. In some places it was a wide stream, in others, narrow, and to the novice, always twisting and turning, inviting innumerable guesses as to which bend in the river was the last. Dr. Stillman recalled in 1849:

We continued ... up the Sacramento — monotonous but always beautiful. Its banks everywhere were bordered with stately trees and festooned with grapevines so dense as to hide from view the back country. The water was so clear that we could see the fish; where it was deep it was a rich green....We arrived in good order the next morning at this canvas city. Dust, men, mules, oxen; bales, boxes, barrels innumerable, piled everywhere in the open air.

Prevalent in Sacramento at the time was a dense undergrowth of blackberry bushes and grapevines. The slough that crossed the area had large white oak trees bearing thick crops of slim, long acorns. Large sycamore trees lined the steep bank and were perfect mooring places for vessels to tie up to; the bank was easily bridged by boarding planks for the discharge of passengers and cargo. The river landing, or Sutter's Fort, became the nucleus for the town and included in mid-1849 up to 20 stores, a hotel and restaurant, a blacksmith shop, and saloons. The scene was described by diarists as chaotic, with merchandise scattered along the banks and covered with old sails. Approximately 200 tents and houses dotted the fledgling town, its population about 2,000 by the summer of 1849.

When news of the need for steamers reached the East Coast, builders responded almost immediately with hastily designed constructions, sending them either on board sailing vessels to be reassembled in the Bay Area or around the Horn under their own steam. The first eight steamboats sent out were small scows or launches from 30 to 50 tons burden. The flat-bottomed sternwheel scow, *Lady Washington,* was

SACRAMENTO. WINTER OF 1849.

Left: *The little town of Sacramento was laid out in 1848. This picture shows it during the winter of 1849, not long before it was struck by a disastrous flood. The riverfront is an orderly place. The river is high and two deep-water sailing vessels have sailed up from the San Francisco Bay, as has the steamer Senator on its regular run. There is neither dock nor levee, no protection from the deluge soon to follow. The damage caused by the flooding river was negligible in comparison to the change wrought by the Gold Rush just about to sweep the city. (TBL)*

Left: *One of the first steamers to reach Sacramento is given an enthusiastic welcome as it draws near the embankment. The illustration shows no wharf or mooring for in 1849 there were neither on the Sacramento waterfront. It gives some idea of the heavily wooded river bank soon to fall to the axe to provide fuel for an increasing number of steamers. (TBL)*

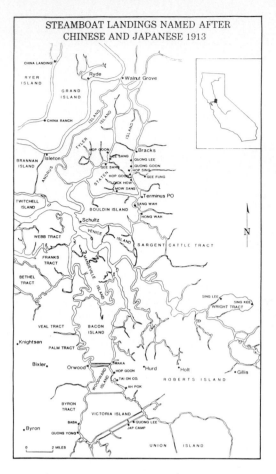

STEAMBOAT LANDINGS NAMED AFTER
CHINESE AND JAPANESE 1913

An active Asian community was involved in farming and in the business of docking and boating in the Sacramento-San Joaquin Delta area in 1913, as revealed by these steamboat landings named after Chinese and Japanese entrepreneurs. Courtesy, Sucheng Chan, UC Press

one of these. Shortly after it arrived and began operating, it snagged and sank on a return trip from Coloma, was raised, refitted, and renamed *Ohio,* and instituted initial regular runs to the town of Vernon on the Feather River. Others were the *Edward Everett Junior* (transported on board the sailing vessel *Edward Everett,)* *Pioneer* (which snagged and sank on the Feather River), and the *Sacramento.* Most of the early steamers experienced varying degrees of disaster on the unpredictable banks and shallow waters of the delta network. It was soon evident that light-draught steamers were essential if freight and passengers were to be ferried from Sacramento City to Marysville or the upper Sacramento. Waters there receded to as little as three to two feet deep in the dry season.

The larger, more comfortable, and faster steamers that left the East Coast under their own power were those destined to make Sacramento City the "metropolis of the mines." Their initial cost approached $100,000; the cost of sailing them around Cape Horn added $30,000 more to their values. Those journeys took from six months to one year to complete. Every precaution was taken to ensure a safe trip by hugging the coastline and stopping

numerous times along the way for shelter and refueling. The lower decks were strengthened with thick planking, and wedge-shaped screens were installed on the forward part of the deck to minimize the impact of pounding waves. The first and most prominent of these steamboats was the *McKim,* of 200 horsepower and bought by the San Francisco firm of Simmons, Hutchinson and Company.

Thereafter arrived the steamboats worthy of comparison to the Hudson River "floating palaces." The first of these was the *Senator,* 750 tons, at a cost of $150,000, which steamed out of Boston by way of Cape Horn. Captain John Van Pelt, with Lieutenant Blair as pilot, made the *Senator's* first run to Sacramento in nine hours, all during daylight. In the first year competition was nonexistent, and it earned a profit of more than $60,000, usually carrying 300 passengers in both directions. Fare was $25 from San Francisco to Sacramento, $30 on the return, and freight took in $40 to $50 a ton. Until serious competitors ascended the river, weekly earnings for the two-trip sailing schedule was a minimum of $16,000. Other steamboats to follow were the *Hartford, El Dorado, Gold Hunter,* and the *New World,* the latter 530 tons and 320 feet in length.

A new era began on the river when the first daily steamboat travel was established by the People's Line. The *Senator* and the *New World* sailed on alternate days, with one leaving Cunningham's Wharf in San Francisco on Mondays, Wednesdays, and Fridays, while the other shoved off on Tuesdays, Thursdays, and Saturdays. Each left Sacramento the day after arriving. The trips took approximately eight hours each way, inducing an editorial writer on the *San Francisco Picayune* (October 1850) to proclaim: "It is not extravagant to say that more substantial, commodious, rapid and well conducted steamers are not to be found on the waters of any other part of the globe."

From the 1850s on steamboat transportation was a crucial factor in the growth of San Francisco, Sacramento, Stockton, and other cities and towns that

Cape Horn is the most southerly island of the Wollaston Group at the tip of South America. Fighting prevailing trade winds from the west, it could take as many as 28 days to round the Horn and reach the Pacific Ocean. Many vessels were destroyed in the attempt, as this picture suggests. The master of this ship, now abandoned by its desperate crew and passengers, had reduced the canvas to prevent damage. Upon leaving the ship, he would have tried to take off the hatch covers so that the ship would sink and not remain in the passage as a hazard. (TBL)

owe their beginnings, partially or entirely, to the quest for gold.

THE PANAMA ISTHMUS: RISE OF COASTWISE STEAMSHIP TRAVEL

William Henry Aspinwall was the grandson of a sea captain and the son of a successful merchant. He and his cousin, Edgar Howland, were partners in the largest trading, exporting, and importing firms of New York. Howland and Aspinwall were foremost shippers, spurring the construction and operation of early clipper ships and doing business in Europe, Asia, and South America. It was Aspinwall who dreamed of fast interoceanic transportation by developing service across the Panama Isthmus, eventually giving rise to the realization of the Panama Railroad. He also hoped to initiate steamship travel on the routes of the Pacific Coast. Yet these extensive undertakings were beyond the capabilities of an individual firm of that time. Investments on such a scale entailed great risks. The oceans defied permanence and could not be depended on for stability, nor could they be parceled out like plots of land. Government subsidies for carrying the mails offered the most logical solution, especially in the role of establishing communication and transportation with the territories and encouraging immigration.

It was apparent the United States had to encourage the deepwater merchant marine generally, and the growth of the Far West particularly. It had to follow England's example and aid the shipping industry. Subsidies were necessary for the most ambitious challenge on the high seas ever confronted by the young nation. In 1845 Congress awarded a subsidy to establish transatlantic mail service, and in November 1847 it approved additional subsidies for mail lines to operate on both coasts. The Pacific Coast award was assigned to Aspinwall's firm. Thus the corporation of The Pacific Mail Steamship Company was born and charged with running a line of steamships from Panama to Oregon.

Aspinwall's vision was obviously a long-range one, imagining a significant civilization gradually materializing in the Far West and spawning numerous communities on the Pacific Slope. In reality, though, the award was granted for service to sparsely populated territories that generated little mail, requiring the vessels to travel a distance of more than 4,300 miles in coastal waters, sometimes calm, other times treacherous, and always laying down graveyards of ships. The great irony was that gold was discovered two months after the Pacific mail award, and it was not

until the end of 1848 that a skeptical East was convinced of the fabulous finds. This was a development Aspinwall or Congress could never have predicted, and one that turned a potentially high risk into an astonishingly lucrative situation. The newly formed United States Mail Steamship Company was awarded the contract for the Atlantic route.

Although Pacific Mail's vessels were steamships, they had from two to three masts and carried sails. Sail plans were varied, the most common being: 1) similar to the Hermaphrodite Brig with two masts, square-rigged at the foremast, with fore-and-aft sails at the mainmast; 2) similar to the Bark with three masts, square-rigged at the foremast and mainmast, with fore-and-aft sails at the mizzenmast. This was the era of the great transition from sail to total steam, which was to last until the

end of the century for the United States. Steam technology was undergoing its most crucial period and severest tests on the high seas. Establishing supply stations that could repair and refuel the steamships along the coasts took considerable time and planning. The vessels were also wooden sidewheelers capable of 10 knots an hour, or 11.5 miles an hour. This was the first stage of development leading to the forerunners of the modern ocean liners that appeared at the turn of the 20th century: steel hulls that were propeller driven with their twin, multiple-expansion and turbine engines capable of more than 22 knots an hour, or approximately 26 miles an hour on the high seas, such as the fateful *Titanic*.

The first vessels of the United States Mail fleet were the *Ohio, Georgia,* and *Falcon,* ranging in tonnage from 3,000 to

Mare Island, across the Napa River from Vallejo, was acquired by the United States Navy in 1854. This picture shows the site one year after its establishment. On the left the frigate Independence is in the floating dry dock. A ferry crosses the river to the island in the center. On the right a river steamer passes a topsail schooner and an elegant felucca approaches the bucolic Vallejo shore. San Pablo Bay lies beyond the island. The name of the island refers to General Vallejo's favorite horse. (TBL)

3,300, each about 240 feet long and 46 feet in beam, with a depth of 33 feet. Those of Pacific Mail were the *California, Panama,* and *Oregon,* the first two built at the famous yard of William Webb and the third at the yard of Smith and Dimon, all of New York. Each of the steamships was from 1,000 to 2,000 tons, 200 feet long, 33 feet, 10 inches of beam, with a depth of 20 feet, driven by single side-lever engines getting steam from two boilers.

Not anticipating immediate increases in the population of the Far West, accommodations on the steamships were conservative: for example, *California* was designed to carry about 55 cabin passengers with 150 to 200 people in the steerage. As soon as the service began operating, the need for more accommodations and larger fleets became apparent.

The *California* was the first Pacific Mail steamship to leave New York, on October 6, 1848, carrying seven passengers and little mail. The mail was for the Brazilian and Pacific squadrons. With 500 tons of coal on board and enough provisions for one year, it headed for the Strait of Magellan with a planned stop at Rio de Janeiro. Problems developed. A crack appeared in the cross-head of the engine; Captain Cleveland Forbes missed Rio, sailing beyond it, and had to double back; the captain's lungs hemorrhaged, necessitating ten days of hospitalization in the city; and adverse gales dogged the vessel all during the 40-hour passage through the strait. When it reached Valparaiso on December 20, 1848, Chileans among others petitioned the captain to take them to San Francisco. News of the Gold Rush had circulated several months before the *California's* arrival, and a steady stream of sailing vessels, after leaving the gold country, had entered the harbor bearing startling amounts of gold. An American bark, the *Tasso*, had stopped on December 5, carrying 3,968 ounces of gold worth $68,000. South Americans, especially Chileans and Peruvians, had a long heritage of mining, and news of a new El Dorado further north encouraged many to try to recapture the wealth of the distant past.

Captain Forbes refused to take on more passengers. His orders had been to pick up no one until Panama, where through passengers, after arriving on United States Mail steamships and having crossed the Isthmus, would be waiting. Little did the captain know that a flood of impatient humanity left by several vessels, many more passengers than he had accommodations for, was waiting to get on board.

From the time the *California* left the East to its arrival in Valparaiso, merchants of that town had been shipping out, along with miners and consignees, everything they believed could be sold in San Francisco—boots, clothing, dried beef, gunpowder, picks and shovels, cutlery, Chilean brandy, soda water, flour, and other commodities.

The *California* remained in Valparaiso 40 hours, taking most of the time to load a new supply of coal on board. A Captain John Marshall was ordered by the company agent to join the vessel, in case Captain Forbes took ill again. Heading into Callao, the next port of call, Captain Forbes was besieged by 80 Peruvians who had paid passage money to the company agents there. Tales of the gold discovery had spread throughout Peru, proclaiming that laborers had become capitalists in no time at all, earning at the placers up to $150 in a single day, and that if one was very lucky, he could realize upwards of $800 a day. All that was needed was a sheath knife to dislodge the gold from the rocks.

Captain Forbes believed he should honor the transactions and take on the Peruvians. He insisted on one condition, though: should ticket holders at Panama

require additional space, the South Americans would have to retire to the unsheltered deck for the remainder of the journey. Their fares, $300 for cabin, $150 for steerage, plus freight charges and agents' commissions, cost the new passengers well over $18,000.

Into the equatorial waters along the stretch to Panama the heat suddenly became pervasive and unshakable. Here were great whales to behold in large numbers, blowing and diving at short distances in their ocean playground. Here were the doldrums through which the sidewheeler ably paddled while sailing vessels could be seen here and there, as though paralyzed, denied nature's motive power. With Panama in sight, 1,300 miles nearer San Francisco, the end of the journey could be contemplated as being a little over a month away. The *California* dropped anchor at the Isthmus on January 17, 1849, two miles off shore. It was then the ailing captain learned that more than 700 people were waiting in the tropical, sultry town, 300 of whom were holders of through tickets to San Francisco.

Panama City was two centuries old. Stone buildings and paved, winding streets represented a stable but small society. There were few accommodations for the instant inundation of impatient travelers. Some stayed in hotels or *pensions* while others set up tent enclaves just outside the ancient city walls, a pattern that was repeated time and again in San Francisco and the gold country. The number of waiting sojourners varied with the frequency of vessels touching at the port of Panama City, and reached as high as 4,000 at one time, until steamship coordination in 1853 improved considerably on both coasts. All those who waited in the early period of the Gold Rush experienced a long, arduous crossing at the Isthmus, beginning at the town of Chagres on the edge of the Caribbean Sea.

The Isthmus was 60 miles across, and before improvements were made along the route, the journey took approximately five days. Gold-seekers disembarked at Chagres from sailing vessels as well as steamships.

General warnings counseled travelers to spend as little time as possible in Chagres, a village of almost 50 bamboo huts, each windowless and roofed over with thatched palm leaves. Situated on the rim of an almost enclosed bay, picturesque hills and forests stretched out beyond the village. Stagnant pools were evidence of the lack of sewers or any means of runoff for human waste. The rapid increase of gold-seekers gave rise to conditions that contributed to disease. Cholera had already reached epidemic proportions on the East Coast of the United States, and it would not be long before someone carried it south. Sickness struck down hundreds who crossed the Isthmus, victims of malaria, dysentery, Panama fever, and the cholera that inevitably arrived.

Travelers began their journey by hiring Panamanians and their canoes to take them up the Chagres River, a narrow waterway banked by a tropical forest. The canoe trip occupied two-thirds of the journey, requiring overnight stops along the way. Mosquitos, fleas, spiders, ticks, unbearable humidity, and torrential rains plagued the crossings. There were no hotels or restaurants. Luggage, usually more than was necessary, was either taken along or transported by the natives on separate trips. The remainder of the crossing was on land; the travelers had to negotiate difficult terrain along a hilly ridge, then down the sloping mountain to the Pacific side, sometimes by mule, mostly on foot.

When the waiting gold-seekers at Panama City learned that the *California* did not have room for all, a volatile situation arose. Complaints were lodged, meetings were held, and strong resentments against the Peruvians developed. There was the belief that the gold, since it was in United States territory, belonged to citizens of the States.

Newly assigned military governor of California, General Persifor Smith, was a passenger on board. He concurred with the prevailing belief and wrote a letter to United States Consul for Panama, William Nelson, insisting that all foreigners be treated as trespassers in the gold country.

Describing a situation where they were carrying off gold "belonging to the United States" in "direct violation of law," the general pledged: "It will become my duty, immediately on my arrival there, to put these laws in force, to prevent their infraction in future, by punishing...those who offend." His instructions were for Consul Nelson to circulate copies of the letter to other consuls in South America. Translations of the threat were published in Peru and Chile and caused much concern, adding to strained relations. A growing anti-South American sentiment had been spawned.

Prior orders issued by General John Mason, the military governor whose office Smith was taking over, inferred otherwise. Mason proclaimed that the gold country was open to all who wished to seek his fortune, without placing restrictions on national origin.

While lighters resupplied the steamer with coal, more meetings were held, verbal and written denunciations of the Peruvians continued, and Captain Marshall went about constructing bunks in the steerage. He informed the Peruvians that they must retire to the open deck for the remainder of the journey. There were no repercussions.

The problem of too many waiting voyagers-in-transit was finally solved by giving preference to those who already held through tickets. Additional passengers were booked until the *California* was full. The remaining people would have to book berths on the sailing vessels that were arriving with increasing frequency. Captain Marshall weighed anchor on February 1, 1849, carrying 400 human beings, twice as many as the steamship was designed to carry. On deck was the customary fare for food: pens holding live chickens, sheep, hogs, and other potential meals shared the open deck with sailing gear of the spar deck and the Peruvians. Many of the additional adventurers were sick with malaria and other fevers.

Landfall was made in Acapulco nine days later. The coastline presented a sharp contrast to the barren coast of Chile. Here

Historic Wharves of San Francisco

The first practical passenger landing stage in San Francisco was constructed in 1848, using the hulk of the old iron steamer *James K. Polk.* It was beached near Clarke's Point where the current Vallejo Street intersects Battery Street. A narrow gangplank ran from its deck to the adjoining shore, and a passenger gangway ladder hung down its side to seaward. Boats from arriving vessels hauled alongside the ladder, and passengers climbed up the ladder, across the hulk's deck, and down the gangplank to the shore. Argonauts landed in this way from the pioneer Pacific Mail steamer *California* in February 1849. Crowds of people would congregate at the very spot when signals from Telegraph Hill announced the arrival of other steamers, such as the *Oregon,* which brought news that the State of California was admitted to the Union in October 1850.

Those early, historic wharves became symbolic evidence of the region's growth in population, cities, and maritime activity. They expanded as the early metropolis mushroomed to accommodate a civilization in an incredibly short period of time. Yerba Buena Cove became saturated with idle vessels waiting for the gold fever to subside, eventually sending seamen back to their decks to resume the business for which they were built. Many of the old hulks became landlocked in the mud as bayfill and wharves walled them into unlikely tombs. This enabled city merchants to gain more land to construct more buildings and burgeoning wharves.

Until the formation of the State Board of Harbor Commissioners in 1863, the city's wharves, actually extensions of downtown streets, were built and operated by private entrepreneurs. Individuals or stock companies recognized the need for

This rectangular brick building was the first U.S. Customs house in San Francisco. It stood on the corner of Clay and Montgomery streets. The draughtsman shows it surrounded by a neat wooden sidewalk. His drawing must have been made shortly before the fire of May 4, 1850, destroyed this building and everything else in the neighborhood. A new Customs House was built in 1854. It was a larger and more impressive building, classical in style with a columned porch, reflecting the growing civic-mindedness of the people of San Francisco. (TBL)

wharves and the great potential in profits the landing stages afforded. As they went about building wharves with unusual speed, the city front grew out over the cove and into the bay like fingers of gigantic hands pointing the way to the future. For more than 12 years owners prospered by charging vessels, shippers, and merchants for the use of their properties.

"The Central Wharf," wrote the first city treasurer, "being the only one in the city in 1848, was the thoroughfare for communication with the vessels, and was crowded from morning until night with drays and wagons coming and going. Sailors, miners, and others of all nationalities, speaking a great variety of tongues, moved busily about; steamers were arriving and departing, schooners were taking merchandise for the mines, boats were crowding in here and there—the whole resembling a great beehive, where at first glance everything appeared to be noise, confusion and disorder."

The more important wharves extended beyond the city front when the filling in of Yerba Buena Cove was finally completed. The following wharves are those initial ones that gave birth to a commerce rarely equalled in so short a time in the history of the world:

Clarke's Wharf or Jetty, whose owner, W.S. Clarke, built a rude timber structure out over the rocks. When the brig *Belfast* brought a cargo of lumber from New York, it unloaded at Clarke's Point. Much of

Hay for San Francisco's horses came into the haywharf near the Berry Street lumber wharf on Steamboat Point. Bales were being loaded onto a wagon from a tarpaulin-covered scow schooner. The scene is in the late 1880s or early 1890s. In the right background is the Pacific Oil and Lead Company. To its left is an empty gas holder. The rest is the lumberyard of Pope & Talbot, a company that had vast holdings of timber in the Pacific Northwest, and shipped lumber to many parts of the world. (NMMSF)

that lumber was used to build the Broadway Wharf thereafter.

Central Wharf or *Long Wharf*, begun April 1849 at Montgomery Street. Commercial Street extended east from Davis 1,400 feet by 57 feet in width. Depth of water at east end, 24 feet. Steamers from San Jose left this wharf at 8 a.m. daily.

Clay Street Wharf, begun 1850. Clay Street extended from Davis east 1,550 feet by 50 feet. Depth of water at east end, 35 feet.

Market and California Street Wharf, begun July 1850. Market Street extended from First Street more than 2,000 feet by 40 feet wide. Depth of water at east end, 20 feet at low tide.

Pacific Street Wharf, begun April 1851. Pacific Street extended from Front east 1,527 feet by 50 feet wide. Depth of water at east end, 26 feet. Steamers from Sacramento and Marysville left daily at 4 p.m.

Broadway Wharf, begun spring 1851. Broadway extended from Front Street, 750 feet by 60 feet wide. Depth of water at east end, 26 feet.

Vallejo Street Wharf, begun June 1853. Vallejo Street extended east from Front Street, flush 1,000 feet by 70 feet with an L opening on main wharf, north 350 feet by 50 feet wide. Depth of water, 25 feet at low tide.

Jackson Street Wharf, begun August 1853. Jackson Street extended east from Drumm Street 700 feet by 50 feet wide. Depth of water, 23 feet.

Washington Street Wharf, begun October 1853. Washington Street extended east from Davis Street 1300 feet, 50 feet wide. Average depth of water, 25 feet.

Main Street Wharf, begun April 1853. From Market Street southeast to Rincon Point, length about 2,000 feet. Owing to the extension of Steuart Street Wharf parallel and to the east of it, Main Street Wharf was available only to a few small craft engaged in supplying wholesalers with wood, hay, and other commodities.

Other wharves with names left to history are Dockham, Rousset, Ryan and Duff, San Francisco, Vigoureau, and Whipple.

was a profusion of vegetation, tropical plants, sugar cane, and fruit trees bearing tangerines and bananas. This ancient city had been a main port for the Manila galleons, and was now considered valuable as a refueling stop for the new coastwise service.

The *California* passed through the Golden Gate on February 28, 1849, five months out of New York. The newspaper *Alta California* greeted the pioneer steamer with high praise:

The California *is truly a magnificent vessel, and her fine appearance as she came in sight of the Town called forth cheer after cheer from her enraptured citizens, who were assembled in masses, upon the heights commanding a view of the bay and in dense crowds at the principal wharves and landing places. She passed the vessels of war in the harbor under a salute from each, returned by hearty cheering from the crowded decks, and at eleven was safely moored at the anchorage off the Town.*

The return to Panama was beset by other problems. Dissension among the crew and the call of gold had sent almost all of the crew members into the Mother Lode. A crew was not secured until several weeks later. Members now received unprecedented wages for those times: painters and carpenters were paid $260 to $300 per month and seamen $120 to $150 per month. The *California* left for Panama with 51 passengers and $300,000 in gold dust. Before completing the return voyage, however, the fuel ran out, and Captain Marshall did what was to be repeated many times in the future on other steamships. He burned whatever parts of the upper structure could be burned without impairing essential operations of the vessel. Spars, bulkheads, berths, cabin structures, and whatever else could be utilized were thrown into furnaces during those years. Because of the resourceful captain, the *California* enjoyed the distinction of being the first steamship to make the round-trip voyage between Panama and San Francisco.

During the *California's* voyage, frenetic activity gripped the world. There were just not enough vessels anywhere to accommodate the army of adventurers intent on getting a berth on seagoing tubs, among them men who had never sailed before, the majority without the faintest idea of what it was to live in confined quarters on deep water for months at a time. The shock of discovery was a sobering one, and few forgot the conditions they had to put up with in those early years: eating food rarely fresh and at times inadequately cooked and going bad; living in poorly ventilated quarters, at times for days in extreme, unrelieved heat; falling victim to violent attacks of seasickness that sent to bed the hardiest of passengers; inhabiting a small society with a wide range of personalities, including some exhibiting disagreeable, anti-social behavior; sharing this microcosm with passengers who contracted various diseases; and finally, either losing one's life in a catastrophic shipwreck or coming within moments of possible death as the vessel miraculously survived turbulent weather.

The coastwise routes gradually became established, steamships and other vessels taking back East hundreds of thousands of dollars in gold dust each voyage, including men whose dreams became realities as they returned with fortunes in varying amounts. The vast majority of the gold-seekers, though, did not strike it rich, were disillusioned, and, having "seen the elephent," acquired the Truth. They had discovered the worst and returned disgusted and poorer in material worth than they had ever been. Yet, many of them were profoundly changed for having taken part in a grand adventure the world rarely affords; for having shared visions of wide-open prairies and powerful vistas at land's end on the Pacific shore; for being where majestic mountains, rich valleys, and precious open space and sky combined to teach them of other freedoms outside the restraints of narrow cultural mores back home. Once having known the Far West, they would help alter aspects of their own society, acting as catalysts to change old traditions. They would acquire a certain strength of character and improved physical attributes, having learned to survive without those amenities Eastern society provided. They would forever dream, talk, and write about the experience in philosophical and nostalgic wonder, attempting to recapture their youth and savor a time of hope and exhilaration that was unlike any other.

Pacific Mail and United States Mail realized excellent profits, and the fact that their lines could not keep up with the demand was additional evidence of the astonishing business. Other lines and individual vessels tried to take up the slack, but their efforts were not enough, and of those vessels available, many were old and leaking hulks. The fantastic demands of the Gold Rush years led to the development of another crossing on the Central American Isthmus in Nicaragua. Growing demands set off an intense, cutthroat competitive war that lasted until 1860.

No major shipwreck of a steamship occurred until July 1851, when the *Union,* operated by the rival Empire City Line, became a total loss after being stranded on a sand ledge off shore, some 300 miles south of San Diego. The 250 passengers, $270,000 in gold dust, and most baggage and provisions were saved. Thereafter, steamships were to suffer those similar tragedies visited upon sailing vessels of the period. The fact that steamships during the intense period of travel up to mid-1851 avoided major disasters gave testimony to the skill their officers and navigators possessed. The dense fogs, shifting currents, and to many commanders, unknown coastal waters, were a continual challenge. The lack of lighthouses was an additional burden to the mariners, for it was not until 1852 that a series of lighthouses were constructed along the coast as a result of Congressional appropriations.

THE QUEST FOR SPEED UNDER SAIL
At different times in history various materials have been developed to their highest potential for specific uses. Whether particular woods, bronze, gold, iron, or other materials, each age discovered imaginative applications to achieve new wonders.

During the 1840s and 1850s, the softwoods of New England were utilized to achieve monuments under sail, those clipper ships of the California, China, and Atlantic trades. Relatively light, from about 1,000 to 2,500 tons, these wooden vessels were natural descendants of an earlier time.

The need for faster vessels was met by those Baltimore clippers, long, low, and flush-decked brigs, schooners, and some barks, which evolved from the Revolutionary period to the 1830s and 1840s. We have seen them as slavers, armed privateers, and opium clippers. Their chief features were great beam, placed far forward, giving them a very fine run from a high bow with plenty of sheer to a low stern. The stem, sternpost, and masts were unusually raked, characteristics that were known to create anxiety in the crews of other vessels observing them from a distance; for they were 'rakish-looking' crafts, sinister in appearance and formidable for their times.

There is some controversy over what constituted the development of the fast clipper ships of the 1850s. Yet, there is general consensus that the design followed logical change and effort until a definite pattern of characteristics evolved. The Baltimore clippper, *Rainbow,* launched in 1845, an exceptionally fast flyer for her day, was representative of that significant break with traditional design, and at the same time part of the evolutionary process.

Three basic designs made up the outstanding clippers of the mid-19th century: the sharp dead-rise, fine-ended Baltimore clipper; the full mid-section minimal deadrise, sharp-ender clipper; and a cross between the two, where the deadrise was marked, but not extreme. What was common to all three was the full-sail plan, utilizing some one and a half acres of canvas overall, representing more than 23 sails to catch the wind. More than one clipper reached speeds of 18 knots an

106 DAYS!
TO SAN FRANCISCO

STANDS STRICTLY A No. 1.

THE CELEBRATED "OUT-AND-OUT" CLIPPER SHIP

WILD HUNTER

THOS. P. HOWES, Commander,

Is now receiving her Cargo at Pier 18 EAST RIVER, and will have

Our Usual Prompt Dispatch.

The "WILD HUNTER" is well known as one of the SHARPEST and FASTEST SHIPS AFLOAT—is of very small capacity, and will finish loading **without delay.** Shippers will oblige by having their goods on board promptly.

CORNELIUS COMSTOCK & CO., 96 Wall St.

Agents at San Francisco, Messrs. DIBBLEE & HYDE.

The Wild Hunter *was built in East Dennis, Massachusetts, in 1855. The advertisement boasts fast loading due to small capacity. On its first voyage it reached San Francisco in 125 days. Its voyages continued from San Francisco in a westerly direction around the world. (NMMSF)*

hour (or some 20 miles an hour), while a speed of 10 to 12 knots for days at a time was not unusual. This amazing swiftness over the great ocean highways was sufficient to enable the ship to pass through patches of calm without being overly delayed. If any slowing down did take place, these mountains of canvas were capable of capturing out of the sky any moving puffs of air, and, like fine-tuned machinery, could generate motion into a driving force. Slapping on more canvas

than any other sailing vessel of any other period in history was common among clipper ship captains. Their ships' daily logs suggest the appearance of a new breed of seamen who drove their ships to the maximum in all kinds of weather, establishing world records while making astonishing use of spanker sails, spencer sails, jibs, topsails, skysails, royal studdingsails, and moonsails.

Although several routes to San Francisco were being developed or improved at mid-century, the overland or Central American Isthmus carriers could not accommodate heavy equipment, machinery, houses, large quantities of furniture, and bulk merchandise. The clipper ship fulfilled those needs. It also offered a tolerable alternative as passage to the gold country, providing fast, direct transportation without changeovers.

For the new breed of seaman as well as the pioneer shipbuilder, clippers demanded new vision, skill, and remarkable risks. Although their striking appearance and splendid records were admired the world over, their designs and handling by skippers in raging seas were bold acts that defied tradition. Clipper owners lived by the maxim that "time was money," and their captains sped over deep water indifferent to those natural elements that mariners usually met with caution or feared. An unpredictable squall, a deep, rolling, and dangerous sea were yet additional fare for motive power, and every part of the ship—sails, yards, masts, and hull—had to meet the challenge or fail. Many a skipper wore the same clothes for days as his ship sailed through tempestuous weather, and he retired only for partial rest, not sleeping, not fully awake, part of him monitoring every movement of the racing ship.

Isaac Webb, a master shipbuilder and teacher, trained three of the foremost clipper builders of all time: Donald MacKay, responsible for *Flying Cloud, Stag-Hound, Andrew Jackson, Flying Fish, Westward Ho!, Romance of the Seas, Sovereign of the Seas, Great Republic, Lightning,* and *Glory of the Seas,* among others; William H. Webb, son of Isaac and responsible for *Celestial, Challenge, Comet, Gazelle, Sword-Fish, Flying Dutchman,* among others; and John Griffiths, builder of *Rainbow,* prototype for the extreme clippers to come. Samuel Hall of Boston is another legendary shipbuilder, turning out *Game Cock, Surprise, Flying Childers, John Gilpin, Wizard, Amphitrite,* and others.

Some of the skippers who were "drivers," made the run from East Coast ports to San Francisco in less than 100 days. These men carved out a special place for themselves in maritime history. They were: Cressy, *Flying Cloud,* and John Williams, *Andrew Jackson,* 89 days; David Babcock, *Sword Fish,* 90 days; Edward Nickels, *Flying Fish,* and Joseph Limeburner, *Great Republic,* 92 days; Philip Dumaresq, *Surprise* and *Romance of the Seas,* 96 days; Robert Waterman, *Sea Witch,* William Brewster, *Contest,* F.W. Cole, *Antelope,* James Foster, *Sierra Nevada,* and Benjamin Freeman, *Witchcraft,* 97 days; George Brewster, *David Brown,* 98 days; Otis Baker, Jr., *Herald of the Morning,* and Samuel Very, Jr., *Hurricane,* 99 days.

The clippers in the first years of their glory returned ample profits to owners, usually paying for themselves on the first round trip, making as much as $50,000 over and above building costs. Freight was as high as $60 a ton, a phenomenal price for that time. No wonder that masters earned as much as $3,000 on the outward passage to San Francisco, and if the trip was accomplished in less than 100 days, the ante shot up to $5,000. Reputations of both masters and builders were at stake. Bonuses for officers were not uncommon, especially after a successful race between these greyhounds of the sea. Many races took place over thousands of miles of deep water.

With the exception of gold, there was little else of value for clippers to take out of the Bay Area. The lack of adequate lading sent the ships on to China, where they loaded down with teas, pottery, furniture, and other goods welcome in England and the United States. They competed directly with the British trade, to

111, 121, 115, 124 & 121 DAYS TO
SAN FRANCISCO!!
Merchants' Express Line of Clipper Ships.
SMALLEST, SHARPEST & FASTEST VESSEL UP

The Well-known and Splendid Little Extreme Clipper Ship
FEARLESS
HOMANS, Commander,
AT PIER 13 EAST RIVER.
The above passages guarantee her SAILING QUALITIES, and as shippers KNOW that she delivers cargo well, no more need be said. She carries but 1,700 Tons, and will be *dispatched immediately* after the "PANTHER."
RANDOLPH M. COOLEY,
88 Wall St., (Tontine Building.)
Agents in San Francisco, Messrs. DE WITT, KITTLE & Co.

the bitter consternation of the empire. After China the clippers rounded the Cape of Good Hope, then traded on the Thames, and finally returned to the Atlantic Northwest—proud, envied, laden with varying fortunes. This remarkable period, the 1850s, saw the development of relatively distinct China and California trades.

A combination of circumstances brought the American clipper activity to an abrupt end. Softwoods tended to soak up water

The extreme clipper Fearless *was launched in Boston at the shipyards of A. & G.T. Sampson in 1853. Small and elegant, it was also fast, as the advertisement claims, with an average time from Boston to San Francisco of 125 days. (NMMSF)*

gradually, and wooden bottoms became waterlogged. Such ships, driven as the clippers were, deteriorated to the point where a fast flyer was reduced to a slow merchantman in five years. Large crews were always needed to operate them, and recruitment was a continual problem. Shipwreck was to take its fantastic toll, while new transportation technology would undermine the domination of the clipper ship. The Panama Railroad, the increasing efficiency of steamships, and the economic depression of 1857 were important factors in the clippers' demise. Steamships would revolutionize scheduling, giving a measure of reliability to departures and arrivals. There was also the renewed, formidable challenge from England. British shipbuilders fashioned composite clippers for the China Trade, constructing iron hulls, covering them with wood planking,

and sheathing the combination with copper. Iron frames and copper bottoms opened a new era in shipbuilding in the 1850s and 1860s and produced improved clippers, such as the *Taeping, Ariel, Thermopylae,* and *Cutty Sark.* These ships would regain England's prominence in the China Tea Trade. London merchants desired swift transport of the first crops of tea leaves, which were the premium harvest, for tea lost its delicate flavor and quality throughout a long voyage.

The introduction of iron was a severe blow to America's shipping. Iron hulls were superior to wooden ones in practically every aspect: stiffer frames, stronger construction requiring fewer repairs and allowing for larger cargoes and greater speed; in addition they were more durable, less susceptible to the ravages of fire, and about one-third the weight of wooden hulls, commanding higher rates for freight. The close proximity of England's iron mines to the sea, as well as the coal that was needed for steamers, gave England added advantages. And since wages were higher in the United States and protective tariffs restricted foreign competition, England was able to produce iron hulls at lower costs. England's *Cutty Sark* was similar in measurement to *Thermopylae*, with the exception that it was a sharper ended vessel. Both claimed to have been the fastest clipper ships in the world.

Events would also add to the demise of the American clipper ship, and in a larger sense, to the decline of the United States as a leading maritime nation. Political conflict at home eventually led to a disastrous civil war and kept the nation absorbed in internal matters for years to come. Ultimately, energies and aspirations were concentrated on healing a wounded nation and the building of towns and cities throughout its frontier. Thus preoccupied, a former vitality and faith were withdrawn from the sea.

Although the era was a brief one, our maritime past will always recall those extraordinary ships carrying mountains of white canvas and navigating the world— names that suggested the mystique of the sea, eternal youth, and like the California Gold Rush that inspired them, an instant promise that was impossible to sustain: *Trade Wind, Witch of the Wave, Syren, Raven, Shooting Star, White Swallow, Flying Arrow, Storm King, Empress of the Seas, Lightfoot, Golden Fleece, Winged Arrow, Competitor, Phantom, Onward,* and *Young America.*

Samuel Eliot Morison in *The Oxford History of the American People,* wrote an appropriate memorial to the vessels that were in large part children of the Gold Rush:

These clipper ships of the early 1850s were built of wood in shipyards from Rockland in Maine to Baltimore. Their architects, like poets who transmute nature's message into song, obeyed what wind and wave taught them, to create the noblest of all sailing vessels, and the most beautiful creations of man in America. With no extraneous ornament except a figurehead, a bit of carving and a few lines of gold leaf, their one purpose over the great ocean routes was achieved by perfect balance of spars and sails to the curving lines the smooth black hull; and this harmony of mass, form and color was practiced to the music of dancing waves and of brave winds whistling in the rigging. These were our Gothic cathedrals, our Parthenon; but monuments carved from snow. For a few brief years they flashed their splendor around the world, then disappeared with the finality of the wild pigeon.

ACROSS THE WIDE PACIFIC

Hawaiians, Australians, and Chinese also responded when news of the Gold Rush reached their countries.

By 1849 the Hawaiian kingdom was suffering from a sluggish economy, dependent as it had been for years on the New England whaling fleet. The years 1847 to 1848 had been poor ones for whalers, and the Gold Rush happened at an opportune time for the islands. Many stores that had previously supplied the whaling industry were overstocked and warehouses were at maximum storage capacity. News of the discovery of gold and immediate needs in San Francisco sent a sigh of relief throughout the islands, and everything considered useful to the goldfields and in the growing metropolis was sent. In addition to pickaxes, shovels, and lamps, playing cards and bibles found ready buyers. Food was the most important export. Cattle, goats, turkeys, and chickens were shipped, along with onions, sweet potatoes, squash, yams, syrup, molasses, coffee, and sugar.

Native Hawaiians, Caucasians who had settled in the islands, and the drifters of the Pacific—beachcombers and sailors who had jumped any number of ships—found berths on schooners, clippers, whalers, and anything else that could transport them to the Golden Gate. San Francisco was just over 2,000 miles away, and vessels made the run in from nine to twelve days.

Facing page: *Built by Donald McKay in East Boston in 1851, the Flying Cloud was purchased by Grinell, Mintern Company of New York. The Flying Cloud made its first voyage to San Francisco in 89 days. Thereafter it served in the China Trade and around the world, calling at European ports on the way. The Flying Cloud was an impressive sight: an extreme clipper with a slightly concave bow, adorned with an angel trumpeter. With towering mast and acres of canvas, it suited its name. The Flying Cloud ended its days with much reduced sail and spars in the lumber trade between Nova Scotia and London. (TBL)*

Hawaii's new prosperity lasted until 1851. It was then that San Francisco became saturated with supplies pouring in from all parts of the world, and agriculture in the Bay Area was beginning to sustain the needs of the region. But another favorable economic climate would return to the islands during the Civil War, when sugar emerged as the king crop and major business.

Interest from Australia took hold slowly. Forty-eight vessels cleared its ports in 1849—ships, brigs, schooners, barks, and whalers bearing the prosaic names of *Eleanor Lancaster, Lindsay, Osprey, Martha and Elizabeth, Eliza, William Hill, Despatch, Plymouth,* and others. The vessels were ballasted with brick for the most part, and salable two or more months later in San Francisco. Their cargoes were tobacco, guns, meat, tools of all kinds, wine, rum, iron, portable houses, and machines for extracting gold from sand. They were items that the rising population of gold-seekers found most useful.

Australia had begun as the penal colony of New South Wales in the 1780s, an outcast land where England sent its "undesirables." Britain was concluding a disastrous war with its American colony, while extending its colonial adventurism elsewhere, straining its resources. Imperialism produced returns for England's aristocracy and privileged merchants, to the detriment of the poorer classes, whose ranks increased alarmingly. The colonists of Botany Bay and other settlements were men and women who were convicted of numerous crimes, the most common being the theft of food and other necessities and the inability to pay off debts. There was a short verse that circulated during the rounding up of colonizers for Botany Bay, and it summed up their condition in a satirical way:

The law doth punish man or woman
That steals a goose from off the common,
But lets the greater villain loose
That steals the common off the goose!

Political prisoners were also among the outcasts, the majority Irish patriots.

Most Australians of 1849 were descendants of that banished colony, and approximately 3,000 sailed to San Francisco by early 1850. Many others were waiting in port towns ready to go. As in New England, Midwestern, European, and South American towns, newspapers and politicians of Australia reacted with alarm and warned of dire consequences should the exodus of young and able people continue.

The journey from Australia to San Francisco took 70 to 85 days. Most vessels took indirect routes, adding more miles to the course in order to pick up favorable trades. Many deaths occurred on these early vessels, and conditions as to food and accommodations varied from vessel to vessel. Complaints over the quality and quantity of food were common. The Hawaiian Islands—where captains hired Kanakas to supplement the crews of usually inadequately manned vessels—were a welcome stopover.

When gold was discovered in Australia in mid-1851 the exodus from "down under" was checked. By 1852 a reverse migration was taking place, and some 95,000 gold-seekers from all parts of the world surged into Australia to explore its much-heralded fields of gold.

News of the "Golden Mountain" or *Gum Shan* in California reached China in mid-1848. When Chinese miners returned to their homeland with gold in 1849, tales of their exploits spread first to the cities, then eventually throughout the maritime provinces of Kwangtung and Fukien. Demands for transportation at China's Treaty Ports of Shanghai, Amoy, Swatow, Canton, and especially the British Crown Colony of Hong Kong, were overwhelming.

There was a limited understanding and acceptance of Chinese by the Western nations, clearly revealed in their imposition of opium and their demands in the 1840s that China open its doors to unrestricted trade. Bankrupt and vulnerable, China was prey to an exploitation that represented the worst of Western imperialism. The concept of extraterritoriality was established in China soley to benefit Westerners. It denied China any legal jurisdiction over foreigners living or trading in the boundaries of her territory. China was forced to accept opium as a legal import, and the presence of Western traders in the China Seas, their activities virtually uncontrolled, strangled China's ability to trade effectively and prosper well into the 20th century.

These circumstances were further complicated by the development of a parallel slave trade that grew to enormous proportions in the 1850s. Due to emancipation proclamation decrees in various countries, mid-century saw the supply of African slaves diminish rapidly and alarmed slave-owners turned elsewhere for cheap or enforced labor. The poor of China would fill the need.

That demand for China's poor, combined with the discovery of gold in California and Australia, created a complexity of circumstances that produced false hope for emigrating Chinese, and they were to become tragic victims to the greed and cruelty of the age. Through deception, widespread kidnappings, and the pretext of legitimate labor contracts, from one-half to three-quarters of a million Chinese men and boys from the Kwangtung and Fukien provinces were transported into bondage on board vessels owned by Americans, Britons, Spaniards, Portuguese, Peruvians, and Frenchmen.

Thus, two types of emigration movements began in China: One consisted of those who migrated to try their luck in the fabled gold countries of California and Australia; the other movement was the traffic that came to be known as the "coolie trade," which lasted well into the 1870s. The uneducated poor of China had little knowledge of foreign lands, and it was a simple matter to suggest that once out of China, all voyagers would at last reach "the Golden Hills." Potential victims were recruited throughout the countryside by an elaborate network of crimps and brokers. Promises of high wages for honest work mixed with the growing tales of gold strikes were effective inducements to attract hundreds of thousands to the port cities of Southern China. The recruited were crowded into barracoons known as "pig pens" and were subjected to intolerable conditions during days or weeks of waiting. Armed guards ensured order and prevented escapes.

Asian immigrants arriving on trans-Pacific steamers had to go through quarantine at Hospital Cove on Angel Island. Immigrants were medically examined while their clothing and baggage were fumigated. The Quarantine Service aimed to preserve public health, but in so doing it served the spirit of the Exclusion Acts, first passed in 1882, which barred Chinese from becoming naturalized citizens of the United States. Courtesy, National Park Service, Golden Gate National Recreation Area

There were five "great" fires in San Francisco between 1849 and 1851, three of them occuring in 1850. The city was not prepared for them and suffered enormous losses, but each time rebuilding began before the ashes were cold. This fire in June 1850 started on the site of the former one and swept to the water's edge, causing massive damage. The mayor then authorized the building of cisterns and wells around the city. Three engine and hook and ladder companies were organized and a bucket brigade law was passed. (TBL)

Once transferred to the vessels that would transport them, the Chinese were forced to remain in the holds. Over 32 American vessels were involved in the trade to Cuba, Peru, and Brazil. Due to its clandestine nature, as the trade became more disreputable, there were certainly a greater number that were American-owned. Famous clipper ships were also involved. Among the fleet were: *Robert Bowne, Winged Racer, Sea Witch, Westward Ho, Hound, Skylark, Waverly, Challenge, Norway, Gov'r Morton, Pioneer, Staghound,* and *Leonidas*. Mortality rates on the voyages ran from 11 to 22 percent.

Congress passed a law in 1862 that prohibited American citizens from participating in the trade, but bold skippers and owners skirted the law for years. The trade was finally brought to a close in 1881 as a result of a determined China. Persistence, firm diplomacy, and beheading brokers and recruiters in town squares proved eminently successful.

The "coolie" trade had a significant impact on the West's perceptions of Chinese, especially those who migrated to the Bay Region. Stereotypes emerged and the belief that most Chinese were virtual slaves was a dominant one. From this, the reasoning went, Chinese took jobs away from Caucasians, or they were an ultimate threat to existing jobs, or they diminished working conditions Caucasians already enjoyed. Little understanding toward them was forthcoming from Europeans recently arrived in California, most of them immigrants themselves. Intolerant attitudes evolved, from xenophobia to racism.

With much agitation from labor unionists and politicians especially, growing antagonisms would eventually lead to the first and only exclusion law Congress has devised. Passed in 1882, it prohibited the immigration of Chinese. This was the backdrop and the substance of Chinese relationships during the latter part of the 19th century in the United States.

The immigrant movement from China to California was dominated by wooden vessels under sail for approximately 15 years. Chinese in the provinces set out for the vessels in Hong Kong, which became the main port of embarkation, in junks,

sampans, Western schooners, and eventually coastwise steamboats. Transpacific vessels were primarily those of the United States, Britain, Scandinavia, and Germany, many picking up passengers on their voyages around the world. Supplies of all kinds were shipped from China on many of the vessels to aid the growing populations of the Bay Area. Foodstuffs favored by the Chinese argonauts and portable houses, as well as granite to erect stone buildings in San Francisco were typical cargo.

Clipper ships also took part in the passenger traffic, discovering lucrative income in transporting Chinese to San Francisco. All vessels carried from 250 to 400 passengers each, and the fare averaged $50 to California. By 1866 approximately 104,986 Chinese had made the trip. Return fare to Hong Kong averaged about $40, and approximately 42,699 returned in the same period. In the 15 years following the Gold Rush, the clipper ships earned some $7 million from Chinese passengers alone, not counting whatever "extras" owners, captains, and mates exacted from voyagers. Non-emigrants, first-class passengers, and cargoes augmented already unprecedented profits.

The crossings took from 60 to 85 days in the early years, and the clippers accomplished the run in incredibly swift time for the period: in 1852 *Challenge* swept across to San Francisco 33 days out of Hong Kong, and the following year *Memnon* took 36 days from the Whampoa anchorage near Canton.

ASCENDANCY OF THE PORT

The Gold Rush port became an international one in every respect. Unlike other migrations, which were invariably homogeneous, with relative sameness in class, nationality, and race, the tens of thousands of people who journeyed to the San Francisco Bay area were perhaps the most unique mix of humanity ever drawn to one place in the history of the world. Here was the biblical Babel turned into reality, an exciting laboratory of social dynamics and at the same time a potentially volatile environment. Living, working, sharing knowledge of the arduous journeys all had made by land or sea, managing the same muddy streets and living in similar tent cities, bearing well or poorly during heavy rains and flood, all participated in a fledgling society profoundly influenced by the diversity of nationalities and races in it.

Here was a universal gathering of men and women building a metropolis the likes of which there were no models to emulate. Here were Frenchmen, Germans, Chinese, Irish, Chileans, Norwegians, Swiss, Peruvians, Filipinos, Swedish, Greeks, Hawaiians, English, Central Americans, Welsh, Mexicans, Italians, Portuguese, Native Americans, American Negroes, and more. Here was a panorama of clothing and hair styles, different cuts of mustaches and beards that would have shocked most communities the world over. Here were endlessly varied designs in commodities, furniture, machines, and houses made by artisans and factories in a dozen different lands. Here were the many languages, and the culinary arts of many cultures which came together to offer a young and vibrant civilization the first cosmopolitan food fare available anywhere. Here was an international populace with all the strengths and weaknesses of human character. San Francisco was truly a microcosm, the first 20th-century city.

During those first years, the city, rather than building beyond the hills of rock, sand, and underbrush, utilized the space occupied by the mudflats and water of Yerba Buena Cove. As though the population was afraid of living too far from the water—and too distant from the boats that would transport it to the gold country—it seemed tentatively poised for any news that would require immediate departures. What distinctions existed between city and cove gradually disappeared. The new settlements of tents, shacks, and other buildings rose as close to the water as possible, with many on hastily constructed piers that later became streets. Piles were driven into the water lots and covered with planking, accommodating houses, cargoes, businesses, and all manner of equipment. Actually extensions of city streets, the water lots, once filled and crisscrossed by adjoining streets, reemerged as the city's downtown section. The historian Edward Morphy quotes a traveller who described the development in 1851:

I was lost in wonder and astonishment at the unparalleled rapidity of the rising of a city....Nearly one-half the city was built on the extensive wharfs, and still the sounding and falling weight of piledrivers, axe, hammer, and saw was heard everywhere employed by speculators in water lots. Immediately after the completion of the few yards of wharf, a frame house was built on it, shaking and trembling in its foundation the piles, at the passing of a vehicle or a horse; and was as immediately occupied by provision and clothing dealers, and liquor vendors or gamblers. All the commercial business was contracted on the wharfs.

Material for landfill was abundant: unwanted cargoes; old hulks; the whole spectrum of civilization's garbage; plus sandstone and shale. The surrounding sand dunes, especially south of market, rose as high as 80 feet, impressive natural barriers in those early years. The dunes and the prominent Telegraph Hill became active quarries. Total reduction of the sand dunes elicited little cause for alarm and provided the growing city with practical, level ground on which to build. Telegraph Hill, however, after being severely cut back by constant excavation for bayfill, the great seawall, and ballast for the vessels that had little of anything to return with in their holds, precipitated protests that prevented its complete destruction.

Estimates of the amount of landfill that was eventually used for some 3,000 acres of Yerba Buena Cove ran from 20 million to 22 million cubic yards. It was actually a good deal more, for the initial estimate was based on filling in a depth of 25 feet of water at low tide. Thirty-five feet was ultimately required to bring each square foot of property up to city grade. The efficient Steam Paddy with its knife-like shovel was a common sight throughout the waterfront. Capable of moving 2,500 tons of fill a day, the seemingly ubiquitous machine continued its relentless assault on the sand dunes and hills for years.

The merchandise that was arriving daily was in critical need of storage space, and until enough became available auctions usually took place at the piers. Master, supercargo (an officer in charge of cargo and the vessel's business transactions), or consignee would choose an auctioneer soon after vessel and goods arrived. With a sign over his shanty reading "auction," the waterfront broker commenced business at the dock. In this way many of these enterprising men sold property worth a million dollars during a year. Increased capital, credit, and the gradual appearance of fireproof storage helped to phase out those outdoor attractions.

The use of vessels as storeships, taverns, boardinghouses, banks, jails, churches, and other facilities was also common. San Francisco's first bank was established on a sailing scow that had been beached at California and Battery streets; a regular exchange, deposit, and forwarding business took place on its deck. The packet ship *Apollo,* after arriving from New York with 62 passengers and freight, was turned into a storeship, saloon, and coffee shop at the Sacramento Street Wharf. Three old hulks were secured by a Richard Chandler and beached near the head of the Vallejo Wharf for use as a coal depot. The *Niantic,* a 14-year-old whaler, was transformed into an elaborate storage facility and saloon complete with a wide balcony and lower structures. The city's first jail was the *Euphemia,* a two-masted brig owned by General Vallejo and sold to the city.

The ship *Panama* became the Bethel Methodist Episcopal chapel in 1851 while anchored off the Sacramento Street Wharf. It was shortly moved to the foot of Mission Street and turned into a more accommodating chapel when a superstructure was built on the deck. The noted port chaplain, the Reverend William

Taylor, founded this early bethel. The *Panama* was eventually hauled up on dry land at Mission between First and Second streets and absorbed into the dock there. Near Vallejo and Battery streets an old iron steamship, *Sarah Sands,* was beached and converted into an inexpensive boardinghouse; it was believed at the time to be the first iron steamship ever built. More than 100 vessels were transformed, most with roofed-over shingled roofs. Appearing like neither ships nor buildings, these strange structures nevertheless represented a practical architectural marriage of the two.

Of the more than 500 vessels in the harbor in late 1850, the greatest number were ships and barques; the rest were brigs and schooners. At least 100 square-rigged vessels were lying at Benicia, Sacramento, and Stockton. Even though the crews and captains of numerous vessels left for the gold country, a fair percentage of men returned shortly after their first disappointing encounter in the Sierras. High wages also induced them to join other crews and head back out to sea. Other vessels entered into various types of trading in the Bay Area, discovering the substantial needs of the growing towns in the East Bay and throughout the Delta.

Those vessels that had made their last voyage, rotting as they were in the mud, or too old and worn to make restoration feasible, were broken up for the much-needed wood, old iron, copper sheathing, metal fastenings, deck houses, and other necessities that were in short supply. Many Chinese found the wrecking business lucrative and engaged in the activity for a number of years. Charles Hare, a native of Baltimore and salvager there, discovered a far more successful business in Yerba Buena Cove: the need for hammering, sawing, and tearing apart old hulks was so great that there were still ample pickings as late as 1857.

Old hulks picked clean and scuttled, others merely scuttled, and still others that were once useful structures locked forever in mud and landfill, were partially or completely burned as a result of one or more of the five major fires that occurred between 1849 and 1851. Old remains of these vessels surface every now and then as a result of new construction in the downtown area.

Shipbuilding followed a logical development with the increasing needs of bay and river transportation. As individuals, the shipbuilders reflected the spectrum of population drawn to the goldfields. Several of the most prominent builders in San Francisco in those early years, beginning with 1849, were Captain Domingo Marcucci from Italy, Captain John North from Norway, Harry Owens from Wales, Austin Hills from New England, and the Dickie brothers, John and James, from Scotland. Their achievements helped to shorten time and distance between the rising communities of the Bay Area metropolis. They built barges, schooners, sternwheel or propeller-driven steamers with the names of *Cleopatra, Belle, Gem No. 1, Success, Hardy, Colorado, Clara, Flora de las Andes* (ordered by Costa Rica), *Susan, Kate Devine* (named after a well known actress), *Capital,* the finest river steamer in its class for the time), *Vallejo, Game Cock, Rambler, Princess, Thomas Payne, Red Bluff, Chrysopolis,* (later known as *Oakland*),

As early as 1851 there were ship repair yards on South Beach. By 1865, when this photograph was taken, there were several small shipyards and marine railways constructing and repairing the ubiquitous two-masted schooners of the bay and the nearby coast. Rincon Point and the U.S. Marine Hospital can be seen in the distance. (NMMSF)

Above: *Stern-wheel steamers with a string of barges in tow were once a familiar sight on the Sacramento River. The San Joaquin #4 was the largest of all California river steamers and, able to pull five barges at once, was said to be the most powerful vessel in America. Courtesy, California State Library Collection, City of Sacramento, Museum & History Division*

Facing page, top: *The sidewheel paddle steamer* Japan *lies alongside the Pacific Mail Steamship Company coaling wharf taking on coal for her next trans-Pacific voyage. The* America, Great Republic, China, *and* Japan *were built from 1867 to 1869. They were the largest wooden ocean-going sidewheel steamers ever built.* Japan *is seen here about 1870 as photographed by Carleton E. Watkins. (NMMSF)*

Reliance, Dart (a pleasure yacht), *Amelia, Washoe, Del Norte, Contra Costa, Julia,* and dozens more from 120 to 950 tons each.

Some $34 million in gold had been exported from the Bay Area by 1851, and in the same year nearly everyone believed the Sierras would provide high yields for at least a hundred years. The following year shipments reached $46 million but were to hit their peak at $55 million in 1853. Gold production declined steadily thereafter. The year 1853 was a turning point for a number of other developments: the so-called stable markets—gold, real estate, storage facilities—were in a state of overspeculation, and all declined in value and in wages, precipitating the first financial panic for California. That year the largest number of Easterners returned home since the beginning of the Gold Rush, all traveling by way of the Panama Isthmus; immigration overland dropped dramatically (to resume in large numbers via transcontinental rails); and shipping fell from 470,000 tons during the high point of gold fever to 197,000 tons by 1857. The brightest prospect of 1853 was the rapid rise of state agriculture, especially the promising harvest of grain and vegetables

from newly cultivated California farms.

By 1854 steamboat operators realized that the increasing numbers of boats on the bay and river networks resulted in less profit and higher cost of operation. A number of these operators formed a powerful association whose capital stock was $2 million at the time. The "combination," as it was commonly called, was named California Steam Navigation Company, and it dominated the inland waterways of Northern California for the next 15 years. The company's members were major operators with such vessels as *Senator* and *World* working the Sacramento run, *Cornelia* to Stockton, and *Antelope, Hartford, American Eagle, Pike, Comanche, Cleopatra,* and others to Marysville and Red Bluff. The monopoly was a formidable one and was at times challenged by towns along the routes. Citizens joined in stock companies to purchase their own steamers, competing against the pervasive combine. The Independent and Opposition lines of delta steamers used the Broadway Wharf in those early years, a location that attracted crowds of people, particularly on special sailing days.

Left: Henry Meiggs, a notorious waterfront entrepreneur, built Meiggs Wharf in North Beach around 1852. Meiggs built his empire in lumber, establishing a mill in Mendocino County. He became a fugitive in South America after accumulating more wealth from the sale of fraudulent real estate in the North Beach area. (TBL)

67

Sails are drying at a lumber wharf. This may be the Third Street Wharf, but the scene is typical of lumber wharves. The hill in the background could be one of the South San Francisco hills. (TBL)

observer in 1857: "I was astonished....Some of the wharves had broken down; others were in a fair way to share the same fate, being veritable man-traps by missing and broken planks, through which, nightly, men were precipitated and engulfed in the muddy waters beneath....Many of the houses erected on the wharves were unoccupied and tottering on their insecure foundations of piles half demolished by the timber-worm."

The California State Legislature passed a bill in 1863 that established a Board of State Harbor Commissioners that would "provide for the improvement and protection of the wharves, docks and waterfront" of San Francisco. The commission took over the piers, but not without being dragged into the courts by some of the pier owners who contested the legality of the law. Some court cases lasted years. Ultimately the state commission prevailed, setting usage fees that would pay for the work on the piers as well as the Embarcadero, the Belt Railroad, and the great seawall. Begun in 1879, the colossal seawall of more than 15,000 feet long by 20 feet across, extending from Third Street to Taylor Street along the Embarcadero, cost over $1,750,000.

No longer offering the notion of instant wealth to the world, the influx of immigrants to the Bay area in the 1860s was in the thousands rather than the hundreds of thousands that had descended during the Gold Rush years. By the 1860s the region was settling down into a period of steady growth, with all the growing pains of rural and urban development. River steamboats and railroad networks were important factors in the continuing growth of communities in Northern California. So too were the inter-bay ferries, such as those between San Francisco, Oakland, and Alameda, where the Oakland Estuary resembled a crowded highway. Alviso in the South Bay was an active port, shipping by steamboat a variety of commodities to San Francisco, including vegetables, fruits, grains, quicksilver, and lumber.

The early years were marred, however,

In the early 1850s regular sailings of Pacific Mail Steamships occurred on the first and fourteenth of each month, a schedule that evolved into a unique San Francisco maritime tradition known as "Steamer Days." During those years the regular semi-monthly departures and arrivals at the Broadway Wharf spurred a great deal of cargo and passenger activity. Friends and relatives gathered at the wharf during those days while merchants engaged in a variety of business transactions.

Individuals and stock companies continued to dominate piers on the San Francisco waterfront, an approach that was taking its toll on the health of the port. There was a haphazard practice to building the piers, and pilings and platforms were given little or no maintenance over the years. They were in a perilous condition by the mid-1850s. Restoration of some piers and the replacement of others were crucial to the port. Edward Morphy quoted an

by social attitudes and prejudicial actions against Chileans, Frenchmen, and especially Mexicans, South Sea Islanders, Chinese, and Native Americans. Laws were passed in the mining districts that expressed the pervasive folly: "Neither Asiatics nor South Sea-Islanders shall be allowed to mine in this district, either for themselves or for others." By the end of the 1860s, the native American population had been further reduced to some 65,000, approximately one-sixth the original populations in California before arrival of the Europeans. The Indians had been violently displaced

road, the reverse actually took place. Before completion of the railroad, demand for labor in California was always greater than the supply. Wages were high, and for recently arrived immigrants, higher than could be earned in the countries they had left behind. With the completion of the railroad, more than 6,000 men who had labored on the enormous project lost their jobs and returned to California.

In the first year of coast-to-coast service, (May 1869 to May 1870) almost 59,000 emigrants traveled over the rails seeking every kind of opportunity in the West.

Sausalito had two ferry terminals in 1920. The Golden Gate Ferry docked on the left, and the Northwestern Pacific Railroad's ferries docked on the right. The two companies merged under Southern Pacific in 1929, and discontinued service to San Francisco in 1937. Courtesy, Sausalito Historical Society

as their land was taken by miners and new settlers; and armed conflict between Federal troops as well as self-appointed posses of settlers resulted in numerable deaths.

After the 1860s mining gave way to agriculture as the major industry of California. The transcontinental railroad in 1869 heralded the dawn of a new era for the country and was to open an exciting future for the Far West. But for the immigrants who had come to work on the

The population of California more than doubled the net increase of the ten previous years. Trainloads of Eastern goods also shared the rails, flooding the market and competing with products manufactured or produced by artisans in the West. When a financial panic hit New York City in 1873, approximately 150,000 more emigrants headed west over the rails. As if to defy the general condition, the Golden Gate Port gained renewed vitality at home and abroad.

IV

California's Bridge to the World

A new west is spread out before us, a west of water starting out from the west of land...San Francisco Bay bows in benediction, with broad anchorage to welcome commerce, and the Golden Gate an ever open door to all the world.
—H.H. Bancroft, The New Pacific, *1899*

Bay Area shipping gradually rose to meet demands from many quarters. The domestic coastwise trades were essential to the continued development of cities and towns. Needs for lumber from Northern California and the Pacific Northwest increased over time. Fishing and whaling, whether in San Francisco Bay, on the coast or in the Bering Sea, became important, thriving industries for Bay Area communities. They were to spur the development of important canneries. Passenger service, for business or tourism, proved popular on the coast. The period of the San Francisco Grain Trade, also known as the California Grain Trade, was phenomenal for its resurgence of magnificent squareriggers at a time when steamships were dominating shipping lanes around the world. The Golden Gate port was the principal terminus for this activity. The China Trade, for the first time in many years, resumed anew with transpacific steamships between San Francisco and Hong Kong, promising substantial profits well into the 20th century.

With the opening of the Suez Canal in 1869, the same year as the transcontinental railroad, the world shrank slightly. Prior to the completion of the canal, the colossal steamship line, Peninsula & Oriental, offered voyagers a formidable route from the Pacific Ocean to England. The trip averaged 55 days with changes in watercraft and stopovers at hotels. The journey went from Hong Kong to Singapore, up the Straits of Malaaca to Pennay, across the Bay of Bengal to Ceylon, by way of the Indian Ocean to Aden, up the Red Sea to Suez, overland to Alexandria, then on to Gibraltar and finally Southampton. Conditions of unbearable heat and unpredictable stormy seas were common along the way. An alternate route was offered by Alfred Holt's Line via the Cape of Good Hope, in which passengers were seabound most of the 66 days to Liverpool. There were stopovers in Singapore, Penang, and Mauritius. Graveyards of shipwrecks around the southern cape of Africa are testimonials to difficult conditions during three centuries of passages until that time.

The Suez Canal simplified travel around the world. It afforded comparatively fast, less arduous journeys to and from Europe via the transcontinental railroad of America or the Panama Isthmus. The situation offered a prime monopoly to the transportation company that controlled the American routes. In little more than ten years, owners of the Central Pacific Railroad—the Big Four, and the Pacific Mail Steamship Company, would reach an agreement to corner that control.

THE SEAMAN'S IMAGE: VOYAGE TO REFORM

The status of men who served America's merchant marine was little different from that given seamen elsewhere. That differences existed between officers and their crews was universally understood, yet the stereotypic images that burdened seamen for centuries have been little understood. Knowledge of the origins are important to gaining insight into the Bay Area as a port of call and into the persistent distortions that existed into the modern period.

Seafaring in colonial America had been for the most part confined to rivers, bays, and coves of the Eastern Seaboard and gradually included coastwise voyages to enlarge the possibilities for trade, fishing, the carrying of timber, and the hunting of seal and whale. Each enterprise was entered into on a small scale, with a family, town, or island sharing expenses. The sailing vessels were relatively small; so too was the size of each crew. The natural hazards of weather and dangerous shoals were antagonists the seafarer learned to live with as he depended on his training and skill to avoid disaster. Early commerce on the sea was primarily a coastwise industry.

In the 18th century an unnatural but common enemy appeared in the guise of the British Admiralty. The officers of man-of-wars impressed colonial seamen when the frigates were short of hands, forcibly securing men either from vessels on the high seas or through the activity of press gangs who were sent ashore to procure men from homes, taverns, or the

Facing page: *The full-rigged ship* Star of Alaska *sails north out of the Golden Gate on its annual voyage to Alaska about 1920. Originally built in 1886 in Scotland as* Balclutha, Star of Alaska *became one of the last great fleet of American sailing ships in 1904 when it was bought by the Alaska Packers Association. Every spring it would carry fishermen, cannery workers, box shooks, tin plate, and crew north for the Alaska salmon season. The* Balclutha *has been restored and preserved at Pier 43. Open to the public, it is under the jurisdiction of the Golden Gate National Recreation Area in cooperation with the National Maritime Museum Association. (NMMSF)*

streets, regardless of their occupations. The Admiralty considered the procedure legal and natural, for "subjects of the Crown" were obligated to serve the Crown in time of need. This attitude, which persisted well into the 19th century, stemmed from the belief that all men who were born English were presumed to be legally and irreversibly English, whether or not they claimed allegiance to or were citizens of the rebellious new nation of the United States of America.

Impressment was a portent of things to come in American seafaring. Historically, the well-being of a seaman was in the hands of the officers, who, on the high seas, were his supreme judges and jury. To an impressed man, the abrupt end to his livelihood, whether earned on sea or land, was a condition similar to enslavement, as he was subjugated to involuntary servitude. This practice, committed anywhere in the world and lasting almost a century, contributed to the increasingly low status that became an inseparable part of the seamen's image. Men-of-war were frequently described as prisons by the men who served them, recalling especially the hard conditions of poor and insufficient food, overcrowded and poorly ventilated

quarters, constant work, meager pay, and frequent floggings. "Where I am it is a prison," wrote an 18th-century seaman who was serving in a man-of-war. "I would give all that I had if it was a hundred guineas if I could get on shore. We are looked upon as a dog and not so good." The vivid ballad, "The Press Gang," describes the common punishment of flogging. Men received as many as 500 lashes at times.

The first thing they did, they took me in hand,
They flogged me with a tarry strand;
They flogged me till I could not stand,
On board of a man-of-war, boys.

They hung me up by my two thumbs,
And they cut me till the blood did run;
And that was the usage they gave me,
On board of a man-of-war, boys.

The months leading up to the Revolutionary War saw an increase in impressment and more severe treatment for colonial seamen, conditions that precipitated unusual protests, similar to strikes, along the Eastern Seaboard. The odious practice was successfully challenged in the War of 1812. Its essential concept, however, would

The corner of Howard and Steuart streets in 1912 was lined with sailors' boardinghouses. Boardinghouse masters served as employment agents for sailors. Men living in the boardinghouses were treated as members of a crew under the orders of the master. (NMMSF)

reappear years later with the emergence of the humiliating act, "to shanghai."

Although the specter of impressment lurked in its unpredictable fashion, life for colonial seamen and, later, Americans of the democracy, was relatively harmonious, living as they did aboard vessels among family, friends, and neighbors. They were, for the most part, homogeneous crews brought together from communities where activity on the sea was a shared means of survival, where children looked forward to seafaring life with awe, pride, and great respect.

Subtle developments would eventually change the nature of American seafaring. Herman Melville in his masterful book about life in a man-of-war, *White Jacket*, bemoans the fact that the United States Navy carried over various practices from the British Navy. He was bewildered that his own new republic would adopt the same procedures and attitudes that were the hallmarks of a cruel and despotic monarchy. Melville's concern was that the U.S. Navy emulated English systems of rank, social attitudes, and punishment. Idealistic and republican, Melville believed that officers of a republican navy should be voted into office by the men who were to serve under them. He also attacked the Articles of War, behavior, and punishment. Melville criticized the pervasive phrase "Shall suffer death," which accompanied the text of numerous infractions of law. "Of some twenty offenses," he wrote, "made penal—that a seaman may commit, and which are specified in this code, thirteen are punishable by death." Flogging was also a carryover Melville bitterly attacked, describing it as a brutal and humiliating act:

We assert that flogging in the navy is opposed to the essential dignity of man, which no legislator has a right to violate; that it is oppressive, and glaringly unequal in its operations; that it is utterly repugnant to the spirit of our democratic institutions; indeed, that it involves a lingering of the worst times of a barbarous feudal aristocracy; in a word,

we denounce it as religiously, morally, and immutably wrong.

Such laws and attitudes, Melville argued, were anachronisms in a republic that had already rid itself of royal privilege and arbitrary rule.

Melville was not alone, for reforms in the United States Navy were inevitable. They required the efforts of many reformers, especially for prohibition against use of the lash. Two years after publication of *White Jacket,* a *New York Times* editorial of September 29, 1852 suggested that problems afloat were due to the "fact that [an] aristocratic system of appointment and promotions, was taken without serious modification from England; and is unadequate to democratic institutions."

Anachronism or no, practices from the old regime continued to influence both the naval and merchant services of the United States. As deepwater trade required larger vessels, longer voyages, and greater investments to meet increased competition and the opening of new markets, foreign seamen began to dominate the forecastles of American vessels by the 1840s. These major shifts changed the earlier social and economic relationships between owners, officers, and crews and the attitudes of society toward seafaring. By the 1880s only 20 percent of all seamen were native born. To accommodate the profound changes, or perhaps to forestall major reforms, codes and attitudes from the old regime found their way into the fabric of the new one. Among others, the aristocracy of the quarterdeck retained its absolute control of the vessel and relegated crews to a near-servile condition, in many respects similar to that of their forefathers. Such rules of law on vessels precluded protection from despotic officers.

Richard Henry Dana, in his celebrated voyage as an ordinary seaman, signalled a growing concern with the statement that "a voice from the forecastle has hardly yet been heard" and complained about the brutality of officers who used the lash unconscionably. "Hell ships" evolved during the same period, whether they were

Richard Henry Dana was born in 1815 in Cambridge, Massachusetts. When he was 19 he shipped as a common sailor aboard the brig Pilgrim *to California. His* Two Years Before the Mast *chronicles his voyage from 1834 to 1836. The book was an immediate success and is considered a classic in American sea literature. During the rest of a very active life as a lawyer Dana championed seamen's rights and wrote two more important books, one of which is* A Seaman's Friend, *a manual of life aboard merchantmen under sail. This portrait dates from 1840 when Dana was 25 years old. (TBL)*

scheduled liners in which men and vessels were driven hard by overzealous and sadistic officers dubbed "bucko mates," or on board whaleships. In addition to the lash, brutal officers utilized brass knuckles and the belaying pin as frequent persuaders.

Ships masters had numerous schemes to keep the costs of voyages down, most of which cheated crews out of their wages or cut deeply into already scanty diets. Ships-masters in the whaling industry had a practice that left men stranded at the last port of call, thereby canceling the mens' wages. Shanghaiing also became prevalent on the waterfronts of the world, recalling the days of impressment; inveigled, drugged, or clubbed unconscious, those trapped men were forced to make up for the shortage of seamen or to fill vacancies left by deserters soured by the dehumanizing system. Shanghaiing escalated to an alarming degree and virtually became an institution by the last third of the century, especially in San Francisco. The business of supplying men for deepwater vessels became corrupted ultimately by the activity of unscrupulous "crimps," early hiring agents who secured men at any cost. The system of exploitation on land was forecasted earlier by Melville in the 1840s in *Redburn: His First Voyage:*

...landsharks, land-rats, and other vermin...make the hapless mariner their prey. In the shape of landlords, barkeepers, clothiers, crimps and boardinghouse loungers, the landsharks devour him limb by limb, while the land-rats and mice constantly nibble at his purse.

Brutality and mutinous uprisings aboard American vessels spawned court trials in San Francisco that received worldwide attention. Such famous clipper ships as the *White Swallow, Crusader, Sunrise,* and the *Challenge,* evoked stories of cruelty and murder that clearly exposed despotic behavior from the quarterdeck.

Communities and governments were mostly indifferent to the seaman's plight, and in major ports his movements were

generally restricted to corrupt sections of town where he became an easy target for the greedy and was exploited mercilessly. Most communities conspired through "understandings" or laws to limit the rights of men before the mast. Such action was taken by San Francisco in 1847, when the port experienced a series of desertions from vessels that touched at its shores, thus creating a precarious condition for the future of the port. Local authorities were in complete sympathy with captains and shipowners, deciding to protect their interests at the expense of crews. The town passed an ordinance that awarded $50 for apprehending a deserter and imposed six months imprisonment on any seaman captured and convicted.

From the 1850s to the turn of the century, newspaper editorials from San Francisco to New York complained about the "calibre" of seamen in the marine service. A common theme was that injustice on board vessels tended to repel rather than attract young Americans to seafaring life, and that the vacuum was being filled by the lowly immigrant, or the "dregs of society." The facts are that the majority of those seamen had fled from countries with highly authoritarian governments, strict religious codes, and static social structures, some leaving occupations that offered great toil and little reward, others leaving home because of famine and lost hope. Many had little or no command of the English language. There were also unsophisticated farm boys attracted by handbills proclaiming insincere promises about adventures at sea and exploring the world, or fishing folk from the islands of the South Pacific who signed ships' articles in cryptic symbols, men whose cultures and religions were seldom understood. The ship's boy on a noted clipper ship details in a letter to the *New York Tribune* of December 3, 1851 the composition of the crew and the tragic consequences of "driving" officers:

Such a set of sailors there never was before on any ship in this wide world. Out of 56 men, only 10 Americans. There are 12 Englishmen, 20 Irishmen, 5 Dutchmen, 4 Frenchmen, 3 Italians, 1 Swede, 1 Russian. Now, maybe you won't believe it, but I tell you, it is the honest truth, out of the 10 Americans, 7 of them are boys...
We have lost 8 men. Three of them fell overboard and 5 have died since; there were 17 sick at one time. When we get to San Francisco, I expect that all of our crew will leave and run away.

The *San Francisco Bulletin* on February 10, 1865 is a representative plea for humane treatment that was heard for more than a century:

Our shipowners complain of the lack of good material with which to make up crews for the merchant service, and yet they countenance and defend a system which tends to drive seamen who have any self-respect out of the service. If they would show by their actions that they regard the sailor as a man, with a man's feelings and a man's rights...and protect him in his rights...they might in the course of time find a better class of men enlisting in the service, and even those at present in it would become better and more efficient seamen than they are now.

Insensitive behavior toward crews was not the rule on the majority of American vessels, in which officers generally treated men with fairness and concern. There are cases where officers spoke out against those who flaunted moral codes of behavior. Yet the especially large number of brutal acts, combined with low wages and poor conditions, were enough to spur the growth of marine-related unions. In 1885 two unions, Steamshipmen's Protective Union and Coast Seamen's Union, amalgamated to become the Sailor's Union of the Pacific, an important voice for men who went to sea. The SUP published the *Red Record,* a treatise edited by one of its officers and editor of the organization's journal, Walter MacArthur. MacArthur's publication presented an irrefutable and profound statement of abuses occurring over the years. It placed before the world forum a declaration of untenable conditions that cried out for reform.

The stereotypes that characterized seamen became locked into the public's consciousness, denying those contributions that members of numerous crews, representing different nationalities and races, have made to the growth and health of the country. Seamen have been looked upon as jolly, irresponsible fools, habitually drunk, mostly brawn and little brain, and unworthy to be treated as first-class citizens. The fact that immigrants continually filled the ranks of crews was a prominent factor in perpetuating this stereotype. At the very least, each wave of population immigrating to the United States was viewed with suspicion. Since 80 percent of America's seamen were foreign born by the turn of the century, they had virtually no political power with which to draw attention to their plight.

Another difficulty was that by the latter years of the 19th century the marine service as an industry was no longer a vital force in the affairs of the nation. The Civil War, Reconstruction, and building of the West all contributed to an intense preoccupation with the land. Shipping in general conjured up images of vessels miles away from land, isolated and detached. The fact that many sailing vessels and

Right: *The crew of the Scottish three-masted ship* Glenholm *poses solemnly circa 1900. The 1916 Lloyd's Register reports that the* Glenholm *was "sunk by submarine 5/15/'15." (NMMSF)*

Below: *During the maritime and general strike of 1934, mounted police herded strikers away from Pier 38 to avoid a confrontation between union members and strikebreakers. The maneuver became a disorderly and violent melee with tear gas, pistols, and cobblestones. Two strikers were killed before Bloody Thursday was over. The strike continued and soon after became a general shutdown of city services. (TBL)*

steamships had disappeared on the high seas compounded the sense of isolation.

Such an act of total loss, with no knowledge of where the vessel sank or how it sank, with no physical evidence of the tragedy, has always been difficult to comprehend. It was also difficult to appreciate the men who would expose themselves to such a possible fate. Henry David Thoreau wrote in his impressive nature book, *Cape Cod*, that the tourist viewed the shore with very different eyes than the inhabitant of the island. The tourist came to see and admire the ocean in a storm, but the island's resident identified the stormy coastline as the place where his relatives were shipwrecked. Experience and perception were ever-growing problems for landsmen in their need to understand those who labored at sea.

Andrew Furuseth, imposing secretary of the Seamen's Union of the Pacific and president of the International Seamen's Union, entered the national scene in 1894. He believed that national legislation was essential to gaining justice for seamen. His life thereafter was devoted to lobbying in Washington, and with the help of Senator Robert LaFollett, he succeeded in getting passed the most significant Congressional law. The Seaman's Act, described as the "Seaman's Emancipation Proclamation," of 1915 was signed by President Woodrow Wilson. As a result of LaFollett's bill, in addition to two earlier laws passed in 1894 and 1898, organized seamen won reforms that were considered virtually impossible 20 years before. The legislation abolished "involuntary servitude," thereby extending protection of the 13th Amendment of the Constitution to seamen; prohibited imprisonment for desertion at home or in a foreign port; obligated shippers and masters to carry adequate provisions on all voyages; made shipowners responsible for any cruelties to seamen; stipulated that a seaman must be given one-half of the wages due him on request; abolished the "advance," the one or two months' advanced wages that were taken from seamen when they were hired, called

"blood money" in the service; and improved safety at sea through various other clauses.

San Francisco would have a long history of labor strife on the waterfront, which also involved the International Longshoreman's and Warehouseman's Union, and other sea-related organizations. It has been estimated that by the 1940s at least one-half of all employees in the city were union members, seemingly eons after the first marine union of San Francisco was organized in 1866 under the name of the Seamen's Friendly Union and Protective Society.

WHALING OUT OF SAN FRANCISCO BAY
On Front, Pacific, California, Sansome, Washington, Commerce, Battery, and Sacramento streets and Central Wharf, the

Andrew Furuseth, left, was one of the mediators who settled the longshoremen's strike of 1934. The president of the Sailors' Union of the Pacific since 1887, Furuseth was a passionate champion of sailors' rights. Known as the "Seaman's Emancipator," he influenced legislation preventing abuses endured by sailors. (TBL)

Shore whaling on the California coast began with this station on Carmel Bay in 1851. In the center of this drawing of a Portuguese station by Captain Scammon is a scaffold from which tackle was suspended. By means of the windlass blubber was pulled from the whale carcass. It was cut up in plank troughs and rendered in the try pots set in the furnace to the right with the chimneys. The rendered oil was stored in the rectangular structure which was covered with brush. The small boats in the bay were used to pursue the whales. Their range was up to 10 miles out to sea. (TBL)

maritime industry's merchants operated through good and lean years. Among others, those early whaling fleets were William Bailey's barks, *Harriet Thompson* and *Rebecca Adams;* G.B. Post and Company's schooners, *Eagle, Prince de Joinville, Francis,* and *Leverett;* Tubbs & Company's *Boston, Ocean Bird,* and *Carib;* and Captain Jared Poole's bark, *Sarah Warren.* The oil refineries on those streets were those of New Bedford Oil and Camphene Works, California Oil Works, and William Bailey. There were also the ships, chandlers, sailmakers, pumpmakers, blockmakers, sparmakers, caulkers, gunsmiths, coopers, clothes outfitters, bakers, butchers, and the numerous other shops and artisans that constituted the backbone of the growing San Francisco industry.

From the voyages of Captain Charles Melville Scammon in the early 1850s to the turn-of-the-century experience of Walter Noble Burns, the apex and decline of West Coast whaling was vividly revealed. A native of Maine, Scammon first went to sea

at the age of 15, and at 23 he skippered a trading schooner along the East Coast. The gold fever sent him in command of the *Sarah Moers,* transporting cargo and passengers around the Horn to San Francisco. Although his initial attraction was gold, the sea called him again. The reasons were eminently expressed in an article he wrote for the *Overland Monthly,* and although alluding to other seafarers, the comments obviously were also about himself:

Among the multitude of adventurers who came hither were a class of industrious, energetic, and hardy men, who, from childhood, had passed their time on board the pigmy fishing-vessels, amid the gales, fogs, and rough seas of the Atlantic, varied only by brief respites at home among friends and companions, who shared their precarious earnings. The change from the life of a mariner to that of a miner was not always congenial to these men, whose hereditary avocations were of the sea. Some restless spirits, unsuccessful in gold-hunting,

A crew of six manned the whale boats used in shore whaling on the California coast. Captain Scammon's picture shows a Greener's harpoon gun mounted on the bow of the boat. Once the whale was caught by the harpoon, bomb lances were shot into it until it was dead. The boat then towed the catch to the shore station to be processed. The captain, mate, and a crew of 14 men typically staffed a station. Each would own a share of all the equipment and would receive a share of the proceeds. (TBL)

longed to be again afloat. For this reason, there was no lack of experienced hands ready to embark in any marine venture, even in those gold-digging days.

In a few years Scammon was to become one of the most famous whalers on the West Coast. He would go on to write a series of short articles for the *Monthly* and to produce an important historical work, *The Marine Mammals of the Northwestern Coast of North America.* The book was based on 16 years in the field as a whaling captain and keen observer of marine mammals. He was most noted, however, for discovering a major breeding ground for the gray whale. It was in 1857-1858, when Scammon was in the employ of Tubbs & Company and leader of a whaling expedition to Lower California, that the significant find was made. He was commanding the brig *Boston,* accompanied by a small shallow draft schooner used as a tender, the *Marin.* The celebrated lagoon that was to bear his name is one of three connected to the Bay of Vizcaíno, some

390 miles south of San Diego. To this day Scammon's Lagoon is still called by its older name on Mexican maps, Laguna Ojo de Liebre, or "Eye of the Jackrabbit Lagoon."

The lagoon is more than 30 miles long, and Scammon and his crew were amazed to see countless gray whales, including cows with calves. There were several Kanakas and West Indians in his crew; experienced and skillful Hawaiian and black whalemen were found in the majority of hunts out of San Francisco.

Scammon returned home with his full load of 750 barrels of oil. Word got out and other whaling captains laid plans to follow the lucky skipper to the fabulous grounds the following year. The discovery marked the beginning of the end for the gray whale. Relentless hunts by fleets of whalers continued into the lagoon and off the coast into the 20th century. It wasn't until 1938 that the international community recognized that the gray was an endangered species, and a ban on further killing was imposed.

The gray whale proved a credible adversary to men in open boats. Although ostensibly a captive, being trapped in a lagoon that allowed little chance for escape to the open sea, it was found to be the most dangerous monarch of the deep. Swift and protective of its young, when threatened the gray was aggressive and attacked boats with its powerful flukes. Scammon wrote about his first hunt:

Early the next morning, the boats were again in eager pursuit; but before the animal was struck, it gave a dash with its flukes, staving the boat into fragments, and sending the crew in all directions. One man had his leg broken, another had his arm fractured, and three others were more or less injured...The relief boat, while rescuing the wounded men, was also staved by a passing whale, leaving only one boat afloat...When the first boat arrived with all its crippled passengers, it could only be compared to an ambulance crowded with men—the uninjured supporting the helpless.

Little wonder then that whalers of the 19th century nicknamed the California gray "Devil-fish," "Hard-head," and "Ripsack." Scammon, on learning that the whale was too unpredictable for an open boat to approach prior to throwing the harpoon, utilized the effective bomb-lance gun. The gun was developed to kill mammals at a greater distance than was possible with a hand harpoon.

From the whaling bark *Russell,* out of New Bedford, regarded as the first whaler to receive registry at San Francisco in 1851, a variety of sea creatures were hunted throughout the years. They yielded oil, ambergris (a base for perfume), hides, bone, attractive shells, and a great variety of food for crews. Sought out in coastal waters and deep water were the sea elephant, sea lion, banded seal, leopard seal, walrus, the sperm, bowhead, right, and gray whales, turtles, and, as Scammon noted when he took the schooner *Henry* south in 1854, "anything else which might come in our way."

The period of the Civil War was disastrous for the country's whaling fleet. On the East Coast, the Union planned to block the main ship channel to Charleston Harbor in 1861 by sinking 25 whalers, called the "stone-fleet." The effort was a failure, since, to the chagrin of the North, a better channel existed in the immediate vicinity. Also, a wash soon opened a deeper channel than had existed before. Captain Waddell, a zealous officer of the Confederacy, commanded the armed raider *Shanadoah,* once an English merchantman in the East India Trade. With a fast, strongly built clipper-ship-rig and propeller of 1,160 tons, and with 240 horsepower, it was purchased privately at Liverpool to aid Confederate forces. It carried on its gundeck eight Whitworth rifle-cannons that helped to reduce Union vessels to firewood. In addition, Waddell burned whalers wherever he found them on both oceans. He and Captain Semmes of the *Alabama,* another Confederate raider, destroyed altogether more than a million dollars worth of whalers and merchantmen. Waddell captured 11 whalers in one day at the Bering Strait and had crews taken off

eight and transferred to three. The Confederate crew of 60 then set all eight whalers on fire. Captain Waddell destroyed six San Francisco whalers in similar fashion, *Covington, Isaac Hawland, Susan Abigail, Sophia Thornton, Edward Carey,* and *William C. Nye.*

By 1866 the nation's whaling fleet was reduced to 199, and in 1871, 31 whalers were abandoned when they became trapped and crushed in Arctic ice. Those from San Francisco were *Victoria, Florida,* and *Carlotta,* the last owned by Hutchinson, Kohl & Company, a financial giant in the city at the time. Arctic tragedies would continue to reduce the fleets of both coasts. Five years later 16 more whalers would end their careers in Arctic ice, and 190 cold and mostly penniless men were brought to San Francisco in the bark *Florence.* Crews that had shipped out with scant money in their pockets earned nothing on such voyages and returned home little more than beggars.

By the 1870s some New England companies had moved to San Francisco to be closer to the whaling grounds, thereby eliminating the expense of sending vessels around the Horn and back again. Fifty whaleships would now operate out of San Francisco Bay. The bowhead whale was the most pursued at the time for its whalebone, or balleen, located in its giant jaw. The long, pliable bone was in demand everywhere for the construction of corsetts to help women attain those hourglass figures that were fashionable in the Victorian Age. When heated, the bone was easily shaped. It was also used for whips, umbrellas, walking canes, and brooms for chimney sweeps.

The 1880s and early 1890s was the peak period of San Francisco whaling, but by the turn of the century the industry had declined, becoming almost entirely dependent on bone. Petroleum products replaced whale oil. Conditions remained relatively unchanged for the men who served before the mast. Walter Burns' book, *A Year With a Whaler,* is about a hunt on board the 128-ton brig *Alexander.* Burns was attracted by an advertisement in the newspaper that read:

WANTED—Men for a whaling voyage; able seamen, ordinary seamen; and green hands. No experience necessary. Big money for a lucky voyage. Apply at Levy's No. 12 Washington Street.

All hands were given wages in the form of a "lay" assigned them when being hired. The lay was part of the worth carried in barrels of oil and bone the vessel returned with at the end of the voyage. Samuel Eliot Morison wrote that "the usual 'lay' for a three boat ship of twenty-one men, about 1804, was three-fifths of the catch to owners, one eighteenth to the master, one-forty-eighth to the 'ends-men,' one seventy-fifth to each able seamen, one eightieth or ninetieth to each negro hand, and a one-hundred-and-twentieth to the cabin boy." The share for crews decreased over the century, and the men actually made less comparatively. Walter Burns was hired and given a 190th lay on board the *Alexander.* His "runner" or crimp carried a pad of paper on which he marked the

The bark rigged steamer Herman, *formerly the missionary steamer* Morning Star, *was built in Maine in 1884. It was purchased by H. Liebes of San Francisco in 1903 as a baleen whaler and renamed. The bottom fell out of the baleen market soon after with the development of spring steel in 1907. The* Herman *was then used in the fur trade and later as a freighter. This picture shows the* Herman *in Alaska in its fur trading days, about 1909, surrounded by ice. The dogsled team used in trading is resting from work. (NMMSF)*

The bark rigged whale steamer Bowhead *has a fine harvest of baleen drying in the shrouds in this 1883 photo. It is anchored in San Francisco Bay. Telegraph Hill, topped by the observatory, is in the left background. The* Bowhead *was built in San Francisco in 1882 and owned by Charles Goodall of San Francisco. It was lost in the ice pack in Alaska in the summer of 1884. (NMMSF)*

articles that Burns was outfitted with: "a sailor's bag, a mattress, a pair of blankets, woolen trousers, dungaree trousers, a coat, a pair of brogans, pair of rubber sea boots, underwear, socks, two flannel shirts, a cap, a belt and sheath knife, a suit of oilskins and sou'-wester, a tin cup, knife, fork and spoon"—all to accommodate one year's voyage. He was also given other clothes when north, to deal with the Arctic cold, and these were added to his overall debt to owners. After being outfitted with what was probably worth no more than $10, Burns was told that his initial debt was over $50, the same amount as his advance. He would soon learn that he would not

earn enough to climb out of debt and receive solid wages by the end of the voyage. A tradition out of San Francisco at this time was the award of the "big iron dollar," as token wages "as fixed and inevitable as fate," notes Burns, at the end of the voyage.

The crew of the *Alexander* resembled hundreds of other crews in the latter half of the 19th century and into the 20th: it included Captain Winchester from New England who became first mate after the voyage to Hawaii, where Captain William T. Shorey, who took a steamer to the Islands, took over command; 60-year-old first mate Landers from Cape Cod; 45-year-old second mate Gabriel and third

mate Thomas Mendez, who spoke Portuguese and had been serving whaleships for 20 years, both blacks from Cape Verde Island; black boatsteerers Longjohn, an expert harpooner from Cape Verde, and Little Johnny, from the Island of Barbadoes; a cook, a steward, a cooper, a Kanaka cabin boy, and three other Kanakas. There was also an international group of deepwater sailors who apparently were shaken when they learned about the low wages and appalling conditions aboard whalers: Taylor, an American; Nels Nelson, a Swede described as the best sailor aboard; Richard, a German; Ole Olson, a Norwegian; and Peter Swenson, another Swede. Seven greenhands completed the total ship's population of 25: a mule skinner who had worked at Western railway construction camps; a cowboy who talked about having ridden the "hurricane deck of a bucking bronco"; a farm boy; a suspected fugitive; a former burglar; an Irishman who had served in the British Army; and an old whaleman on his seventh whaling voyage.

The *Alexander* took one of two routes that other whalers had followed since the mid-1850s—down to Lower California to Scammon's Lagoon, Turtle Bay, Ballenas Bay, and the Bay of Magdalena. The waters along the way were alive with mackerel, rock bass, bonito, and many other kinds of fish. Several whalers on the *Alexander* considered jumping ship, although like hundreds before them, they learned that the barren plains of the lower peninsula offered only death from exposure and starvation. The whalers then headed out to catch the trade winds for Hawaii, hunting sperm whales, and eventually winding up in the Arctic in the summer season, chasing bowhead and humpback whales. New England vessels would take the time at Lower California to overhaul ship and prepare boats for the Arctic hunt. Whalers out of San Francisco utilized the time on the southern coast by allowing the greenhands to practice managing the whaleboats—also by sealing, elephanting, and catching the gray when available. Whales became so scarce toward the end of the 19th century that smaller whales, once ignored, were also chased.

Walter Burns writes about the irresistible attraction of Hawaii and the surrounding islands, especially for those whalemen who had a strong desire to jump ship. They soon learned, however, that island authorities restricted seamen's movements. There was also a standing reward of $25 for anyone who turned in a runaway. *Alexander* returned to San Francisco November 1891, with 200 barrels of whale oil and 6,500 pounds of balleen.

Winter months in port were spent at a number of places in San Francisco Bay. Islais Creek near Third Street and the

Tubbs Cordage Company's large plant was one refuge. The Oakland Creek, called at times "Crik," cemetery, and Brooklyn Basin, was a protective estuary past Jack London Square and Broadway. In 1885 such vessels as *Eliza, Ocean, Arnolda, Helen Mar,* and the *Sea Breeze,* laid up there. It was not long before owners of vessels began towing their properties to Dakota Town or Dakotaville to end their whaling careers forever. At the isolated beach just south of Candlestick Park, old hulks were stripped of whatever was salvagable, then the once-active whalers were set afire. Other graveyards were at the old China Basin near Third and the Townsend Street

Looking like reeds at the water's edge, whalebone is drying in the Pacific Steam Whaling Company's yard in the Potrero District of San Francisco in the late 1880s. Drying prevented spoilage. Tied at the company's docks are the bark J.D. Peters *and the steam whaler* Orca. *(NMMSF)*

Depot, and at India Basin off Hunter's Point.

Several developments combined to bring an end to United States whaling. The country's first petroleum company was organized in 1857, and petroleum products would replace whale oil, sperm oil, and spermaceti wax as illuminating oil, lubricants, and raw materials for candles. Use of cottonseed oil followed shortly. In 1871 a Norwegian, Svend Foyn, invented the first viable harpoon gun. Until then, the sperm, bowhead, and right whales had been the primary prey of whalers. Foyn's gun and an emerging Norwegian steamship fleet allowed hunters to take on the larger "finner" or rorqual whales. The "killer" steamboats were destined to overtake the activity of the United States' whaling fleet.

Steam whalers were expensive vessels, costing more to build and operate than wooden ships. The average cost of a steamer was $80,000, while the common whaler cost $20,000. Practically no American shipper would commit the necessary capital. But there were at least two firms operating steam whalers out of San Francisco from the late 1870s to the 1890s, the Pacific Steam Whaling Company and Goodall & Perkins. Pacific Steam's *Mary and Helen* was the prototype steam whaler built in 1879. Some of Pacific's fast steam whalers were *Orca, Balaena, Beluga, Narwhal,* and *Thrasher.* But when the price of whalebone collapsed about 1908, Pacific Steam began in 1910 to phase out and lay up its remaining vessels.

Finally, continued hunting forecasted an ominous future for the mighty leviathan of the deep. A prevailing belief among members of the International Whaling Commission is that in order for whales to gain in numbers beyond the pall of extinction, years, and probably decades, are needed. Today, eight species are on the endangered list—the gray, sei, fin, blue, humpback, right, bowhead, and sperm; the Asian gray has been hunted to extinction.

GRAIN AND THE CANNERIES: SQUARE-RIGGER'S EPITAPH

California, and the San Francisco Bay Area in particular, could be considered one of the last areas of the world to generate and supply the penultimate movement of great Cape Horn square-riggers. They were the Down-Easters, what Howard I. Chapelle labeled the highest development of the sailing ship. The California Grain Trade spurred the need for those magnificent square-riggers that embodied a combination of the best of the packet and the clipper. They were not ships built for speed, but rather for large cargo-carrying capacity, unusual strength, seaworthiness, and commendable speed for the continent-to-continent passages by way of Cape Horn, which was invariably called "Cape Stiff."

Isaac Friedlander, the son of German Jewish parents, settled in San Francisco in 1849, and after a time earned a fortune through investing and speculating in the Grain Trade. The crop year of 1866-1867 was an exceptionally abundant one because of high rainfall and increasing acreage of wheat in California. Friedlander was aware that European markets were in special need of grain, but there were no current means of transport, especially for Californian and other Western grain. No transcontinental railroad existed as yet, and it would be years until the technology for transporting grain via rails was fully developed. There was also no regular service from Europe to San Francisco, as there was in the Atlantic. The hard, dry, white grain that grew in California was capable of withstanding long ocean voyages and was favored by British millers. If large volumes of the wheat could be grown by using the latest farm machinery, brought to San Francisco, then loaded on square-riggers for Liverpool, the terminus for various markets in Europe, a golden era of commerce was possible for California. Those who would benefit from such activity were numerous—growers, farm and ship suppliers, shipbuilders, timber industry, deepwater men, the produce exchange of San Francisco, and a dozen other auxiliary businesses of the Bay Area and around the world.

The trade received its impetus when Friedlander chartered vessels, guaranteeing them valuable cargoes out of San Francisco

A European ship is unloading its coal into the giant hopper in this 1886 photo of the Howard Street Wharf. The ship's yards and rigging, worked by the smoking donkey engine at the left, provide the tackle for hoisting and tipping the coal tub. The horse carts are loaded with coal from the hopper. Once the ship is unloaded it will take on grain for the homeward voyage. (TBL)

and affording them the opportunity to transport to the Bay Area coal and general merchandise. The Grain Trade flourished for some 20 years, well into the 1890s. Friedlander, who was called the "Grain King," managed a worldwide operation, from production to shipping arrangements. He employed men in the field to survey numerous farms and to project how much wheat would be available at harvest time. Friedlander then ordered his charters in accordance with need.

The grain also went to Australia, China, France, Spain, and Italy. Those years saw a phenomenal increase in grain shipment, from six million bushels in 1860 to 40 million in 1890. In 1877, however, Friedlander chartered more vessels than was required, went heavily into debt, and finally went bankrupt. Although he dominated the trade until his misfortune occurred, he did not monopolize every phase of the grain trade. Other exporting firms took part in the enormous daily activity, with business increasing

every year.

The Down Easters were built in the United States, most of wood, some of iron. The majority came from Maine, where towns like Thomaston, Searsport, Rockland, Bath, Freeport, Yarmouth, and Eastport were alive with the sounds of individual shipyards, their master shipwrights turning out unique monuments of sail. The names of the master builders, although not as famous as a MacKay or Webb, ring nevertheless with a commitment to excellence before wind and wave. There were, among many others, Samuel Watts of Thomaston, Arthur and Edward Sewall of Bath, Enos C. Soule of Freeport, and Lyman Walker of Yarmouth. Down Easters were also built elsewhere in New England: Newburyport of Massachusetts, Portsmouth of New Hampshire, and Mystic and Stonington of Connecticut.

Although the Cape Horners, which included half-clippers, medium clippers, or "full-modeled cargo carriers with no pretentions for speed," were active in the

Above: *The three-masted San Francisco bark* Golden Gate *is at a dock near the end of Montgomery Street, circa 1880. The mound of earth in the left background is intended for the construction of the seawall which was gradually being built, and changing San Francisco's shoreline. (NMMSF)*

Facing page, top: *The French iron bark* General de Negrier *at the Oakland Long Wharf is loading grain brought down the San Joaquin River. (NMMSF)*

Facing page, bottom: *The demand for California grain continued into the 20th century. This 1902 photograph shows several British vessels waiting at anchor in the Carquinez Strait to load grain at Port Costa. (NMMSF)*

Grain Trade from 1860 to 1892, the majority were Down Easters and medium built. As they had for the famous clippers, shipbuilders utilized timber from their own New England forests, constructing the frame of the Down Easter—stem, stern-post, breast-hooks, and other critical parts—of white oak. Pitch-pine was used for deck beams, inside lining, and outside planking, while massive logs made up the keel and keelsons. Knees were from the Maine hackmatack, fastened with locust wood-tree nails. Yellow metal, copper bolts, or iron bolts were commonly used throughout. Oak, white pine, and polished hardwoods made up the deckhouses. The overall result was simplicity of form and trim appearance. The Down Easters resembled the earlier clippers, with the bowsprits seeming to grow out of the sheer rather then being placed on top of it. The main differences between the clipper and the Down Easter included a line that was less sharp, almost no dead rise, and full-bottoms for the large cargo-carrying holds.

The British Cape Horners were constructed mainly of iron, although a few were of wood, and there were a handful of

steamers. They dominated the trade during the entire period. There were also Germans, Norwegian, French, and Italian Cape Horners. An example of competing relationships can be derived from a comparison during one of the most active periods. From 1881 to 1885 those vessels engaged were: 959 British; 418 American; 80 German; 20 Norwegian; 23 French; and 12 Italian. The "shipentine" vessel was developed at the beginning of the wheat period, having four masts: foremast, mainmast, mizzenmast, and jiggermast.

Over the years there was a steady regard for reducing overall operating costs and cutting the number of men needed for crews to operate ships. The change in crew numbers from the 1830s to the days of the Grain Trade was significant. Labor-saving devices for operating sails and other parts of the ship emerged over the years, although it is also true that much hard work was expected of each man regardless of the period. The huge topsails on large ships in the 1830s were extremely difficult to handle during storms. Reefing (reducing the sail area by folding, rolling, or tying up part of the sails) was a risky and time-consuming business for men who

Ten Times Round the Horn At Chain Locker Saloon

*As I was walking down London
    Road, I came to Paddy West's Inn.
He taught me the ropes of a seafarin
    man as he filled my glass with
    gin.
He said: "There's a ship a-waitin, my
    lad, and on her you'd quickly
    sign;
Her mate is a blackguard, her
    bosun's worse, but she would suit
    you fine."*
                    —Capstan sea shanty

During the 1880s on San Francisco's
Barbary Coast, Mike Connor stands
out as an imaginative boardinghouse
master whose reputation among
seamen made him a virtual folk
legend. Connor moved his early
establishment from East Street (now
the Embarcadero) to Bryant and
Main, calling his new enterprise the
Chain Locker Saloon. Although
Connor did not have a sea shanty
dedicated to his antics, one was
written about his counterpart, Paddy
West, an innkeeper in Liverpool.

Both proprietors ran mock
seafaring schools where any
"landlubber," the unemployed, or
young men with the romance of the
sea in their hearts received lessons
before a slightly different mast.
Rather than learning the trade
aboard a squarerigger or schooner,
the students, at times slightly
inebriated, undertook lessons in the
parlors and backyards of the
saloons.

Sea captains were always looking
for able seamen in those days.
Shipping was steadily declining in
the last three decades of the century,
and men were turning away from
the sea with its rigorous life and
little reward. There was a shortage
of the experienced deepwater sailor,
especially along the shores of the
West Coast.

The experienced sailor possessed a
world of practical knowledge. As
Herman Melville wrote: "The business of a thorough-bred sailor is a
special calling, as much regular trade
as a carpenter's or a locksmith's.
Indeed, it requires considerably
more adroitness and far more
versatility of talent." But in Mike
Connor's time, a sea captain was
content to get a man who had at
least furled sail, taken a turn at the
wheel, crossed the line (equator),
and made the perilous Cape Horn
passage. These requirements were
"learned" at the Chain Locker
Saloon and Paddy West's Inn.

*Now, when I had my drink, my
    boys, the wind began to blow,
He sent me up in the attic, the main
    royal for to stow.
But when I got in the attic, no main
    royal could I find;
So, I turned around to the window
    and I furled the window blind.*

Connor and West were also
crimps and sometimes shanghaiers.
Crimps were those early hiring
agents with few scruples. When they
secured a berth for a man going to
sea, they required two month's
advance of his wages, "blood money"
payable from the captain on the
spot. Wages out of San Francisco
were $25 a month, and as a result of
deals made between boardinghouse
masters and some deepwater captains
desperate for men, the seaman
generally wound up $40 to $55 in
debt. His first two months outward
bound were a "dead horse" hanging
about his neck, requiring him to
work them off before his wages
turned free and clear.

Potential sailors to Connor and
West were as good as silver coins on
their counters. The backyards of the
Chain Locker and West's Inn had a
mast complete with halyard and jib,
a ship's wheel, and inside, a very
special rope and cow's horn placed
on a table. Each of the proprietors'
wives waited with a full bucket of
water and produced a glorious spray
when the "student" took the wheel.
The lessons in seafaring, if not
strictly authentic, were nevertheless
notable for a certain amount of
inventiveness.

*Now, say that you're to the
    starboard, boys, to Frisco you'd be
    bound.
Old Paddy, he called for a length of
    rope and he laid it on the
    ground.
And we went over and back again,
    and he says to me, "That's fine!
Now, when they ask were you ever
    at sea, you can tell 'em you've
    crossed the line!"*

*It's Paddy, he pipes all hands on
    deck, the stations for to man.
His wife, she stood in the doorway,
    with a bucket in her hand.
His wife let go of the bucket, the
    water flew on its way;
"Clew up the fore t'gallant, my boys,
    she's taken in spray!"*

*"Now there's one more thing for
    you to do before you sail away.
That's to step around the table
    where the bullocks horn does lay.
And when they ask were you ever
    at sea, you can tell 'em, 'Ten times
    round the Horn!'
And by Jesus, you were a sailor
    since the day that you was born!"*

The crew of the German windjammer Elfrieda in 1912 is performing an ancient ritual in a "crossing the line" ceremony, celebrating crossing the equator. The cast included King Neptune, Queen Amphitrite, and others of the salty court. (NMMSF)

Mike Connor liked to boast that he was a religious man who could "swear on the bible" he "never told a lie." He continued to make that claim while supplying ships' captains with what he characterized as "prime seamen" who not only braved mighty sea gales but also carried discharge papers in their pockets. (Mike had gotten the papers from the bodies of dead seamen down at the morgue.) And he challenged every skeptic with the facts that his "landlubber" had indeed rounded the Horn, taken a wheel, and been aloft!

*So, put on your dungaree jackets
and walk up looking
your best.
And tell 'em that you're an old
sailor man who came from
Paddy West.*

Whether by design or accident, Mike Connor of San Francisco and Paddy West of Liverpool became similar, unique legends in the folklore of the sea.

went aloft. Captain Robert Forbes devised a rig with double topsails in 1841, a most welcome labor-saving invention. In 1854 this rig was improved to require less work aloft. In 1874, double topgallant yards and double topsail yards were used, further cutting needs aloft. Block sheaves furnished with roller bearings and hand-operated drum winches were additional labor-saving devices.

An example of the reduced size of crews can be found with reference to the *Great Republic*, which also operated in the Grain Trade. It was the largest ship in the world when built in 1855. Its builder believed the ship required 100 ablebodied seamen and 30 apprentice boys to operate the massive shipentine. Unfortunately, before its maiden voyage became a reality, it caught fire and burned to the water's edge. It was rebuilt, with the weather deck eliminated, and all spars and sails cut in size. The tonnage was reduced from the original 4,555 tons to 3,356 tons; economy and practical handling was intentionally sought. Captain Limeburner, its skipper on the eventual maiden voyage, used 50 men and a few boys, half what was needed before the fire. By the 1880s a Down Easter typically carried a crew of 25 to 35 men.

The crews remained international in scope, men joining from the major ports of the world, including San Francisco. The great majority of ships-masters came from New England, and a large number came from individual towns. Searsport, for one, sent no less than 145 captains. The impressive grain ships displayed forests of masts throughout the San Francisco Bay Region, as they stood by at North Point, Howard Street Wharf, Oakland Long Wharf, in Richardson Bay, and in the Carquinez Strait at Martinez or the warehouses at Port Costa.

Several factors combined to end the substantial participation of United States square-riggers in the Grain Trade. Iron ships were favored by the British insurer, Lloyds of London, which sent rates for the Down Easters sky high. Although there was guaranteed cargo for the British ships, those of the United States had a difficult time finding cargo at European ports outwardbound. Returning home across the Atlantic was often made in ballast. Costs for operating American vessels remained higher than their European counterparts. And the Grain Trade, in general, began to decline. As a shift in world markets took place, prices edged downward, and the soil that maintained the wheat degenerated after years of intensive overuse.

THE ALASKA PACKERS

Many of the British square-riggers entered the West Coast fishing and canning industries, purchased by an alliance of individual companies known as the Alaska Packers Association. Eventually nine steel square-riggers that were built in the United States also joined the fleet. The sturdy square-riggers fulfilled manifold needs, such as transporting cannery workers and fishing crews up to Alaska, the site of the canneries and fishing waters. The passage, about 2,500 miles, took 25 to 40 days. The salmon run began in the early part of July and lasted for some two or three weeks. The season closed when the catch was cooked, canned, labeled, and packed ready for market. Cannery workers, fishermen, and the cargo of newly canned fish returned to San Francisco on the square-riggers, usually racing against one another for the homeward voyage of some 20 to 30 days. Once through the Golden Gate and docked, the cargoes were transshipped via trains and steamers to other parts of the world. The vessels were also used as floating warehouses.

The Alaska Packer's enterprise was a successful one, beginning in 1893 and lasting until 1930, 37 years on the West Coast, providing San Francisco Bay a special heritage.

The men who sailed the ships, fished, and operated the canneries—like the whalers, fishermen, and other mariners before them—also represented the spectrum of nationalities and races—Scandinavians, Italians, Chinese, Japanese, Mexicans, Filipinos, Portuguese, Blacks, Germans, and more. Most had settled in San Francisco, Seattle, and other cities on the coast.

The square-riggers that were purchased for the cannery industry were renamed for the Alaska Packers Association's Star fleet. *Balclutha*, built in Glasgow in 1886, had been a regular sight in the years of the San Francisco Grain Trade from 1886 to 1889; it had gone from the Cape Horn experience to the transpacific Lumber Trade, then became a cannery supply vessel for the Association in 1902. It was renamed *Star of Alaska*, then *Pacific Queen*. Other vessels in the coastwise trade were *Star of Finland*, formerly known as *Kaiulani*; *Star of Greenland*, formerly *Hawaiian Isles*; *Star of Iceland*, formerly *Willscott*; *Star of Lapland*, formerly *Atlas*; *Star of Shetland*, formerly *Edward Sewall*; *Star of Zealand*, formerly *Astral*. An average of 30 square-riggers a year went north from their base in the Oakland Estuary. Once in San Francisco Bay, the ships were cleaned and fumigated before being sent to the Oakland Creek where they were laid up for the winter, overhauled, and made ready for the next season.

In 1912 the Association was operating four canneries in Alaska and had a fleet of 9 ships or barkentines, 11 barks, 3 schooners, and 62 small steamers used as tenders. Operations would eventually be handled by steamers. Maintaining the square-riggers was becoming costly and it was getting more difficult to find competent crews in an era that was overwhelmingly dominated by steam. The square-rigger would fade from active participation on the sailing lanes of the world, except for the training ships of various maritime nations and for occasional calls to duty in time of war. Its memories have been kept alive, however, by the men and women who sing its praises in a multitude of ways.

FISHERMEN AND SAILORS: THE CHINESE HERITAGE

Chinese fishing villages and camps were located in San Francisco Bay, Monterey Bay, in the Delta Country, as well as at San Diego and north at Oregon and Vancouver Island. Fishing is a quiet and unobtrusive activity and was perhaps not as dramatic or attractive as the call of gold, yet the Chinese would establish fishing camps and villages during the Gold Rush in out-of-the-way coves along the Bay.

There is a fascinating painting of a Chinese fishing village in San Francisco situated at a small cove. It depicts a bluff around the cove, with the fishermen's houses beginning at the beach and cluttering the sides and top of the bluff. The houses nearer the water are on stilts. The scene is a common one on the coast of southern China, reminiscent of hundreds of Chinese fishing villages there. The location of the village in this painting was identified as being in the south beach of San Francisco between Steamboat Point and Rincon Point, where the presence of Chinese residents was confirmed by the 1860 census. This was most probably the first fishing village established between 1850 and 1852 at the approximate shoreline between First and Second streets on Bryant (a distinctive cove was situated at Bryant and First). A careful study of an 1857 Coast Survey shows a small village of some two dozen houses; and an 1859 soundings Coast Survey chart shows the word "China" and a wharf clearly marked. The location is the same on both maps. Another map indicates an elevation in the area quickly rising to 20 feet at the beach and 40 to 80 feet behind the village, suggesting that the bluff somewhat

encircled village and cove. The settlement was secluded from the bustling activity around, especially that taking place just north at Rincon Point, the southern boundary of Yerba Buena Cove.

We know that there were about 150 fishermen, some two dozen houses, and 25 boats in the village. The painting suggests a combination of sampans and junks. Sampans are a flat-bottom craft designed to work inshore and are quite easy to pull up onto the beach like any rowboat or canoe. They were built by the fishermen of the village, using rough redwood, and they ranged from 14 to 25 feet long, 36 to 48 inches across, with identical narrow transoms at each end. Some sampans are completely open and others are partially covered over, allowing for various kinds of living arrangements. One type was propelled by sail and oars, the other by oars alone.

Junks also varied in size and design, from the enormous oceangoing vessels in China that had room for 600 people, to the small coastwise and riverine junks used for fishing and trading and as houseboats. Most have a steep sheer, high stern, broad beam, and shallow draft. High matting sails are used, simple to operate and requiring small crews.

The characteristic sail of China is the balance lug. The sail is shaped in a variety of ways, from being peaked to being

This painting by Mathilda F. Mott depicts what was probably the first Chinese fishing village in the Bay Region, at South Beach in San Francisco about 1852. The people of this village moved from South Beach around 1856, when their cove was no longer so isolated, and ambitious San Franciscans pressured villagers for their real estate of increasing value. Courtesy, Fine Arts Collections, California Historical Society, San Francisco

These two fishermen were aboard their fishing vessel on San Francisco Bay in the 1880s. The Chinese usually used the sampan for shrimping, staking out nets across the tides so the shrimp could be caught as the water rushed against the nets. (NMMSF)

flattened out into a square-headed lug. The sail is stiffened by battens of bamboo, each connecting and forming part of the sheet. Thus it is very flat. Riverine and bay sails are usually flat-headed, narrow, and very tall to take advantage of whatever breeze is in the vicinity. The number of battens on a sail vary greatly, sometimes 20, 30, and more. The batten also simplifies reefing; it allows more time to keep on sail, and when needed, can be reefed quickly; sailcloth can be of relatively weak material, for the strain of wind is evenly distributed over battens and sheets; battens also enable a man to go aloft, as he would use the rungs of a ladder to ascend. The Chinese sail has been called one of the most efficient in the world.

Like the sampans, the junk has no keel, using a large rudder for stability. The rudder is attached at the stern and could be lowered or raised when needed according to the depth of the water. The rudders were unusually large in relation to the overall size of the junk, and the sight of rudder, hull, and sails on San Francisco Bay and tributaries added another dimension to the international nature of the port. The largest junks were 59 feet

long, although the most common were 45 feet long, 12 feet wide, and 4 feet deep, carrying from one to two sails.

The fishing village south of Rincon Point disbanded by 1865. An expanding city, speculation in real estate, and waterfront development no doubt crowded out the fishermen, who most likely moved on to safer and more isolated areas. An intriguing real estate venture took place when the Pacific Mail Steamship Company built a new dock in the South Beach Area. It chose the waterfront at First Street and Brannan, approximately one block away from where the cove of the early fishing village had been situated. The steamship company and the Chinese would have many future close ties. The whole area, village, cove and mail dock, was eventually filled in and closed off by the great seawall.

Chinese shrimp fishing villages and camps were also established at China Beach, Point San Quentin, and Hunter's Point in San Francisco; Point San Bruno; Point San Mateo; near Redwood City; at Burlingame; Point Richmond in the East Bay; Point San Pedro and Tamales Bay in Marin County; and at Newark in the South Bay.

When the transcontinental railroad was complete, the population of the villages increased with men who had just lost their jobs. Many remained and earned their living by fishing. By the late 1880s approximately 30 fishing villages ringed the bay in practically all Bay Area counties, and the overall population was as high as 4,000 during the fishing seasons. The two largest villages in Northern California were at Point San Pedro in Marin County and the settlement at Monterey Bay. Both were extensive communities of several hundred people each that included at least one general store, a temple, a gaming house, and, in Marin County, a school.

Laws were passed against the bag nets the fishermen used for catching the shrimp. Such regulations were justified in the name of conservation; but, on the other hand, they were being passed during periods of intense anti-Chinese feeling. In 1892, when the Chinese Exclusion Act was

This Chinese fishing junk sailed San Francisco Bay about 1895. By 1885 over 50 Chinese shrimping vessels, sampans and junks, operated on the bay, employing as many as 4,000 men in various aspects of the harvesting and processing of the bay shrimp. (NMMSF)

renewed, the graceful junks and sampans—several hundreds of which had been built in the Bay Area over the years—were considered "alien vessels."

Shrimping had been a big business in California. In 1895, for example, the shrimp catch was worth $162,749, about $40,000 more than the state's salmon catch. It was not long after that most Chinese fishing communities went into a decline. Anti-Chinese legislation and ever tighter restrictions made it extremely difficult for the Chinese fisherman to continue. Another factor was the steady pollution of the bay and bay fill, reducing shoreline that was used for shrimp beds. China Camp in Marin County, once one of the largest villages, is the last to survive and has been designated a California State Park. Frank Quan, literally the last of the shrimp fishermen in the bay, is a descendant of those fishermen who were part of a community that was an active, thriving enterprise of the Bay Region.

It is fascinating to remember that the bay at one time had many junks and sampans moving here and there, harvesting their shrimp, drying it on the beaches and hillsides, taking it to market, and sending much of it by way of the Pacific Mail

steamers to China. Larger junks have stood off Monterey Bay and would eventually take their catch of abalone to market in San Francisco, where a portion of it would be also shipped to China. Sandy Lydon, scholar of Chinese fishing in Monterey County, tells us that local tradition speaks of huge ocean-going junks taking the catch directly from that bay to China. When the abalone was scarce, the Chinese south of San Francisco, who had universal tastes, caught the great variety of food offered by the bountiful ocean: shad, salmon, smelt, squid, halibut, flounder, mackerel, rockfish, herring, yellowtail, sardines, cod, and sharks.

Chinese have also served numerous vessels that plied the waters in and out of San Francisco Bay. As seamen, the Chinese were the backbone of the great movement of transpacific ocean liners from 1876 to 1916.

With the aid of a $500,000 Congressional subsidy, the Pacific Mail Steamship Company made its first transpacific run in 1867. Seven years later the Occidental & Oriental Steamship Company, incorporated in California, arranged to charter ocean liners from the popular White Star Line of Liverpool and made its first transpacific

Steerage passengers confined to the vessel's deck are seeing America for the first time. (NMMSF)

run in 1876. Thus, the significant movement of transpacific voyages began, and by 1916 their combined fleet of some 27 vessels had made more than 1,000 round trips between San Francisco and Hong Kong, via Yokohama.

The steamships were large, ranging in weight from 2,600 to 5,000 tons, and utilized steam and sail for motive power. During the years of operation, they carried all types of cargo, immigrants, tourists, members of the clergy, government representatives, naval officers, students, and others eager to reach their destinations with dispatch. They were part of the critical transition from sidewheelers to propellers and from sail to steam. The early wooden sidewheelers were the largest ever built anywhere. They were primarily steamships with auxiliary sails, while the British mail ships resembled sailing ships with steam merely added. The maritime industry was still dubious about eliminating sail altogether, and it is a fact that several

of the vessels depended entirely on sails when they ran out of the wood and coal that fueled them.

Although representing a unique naval design, the sidewheelers were practically obsolete by the time they were built. Their most serious defect was a high susceptibility to fire. The wooden hulls were of strong construction, able to withstand gales and typhoon seas. Each carried from two to three towering masts with sails and a 1,500-horsepower engine, with a driving paddle wheel 40 feet in diameter. The coal bunker accommodated 1,500 tons, for each vessel burned approximately 45 tons of coal a day. Those first sidewheelers were called "floating palaces" and had three full decks. They were the *Colorado, Japan, Great Republic,* and *America.*

The later steamships, like those of Occidental & Oriental, were the most advanced for their time. E. Keble Chatterton, a leading British maritime historian, wrote of the *Oceanic* that its designers had simply thrown "convention to the wind and set going a completely new order of things in the steamship world." They had endowed the *Oceanic* with a revolutionary length of 420 feet, introduced a new type of watertight door, and extended its saloon, which had a library, grand piano, and two fireplaces, across the width of the ship, allowing for good lighting and easy observation through the large portholes to the outside. For the first time the saloon and staterooms "were placed not at the stern of the ship," according to maritime historian E.K. Chatterton, where the vibration and jarring of the propeller were most felt, "but amidships and forward of the machinery." When launched in 1871, its four imposing masts, three carrying enormous square sails, and its 3,000-horsepower, four-cylinder compound engines, gave it the ability to maintain almost 14 knots (or approximately 16 statute miles an hour) over the great ocean routes. The other early steamships for Occidental & Oriental were the *Belgic* and the *Gaelic.*

Operation of each of the steamships with engine room, cabins, steerage, saloons, and masts, required sizable crews that ranged from 70 to 175 members. After 1900, larger steamships weighing more than 11,000 tons, such as the *Korea* and *Siberia,* and the *Mongolia* and *Manchuria,* weighing more than 13,000 tons, required crew sizes of 260 to 300.

The two steamship companies came to a cooperative arrangement after the owners of Occidental, California's "Big Four" (Leland Stanford, Charles Crocker, Mark Hopkins, and Collis Huntington), challenged Pacific Mail on the route it had already been servicing for nine years. The threat amounted to a rate war, and it was the most serious threat confronted by Pacific Mail since the early coastwise days. The Big Four controlled the continental railroad as well as much of the inland water transportation of Northern California, and hoped to gain a far-reaching monopoly by launching its own transpacific steamship line. The

mutual agreement had the two companies sharing the Pacific Mail facilities and docks, alternating sailing schedules, and becoming the major transporter of Chinese immigrants and trade in the Western Hemisphere. For 30 years the companies provided an average of 32 round voyages a year. Occidental ended operations in 1907, and Pacific Mail stopped temporarily in 1915, when thereafter, Chinese sailors were no longer hired as crew members.

The officers of all the steamships were Caucasian, while remaining crew members were Chinese. A representative crew list from the *City of Tokio* in 1884 reveals the Chinese crew included two boatswains, 24 seamen, 24 firemen, and 30 coal passers, in addition to cooks, stewards, cabin boys, WC boys, storekeepers, bakers, porters, pantrymen, and waiters. Caucasians were captain, chief, second and third officers, four engineers, purser, surgeon, clerk, carpenter, three quartermasters, stewards, and stewardesses.

The number of individual Chinese positions held over the 30-year period was 78,433 and the average total sum—considering the years before 1867 and after 1906—was over 80,000. Some seamen were undoubtedly hired for more than one voyage; yet a high percentage were not, since thousands of seamen were available for hire in China, and Hong Kong was a major "free port," the "Emporium of the East" that attracted steamships and ships under sail from all over the world. San Francisco was an attractive port of call for many reasons, and substantial Chinese communities had taken roots throughout the West, especially the Bay Area. In the early days the majority of seamen were recruited in Hong Kong, but as years passed, many received various immigration papers.

G.R.G. Worcester, in his monumental work, *Junks and Sampans of the Yangtze,* wrote the following about the Chinese sailor: "(He) appears to flourish not only in his country, but abroad...Chinese were employed very successfully as sailors by the early East Indiamen; so they were initiated to the foreign style of ships and gear a

and the growing immigration restrictions of all Chinese, ended a unique period in the maritime heritage of the Bay Area.

Officers and crews of the transpacific steamships were proud men operating vessels that represented outstanding developments for deepwater. Those years would also represent the highest numbers of immigrating Chinese to the United States. This was the time when the greatest hopes for the coveted China Trade evolved. Approximately 300,000 Chinese traveled to San Francisco from 1850 to 1915, and half that number returned to China in the same period. The steamship

Above: There is a cheerful sense of community in this picture of Italian fishermen in the early 1890s. The scene is the Taylor Street Wharf in San Francisco. Fishing boats are pulled out of the water for painting. The group of men in the foreground are mending a net and swapping tales. The disk-shaped cork floats on the net are familiar to present-day beachcombers, reminders of this aspect of San Francisco's heritage. Courtesy, National Archives

Right: Jack London, the noted Oakland author, took this photo and the one on the following page in 1904, homeward bound from his stint as a foreign correspondent on the Russo-Japanese War. This is a rare view of Chinese seamen at work on an American steamship, the Pacific Mail's Siberia. Courtesy, Robert J. Schwendinger, Jack London Estate

very long time ago...Their courage and skill in navigating and handling their own junks about the China seas is well known. Such work for generations past amid perilous conditions has evolved a hardy race of seamen, whose skill and resourcefulness is second to none in the world."

Unfortunately, the Seamen's Act of 1915 was not only designed to rectify past injustices for seamen, but also to keep Chinese from working on vessels in the United States Marine Service. The Act,

companies fared well and earned good dividends for their shareholders, and rigorous timetables were kept.

The maritime community recalls the period with an exhilaration that echoes the clipper days. Roy Anderson, in his *White Star*, writes that W.H. Smalliman, an officer of the *Oceanic*, recalled: "No merchant ship ever sailed the seas that was so embowered in sentiment as the *Oceanic*. All the time we had her at San Francisco she was a great favourite of the travelling public and of people who took interest in ships. She

was the first modern steamer that floated on the waters of the Bay of San Francisco and even to this day the old mariners speak of her beauty and smart lines. She was just as much of a clipper-ship as she was a steamer. And, oh my, how that ship could sail!"

THE ITALIAN HERITAGE

The call of gold probably attracted the first Italian fishermen to San Francisco, yet at some point these men decided that the practical and dependable gold was the fishing resource of the bay and coastal waters. At first, these immigrants, such as the Genovese, came from Northern Italy, primarily the province of Liguria; then Sicilians, Calabrians, and Neopolitans came from the south. Their occupations for the most part had been tied to the sea and like other immigrant groups, their expertise proved eminently useful in the waters of California.

Many of the early Italians came on vessels direct from Italy and France and disembarked at the North Point Docks, built in 1853 from Sansome Street and just below Telegraph Hill. This "North Beach" area evolved into the Italian quarter of the city.

The fishermen in the 1850s were generally scattered among the growing wharfs of Cunningham, Law's, and Vallejo Street, until an early center for the fleet of *feluccas* developed at the foot of Telegraph Hill, and later at the Filbert Street Wharf, which was called "Italy Harbor." In 1900 a final move was made when the State Harbor Commission provided "Fisherman's Wharf" at the present site of Taylor and Jefferson streets.

In 1871 men such as Pietro Aiello decided that New York Landing (presently Pittsburg), was a good place to settle in, as well as an inviting port for fishing. We are told by John A. Buffo, teacher and scholar, that Aiello probably identified the appearance of the shoreline at that part of the Carquinez Strait with his own Mediterranean homeland and Sicilian town, *Isola delle Femmine*. Not too long after, these hardy fisherfolk also settled around Monterey Bay, San Diego, and other places, keenly aware of the rich potential of the sea.

That early sturdy fishing boat, the felucca, has Mediterranean origins. It had a shallow draft bottom, long, narrow cockpit, and triangular lateen sail, one or two in the traditional brown color. The boats were usually painted white, and many had wide bands of bright colors along the

Chinese passengers from steerage and cabin classes gather on the main and upper decks of the Siberia. They wear a mixture of modern and old world dress for their arrival in Honolulu. Courtesy, Robert J. Schwendinger, Jack London Estate

97

topsides, from the rail cap to one stroke below the plank-sheer. The decks were painted yellow, green, or blue. They were made of oak and cedar. Oars were also used, and when sailing along the coast, they carried from 500 to 1,500 pounds of ballast.

The felucca would give way to the Monterey Clipper about 1912, a bigger and more durable fishing boat with a clipper bow, able to accommodate larger crews and overnight living. The hand-started gasoline engine would also appear, invented by San Franciscan Frank Hicks. The engine freed the boats from their dependence on the whimsical wind and gave the fishermen a freedom of movement previously unknown.

The Italian fishermen caught a variety of fish—herring, oyster, salmon, crab, perch, striped bass, rock cod, tuna, sardines, and to a lesser extent, shrimp. They fished in a wide range of waters, from the Sacramento and San Joaquin rivers to San Francisco Bay, and between Monterey and the Golden Gate. Their catch was brought to the markets in San Francisco and sold to

brokers who controlled aspects of the market, and who at times exploited the fishermen severely. The fishermen were small-scale entrepreneurs for the most part, individual owners of boats who were vulnerable to greedy wholesalers. The need for some form of protection was inevitable, and the fishermen banded together in successive organizations: The Fishermen's Association, the Fishermen's Mutual Aid Society of San Francisco, the Crab Fishermen's Protective Association, Rock Cod Association, and others. At times, tempers flared over the Crab Trusts of brokers, and volatile "crab wars" ensued, the price of crabs plummeting to five cents apiece.

Local government would also create conflict with the passing of discriminatory laws against ethnic groups. In 1864, the San Francisco supervisors moved against the Chinese by requiring them to pay a quarterly license fee of $25.00. Many Chinese street sellers bought fresh fish from Italian fishermen and the arbitrary license threatened a range of economic relationships. Italians protested, striking and forming their first union.

Fishing season for the crab-fishing fleet went from November through August, the fleet usually leaving the wharf with the tide. Fishing gounds, where the boats anchored, were three to six miles outside the Golden Gate. The boats returned in mid-afternoon with as many as 48 crabs apiece. The sardine fleet had larger vessels, schooners and trawlers with deep after-holds, in which Slavonians, Norwegians, and Italians worked the coastal waters as far north as Alaska and as far south as Mexico. These vessels were powered with 200 to 300 horsepower diesel engines and the season was usually August through February. Bottom-fish vessels used the *paranzella* net, which was managed between two boats and dragged along the ocean floor. The nets trapped rock cod, flounder, sand dab, sole, and at times starfish, octopus, and shark.

The sardine catch was described as a "silver harvest," for the schools of fish were caught on moonlit nights, and they gave off an iridescent flash as they moved through the water. The iridescent effect was most vivid when the catch was being hauled on board, the moonlight heightening the silvery color of the sardines. The *lampara* net was used until about the 1930s, an invention brought over from Italy. It was a closely woven bag, in the center of which were attached two wings. The net was laid out around the school of fish, and when the lead line and two wings were hauled in, the fish were forced into the center bunt. The *purse seine* net was adopted by the larger vessels; capable of holding a greater catch than the *lampara* net, it is maneuvered in a circle by means of a skiff, then drawn together similar to the action of a drawstring on a tobacco pouch.

Cannery Row in Monterey was famous for its sardine canneries. At the high point of the industry there, 69 mainly Italian-owned boats kept 19 canneries operating, employing some 3,500 people. Women were in the majority at the canneries, among Chinese, Japanese, Mexicans, and others. In one year, 235,000

tons of fish were processed. At the height of the sardine fishery in San Francisco Bay in the 1930s, the fleet amounted to 466 boats. The total number of fishing vessels in California overall at the time was 2,453.

The early 1950s were disastrous for California's sardine industry. The species declined rapidly, until the fish was no longer available. Numerous theories have been offered for the phenomenon—over-fishing and polluted waters as well as the fallout from atomic bomb explosions. Whatever the reason, the disappearance of such an enormous resource was especially hard on the Italian community. Readjustment took years for many fishermen.

The Italian fishing experience is still with us. One need only visit Fisherman's Wharf or watch the boats go out each season to see evidence of the area's Italian maritime heritage. Although the fleet is not as large as in prior years and the industry has changed considerably, one only need to peruse the telephone books of San Francisco, Monterey, Pittsburg, and Martinez to find the names and descendants of these pioneer fisherfolk.

Circular crab nets are ranged on one side of the pier; large nets are hung on the rail to dry. The feluccas are at home in their sheltered Taylor Street dock after the day's work. The strong patterning of diagonal masts and gaffs gives this picture of 1890 an exotic flavor. A British iron grain ship rides at anchor out in the bay. Courtesy, National Archives

V

The Modern Port

The sea and the earth are unfaithful to their children; a truth, a faith, a generation of men goes—and is forgotten, and it does not matter. Except, perhaps to the few of those who believed the truth, confessed the faith—or loved the men.
—Joseph Conrad, The Mirror of the Sea, 1905

The latter half of the 19th and early 20th centuries were important years for shipbuilding on the West Coast. It was a time when shipyards came into their own, producing unique regional vessels for the growing industries of the West. Practical vessels were developed and indigenous materials were used. Various cargo required carriers of particular design.

The lumber schooner went through several stages before arriving at the most practical for the long, rugged redwood coast, and the vast deepwater of the Pacific Ocean. The single deck, two-to-three mast schooners commonly referred to as "doghole" schooners, were suitable for a time. Hulls were broad and beamy, carrying cut lumber in large holds and, usually, bigger loads above decks. They were able to maneuver into numerous coves along the coast which had "landings" or "outports," where they were loaded from ingenious contraptions. The vessels took lumber from long apron chutes extending out over the bluffs or from "under the wire," picking the lumber off aerial tramways. Some outports had a wharf or a mill on the site, or lumber was placed in a box-like vessel and floated to the schooner, or the wood was shuttled by small tugs. Many of the outports were extremely tight and the loading process was potentially dangerous. Here was a coastline whose wind chart is studded with wind roses, symbols of weather activity that characterizes the northern coast. Here is a lee shore where a "blow" could charge down from the Northwest, and, aided by a rough sea, invariably dash unsuspecting sailors against the rocks. The size of the outports increased the danger, and they were described by the incredulous as being only big enough for a dog to turn around in. Fog was another adversary, especially in summertime. And, since there was no railroad of any consequence going south, these schooners performed multiple services; they also carried mail, produce, and passengers to and from the city by the Golden Gate. Utility chutes built near the lumber companies' chutes accommodated the more mundane cargoes. Sturdily built,

with shallow draft and extra wood on the bottom for additional strength and weight, the schooners managed the course without ballast, a plus for vessels carrying virtually nothing in one direction.

Redwood is an exceptional building material—water resistant, rot resistant, and a "slow burn." The city that had experienced many fires, that refused to die and continued to grow, along with the ever-expanding communities of the Bay Area, placed heavy demands on the timber. The earthquake and fire of 1906 and the tremendous need for more wood kept the pressure on for increased logging. The railroads, at first regional short lines which were extending hookups north, south, east, and west, also demanded redwood for railroad ties. In addition to supplying the early needs of the mines, the wood provided other products: shingles, sidings, shakes, paneling, flooring, fence posts, pilings, cigar boxes, coffins, and many others.

REFINING THE SPECIALIZED CARRIER
The discovery of Douglas fir and its outstanding use as a shipbuilding material led to an important shift in lumber centers from San Francisco to the northwest corner of California, Oregon, and Washington. As a shipbuilding material it afforded unusually great lengths, had strength, was light, and when processed correctly, resisted dry-rot. The magnificent schooners that were built of Douglas fir were comparable to the best ships of the East made from oak.

Now the entire coast from Northern California to the Pacific Northwest with its vast stands of coastal timber would be available for foreign as well as domestic markets. Shipbuilding yards rose nearer the sources of redwood, Douglas fir and other species, and the development of larger, faster coastwise and transoceanic schooners and barkentines provided another step toward the development of the timber industry. As though an appeal went out to satisfy the needs of the twin industries of shipbuilding and timber, burgeoning population centers formed in the Puget Sound area, on the Columbia River, and at Coos and Humboldt bays.

Facing page: *The Excelsior was a coastal lumber schooner, shown here moored at John Rosenfeldt's Sons' coal wharf. The Excelsior is taking on passengers for Skagway during the Alaska Gold Rush in 1897. When the gold fever subsided the little steamer went back to transporting lumber. Its career was brought to an end in 1916 when it collided with the passenger steamer Harvard in the Golden Gate. The Excelsior sank in fairly shallow water. Rescue attempts failed and the Excelsior was carried out on the tide near Point Bonita. (NMMSF)*

Facing page: *The steam schooner* Whitesboro *is moored at the L.E. White Company's chute at Greenwood Landing on the Mendocino Coast. A load of lumber is on the rails going toward the chute from the top of the bluff. The car is controlled by a cable. At the point where the trestle levels off there is a switch. With this cable and switch arrangement, a car going down the track could pull a car on the other track up to the top of the bluff.* (NMMSF)

Left: *The lumber schooner* Big River *enters San Francisco Bay, hold and deck stacked with roughly sawn planks obtained from the mills of Humboldt and Mendocino counties. The broad beam and sturdy build of the lumber schooners made it possible for them to sail back up the coast without ballast against the prevailing northerly wind.* (TBL)

Left, below: *George Davidson of the United States Coast and Geodesic Survey said of Newport Landing in Mendocino County that it was "one of the most contracted anchorages on the coast." The lumber schooner is moored facing seaward. The stake in the center foreground holds the stern mooring line. There are other lines on buoys and submerged rocks on all sides. It was difficult to make a vessel secure in a situation such as this, and when Fort Bragg Harbor opened in 1887 Newport Landing was abandoned.* (NMMSF)

The Black Heritage of the Bay Area

The black heritage of maritime history in the San Francisco Bay Area spans over a century of involvement, at times invisible, yet ever present. One of the earliest-known black seamen was Allen Light, who sailed during the time of the Mexican Republic.

Light served on the same ship as did Richard Henry Dana. When the brig anchored off San Diego in 1835, Light jumped ship, saying farewell to the poor living conditions and moody officers of the *Pilgrim*. He was a good marksman and immediately made an alliance with hunters of sea otters, George Nidever, Joseph Walker, and a Kanaka called Sparks. They were successful in their forays after otters in the Channel Islands, but knew they eventually had to become citizens of the Republic if they wished to hunt legally. They took their vows. Allen Light, who was now called "Black Steward" by his colleagues, became a Mexican citizen in 1838. The authorities in California were

attempting to reduce the wholesale killing of otters, realizing that the mammal needed protection from extinction. The *contrabandistas*, Russians, English, and New Englanders, continually engaged in illegal hunting, at times precipitating armed conflict. Allen Light was appointed special commissioner by the Mexican governor and was instructed to use force, if necessary, to prevent the illegal activity. By 1843 Light had settled comfortably in Mexican California, becoming an employer in the otter business.

From the early days of whaling in the Pacific Ocean, New England whalers discovered that it was to their advantage to leave on the outward-bound voyage with small crews and supplement them in the West Indies or to have transplanted Portuguese from the Cape Verde Islands on board. Here were experienced whalemen and fishermen. After some time, it was a common sight to see black men as "harpooners" as well as serving

other critical roles. By the turn of the century many of the laborers on whalers were black teenagers.

William Alexander Leidesdorff was a native of the Virgin Islands. His mother was black; his father was a Dutch planter. He spent some time in New Orleans where he made his fortune as a cotton broker, then immigrated to San Francisco in 1841 while captain of a schooner. He became a citizen of stature, building the first hotel in the city and a large warehouse at Yerba Buena Cove. He acquired land on the American River, became the first treasurer of the new city government, ordered the first steamer to ply the waters of San Francisco Bay, was a member of the first school board, and served as a United States vice-consul. A street was named after him. He died prematurely in 1848, struck down by typhus.

Captain William T. Shorey was a native of Barbados, who, at the age of 24 moved to San Francisco in 1883. Having been to sea since he

was 14 years old, much of his experience was on whalers where he learned navigation. Shorey settled in Oakland and was to become one of the Bay Area's well-known skippers, master of the *Harriman, Andrew Hicks,* the *John and Winthrop,* and the *Alexander.* He was known to have all-black crews as well as interracial ones, and also took his wife along on voyages. He died in 1919, after a long career in the maritime industry.

Captain Michael Healy was a member of the Revenue Service, forerunner to the Coast Guard. He rose in the ranks to become captain of the *Bear* in 1883. A steam barkentine, the *Bear* patrolled the Pacific Northwest from Alaskan waters to the Arctic Ocean. He enforced quotas on sealers, was involved in crucial rescue efforts, and attempted to protect native populations from unscrupulous mariners. He and Captain Shorey are believed to have been the only black captains on the West Coast in the 19th century.

The black heritage was strongly felt during World War II when the population of the Bay Area increased with a large black migration, principally from Louisiana, Texas, Arkansas, and Oklahoma. Opportunities for employment had opened up in the shipyards of the Bay Area, the

most noted yard in Marin County, called Marinship. In 1942, the black workforce of the Bay Area constituted three percent; by 1945 it had increased to more than 10 percent. There was an overall 22,000 employees at the Marinship plant alone. Black shipyard workers there became intimately involved in turning out the remarkable Liberty Ships, among others, during the war.

The most significant development for organizing black seafarers was the founding of the Marine Cooks and Stewards Union in 1901. Blacks as well as Chinese were barred from other unions. Those service positions on vessels — cooks, stewards, and others — were traditionally filled by blacks,

Chinese, and Filipinos. With the formation of Marine Cooks and Stewards, men and women finally found an important voice and protection for the union's members. Still a viable and integrated organization, the union is an arm of the Seafarers' International Union.

In the 1930s, blacks would also become an integral part of the longshore experience in the Bay Area. They were integrated into the West Coast Longshoreman's Union as part of a policy laid down by Harry Bridges, leader at the time. By 1950, about one-quarter of West Coast longshoremen were black, and in San Francisco, the percentage was just under one-half.

Facing page, top: *On a placid day on the bay about 1900, the scow schooner* Regenia S, *built in 1893, sails by the Embarcadero. In the late 19th and early 20th centuries scow schooners were the primary means of bringing goods from the areas around the bay to the markets of San Francisco.* (NMMSF)

Facing page, bottom: *Well into the 20th century, the lumber companies of Northern California and the Pacific Northwest continued to be major shippers and shipowners. Here, the steam schooner* Svea *unloads its cargo (it was able to carry 700,000 board feet) at the Hogan Lumber Company at the foot of Alice Street, Oakland, about 1915-1920. Thanks to federally funded dredging and wharf-building, Oakland at that time enjoyed increased shipping activity. Courtesy, Oakland Public Library.*

Left, top: *There were many shipyards around San Francisco Bay. This one in Oakland Creek is building a steam schooner. Its stem post rises straight from the solid keelson which runs the length of the hull like a spine.* (TBL)

Left, bottom: *The American bark* Majestic *is hoved down at the Beale Street Wharf while workers recaulk the hull. The copper sheathing has been peeled back for this operation, and once the hull is recaulked it will again be sheathed in copper. Copper is a good material for this purpose because it repels shipworms.* (TBL)

Around 1885 the focus of West Coast shipbuilding would return to San Francisco to fill a particular need. It was here that the steam schooner—the ultimate "dog-hole" vessel—was built. Here were the necessary iron foundries and machine shops for constructing these workhorses of wood, iron, (and eventually steel), that were propelled by the steam plant. No longer captive to the capricious wind, the more powerful and larger steam schooner carried heavier loads, accommodated more passengers, and completed voyages in shorter time. Yet the builders of these marvelous vessels were conservative designers: the early steam schooners were built with auxiliary sails.

The beamy, shallow-draft hull remained a design characteristic of the schooner to achieve good cargo-carrying capacity and access to difficult ports, but other design features evolved. The most significant was the changeover from the single-ended design, with deckhouses at the stern, to a double-ended design, with deckhouses amidships. This allowed for more efficient loading machinery, thus cutting time in port.

The active lumber trade to Hawaii, Australia, China, and the west coast of South America utilized at first large schooners carrying as many as four to five masts, followed by the barkentine rig which became the favored vessel, with square sails on the foremast only. Such an arrangement was more adaptive to the open ocean, and it improved speed. The coastwise vessels were mostly from 100 to 400 tons while the deepwater sailers were usually over 500 tons.

Ships of the National Maritime Museum.

The numerous shipbuilders along the coast at such places as San Francisco; North Bend, Oregon; and Hoquiam, Washington were all inextricably tied to the maritime heritage of the West Coast. A few of the foremost builders in California were Matt Turner, Thomas Henry Peterson, and Hans D. Bendixson. Turner sent down the ways early brigs, barkentines, and schooners at San Francisco, Benicia, and Eureka. He built a total of 201 vessels, such as the brigs *Claus* and *John Spreckels,* and four-masters *La Merced* and *Cronkite.* Peterson turned out two-to four-masted schooners, steam schooners, and tug boats, at San Francisco, Mendocino County, and Washington State. They included the three-masters *James Townsend* and *Peerless,* and steam schooners *Lakme* and *Luella.* Bendixson built over 100 vessels from 1869 to 1900, with two-to five-masted schooners and steam schooners for the lumber, fishing, and Tahiti Island trades, in addition to barkentines, a battleship, and a six-master which had been converted from a two-master, all at Eureka or Fairhaven in Humboldt Bay. Bendixen is the builder of the steam schooners *Wawona* and the *C.A. Thayer.* The former is currently in Seattle awaiting restoration as a floating museum. The latter is in San Francisco at Historic

The coastwise lumber trade was remarkable for its high concentration of Norwegian, Swedish, and Danish seafarers, approximately 40 percent overall. They were called affectionately or pejoratively the Scandinavian or "Scandahoovian" Navy. They and other nationalities and races raised their rough and dangerous calling to an art.

The oil produced from Southern California wells by the end of the 19th century was being moved, for the most part, by barges. Sailing vessels would also help, such as the *Falls of Clyde,* once owned by the Bishop Museum of Hawaii but recently secured by a private fund-raising group in the islands. The

steamer *Whittier* heralded in the age of tankers in 1903. Development of these huge floating vessels went through various stages for safety and reliability. Their carrying capacity increased from 20,000 deadweight tons to a supertanker load of 200,000 to 300,000 tons of crude oil which was stored in as many as five gigantic tanks. The latter are the largest of any man-made objects afloat, reaching lengths of more than 1,000 feet and 160 feet across. These enormous tankers have challenged builders and seafarers with a technology unlike any other on the open sea. Much too large for seaports, the supertankers have been accommodated with pipeline terminals anchored as much as ten miles

A 154.   O. S. S. Cos. Steamer, "Mariposa," Capt. Howard.

off the coast. Tankers entering the Golden Gate to dock at the long wharf of Point Richmond are smaller and have been calling there for years. Once Standard Oil's facility, it is now part of Chevron U.S.A.

Modern specialty carriers have changed the nature of crew life, having virtually eliminated traditional turnaround time in ports of the world. The crew of a supertanker might not visit land for months at a time, and many modern containerships achieve the incredible turnaround time of 48 hours in port. New relationships have evolved, no longer associated with wood, masts, yards, lines of hemp, sails, wind whistling in the rigging, or the conventional expectations that grew

out of the steamship experience for more than a century. No longer sharing cramped forecastles, their living quarters always subjected to the vagaries of weather and inadequate hygiene, with perennial diets of "salt horse," beef or pork pickled in brine, and meals usually devoid of fresh greens and vegetables, crew members aboard space-age carriers now enjoy air-conditioning, individual or semi-private staterooms, and balanced diets that would be welcomed in many homes on land. Although the lot of the seaman has improved immeasurably, the camaraderie that was known from living and working together, however uncomfortably, is presently rare. The clockwork fashion of modern carriers keeps

Facing page, top: This view of the North Beach area shows the development of the city at the end of the 1880s. (TBL)

Facing page, far left: The John D. Spreckels Company was not only the ticket agent for the Oceanic Steam Ship Company, but also sailed its own fleet of wooden vessels to Hawaii in the sugar trade. (TBL)

Facing page, left: The launching of this troop transport is a gala occasion at the Moore and Scott Shipyard in the Oakland Estuary. Courtesy, Oakland Public Library

Above: This view of San Francisco in 1883 shows a portion of the seawall on the left, and from left to right the Union Street, Green Street, and Vallejo Street wharves. (NMMSF)

Left: Robert Louis Stevenson chartered the yacht Casco from Dr. Samuel Merritt in 1888. The schooner had been built by Mears & Havens. Detail from The Casco, by William Coulter, from the Oakland Museum

The last surviving scow schooner sailing on San Francisco Bay, the Alma *was built at Hunters Point. The* Alma *sailed the bay until 1919. Then, dismantled, it was used as a salt barge and later as a shell dredge. In 1957 it was brought to the San Francisco Maritime State Park at the Hyde Street Pier and restored. Here it is in the 1970s out for a sail on the Master Mariner's Regatta Day. Further restorations have been completed on the* Alma *by the National Park Service and the* Alma *is a common sight on the bay. Courtesy, National Park Service, Golden Gate National Recreation Area*

crews busy on schedules that generally prevent the kinds of interactions men of the past commonly engaged in through unified efforts on board square-riggers and steamships. It appears that man and vessel are leaving behind an ancient relationship. For in the actual physical encounter with vessels of the past, man and ship became one, each an extension of the other, and together they were art forms taking their place in the natural order of the world. Yet, a new order of high technology seems to have come to commerce on the sea, and prospective merchant seamen must acquire new skills for the enormous carriers that are essentially run by computers.

The Hawaiian, Far East, and coastwise traffic of cargoes and passengers represented efforts to expand markets for stateside products and tourist travel. Steamship lines and agents in the San Francisco Bay Area have touched virtually all parts of the globe, at one time or another exporting and importing a tremendous variety of items. During a typical month in 1948 Bay Area vessels departed for Japan, the Philippines, Dutch East Indies, both coasts of South America, the Caribbean, Canada, the British Isles, Holland, Sweden, Hong Kong, Indonesia, Australia, New Zealand, India, Pakistan, Belgium, Germany, South America, and Italy. In the same year over 150 shippers and agents were operating throughout the metropolis, in addition to dozens of operators working the bay and its tributaries. Those companies that have a stake in the heritage of the Golden Gate are the Dollar Steamship Lines, which

purchased Pacific Mail's fleet of 535s (the length of vessels in feet), when PM went out of business in 1925; the American President Lines (successor to Dollar); Matson Navigation Company; Oceanic Steamship Company (founded by John D. Spreckels); Pope and Talbot, which expanded early, utilizing its vast timber holdings of the Pacific Northwest to export lumber around the world; Admiral line, and others on inland waterways as well as deepwater.

The highly efficient, specially designed cargo carriers of the space-age era include containerships, LASH or lighteraboard vessels, CB carriers, and roll-on, roll-off or trailer ships. These are known as the intermodal class of oceangoing vessels, using, among others, steam turbine technology.

The ports of the Bay Area, each in its own way, has accomplishments best suited for its geographical position and time. Each has access to rails, and continues to expand, perhaps to achieve a regional capability that will surpass other areas of the nation. The ports of Oakland, Alamenda/Encinal, Redwood City, Richmond, Benicia, Stockton, and Sacramento have deepwater capabilities of 30 to 35 feet. Together, with San Francisco, they have an edge on Pacific Basin commerce, the wave and promise of the future.

The San Francisco Bay Region has been blessed not only with incomparable scenic beauty and a gentle Mediterranean climate, but also serves as the major cultural center of Northern California. Here is where a unique maritime heritage is being cared for through preservation, research, and public programming. That heritage is an infinitely varied one and speaks to us of centuries of communion with the sea. On the Pacific Rim of the world, that heritage has been made richer by the human web of golden threads—cultures, races, and many national origins. The international port of call symbolizes a world view, and further insight into its past will surely unveil keys to a future in need of global cooperation and understanding.

Preceding page: *This vessel from Boston is loading hides on the California coast. The ox cart brings the hides to the beach where the stiff-cured skins are carried, several at a time, on the heads of sailors who wade to the ship's boat which ferries the hides out to the trading vessel. The California settlers from Mexico and the mission fathers were eager to trade hides for manufactured goods. The hide and tallow trade brought Jacob Leese to Yerba Buena in 1837, where he became one of the first American settlers. Courtesy, Automobile Club of Southern California*

Right: *The painter William Coulter was participating in rescue work during the fire which followed the great earthquake of 1906. This painting was made from sketches he did from a ferry in the bay. The Ferry Building tower which survived the quake is on the left near the water. A two-stack passenger liner is in the distant left; a ferry comes from the direction of the Ferry Building toward a British grain ship and a large down-easter in the center left. The U.S. Army Barge Office on Meiggs Wharf is a small tower on the shore to the right. Several small launches and rowboats are evacuating people from the burning city. Courtesy, San Francisco Commercial Club*

From the rocks of
Rincon Point in the
right foreground to
Telegraph Hill in the
background, this view of
San Francisco shows
great maritime activity.
The vessel on its side in
the foreground is being
repaired. Further along
the beach a steamer is
being reassembled. Built
on the East Coast, it was
brought around Cape
Horn in sections on the
deck of a sailer.
Ocean-going vessels lie at
anchor in the distance.
(TBL)

Above: *Vessels of the Pacific Steam Whaling Company brought their harvest of whale oil and baleen from the western Arctic to their refinery, the Arctic Oil Works in the Potrero District in South San Francisco. The large building on the right is the refinery, and storage tanks are on the left. Baleen was dried in the yard. Steam whalers are moored to the pier. The operation thrived from the mid 1880s into the first decade of the 20th century. (TBL)*

Right: *William McMurtrie, draughtsman for the U.S. Coast Survey, drew this scene in April 1850. This view of Yerba Buena Cove from the north on the slope of Telegraph Hill provides a striking contrast to the painting of June 1849 on page 118. Considerable building has occurred in town and along the waterfront. The most prominent feature of the waterfront, the Long Wharf, can be seen in the center. The storeships Apollo, center, and Niantic, right center, can also be seen. The artist barely begins to suggest the vast number of ships in the harbor at the time. (TBL)*

Above: *Depicted here is another view from Telegraph Hill looking across to Rincon Point, this one in mid-1850. The advancing wharves: Pacific Wharf, Long Wharf, and the beginnings of Market Street Wharf, nearest to farthest in the right center, bespeak the rapid construction of the waterfront. Cunningham's Wharf can be seen in the left foreground at the foot of Telegraph Hill. A few of the city's remaining vaqueros can be seen in the foreground. (TBL)*

Above: *By June 1849 there were already many abandoned ships in Yerba Buena Cove. There is little else to suggest in this quiet scene the soon-to-be booming metropolis of San Francisco. The view is from the southern shore of the cove, looking across to Telegraph Hill. The American ship Philadelphia is aflame, center right. (NMMSF)*

Facing page, bottom: *Hay scows were a familiar sight in San Francisco Bay until the advent of motorized trucking made them obsolete. They brought hay and agricultural produce from the rural areas surrounding the bay into the city. This painting by Gideon Jacques Denny shows one of them loaded high with hay or straw. (NMMSF)*

Above: *In 1859 the Army acquired Alcatraz Island to use as a military prison. In 1863 it was fortified against possible Confederate attack. This view from the 1860s shows the fort and, on the north side of the island, the lighthouse which was built in 1854. Angel Island forms the backdrop; further back on the left is Mt. Tamalpais. The sun is shining on Contra Costa County across the bay. The steamer Princess crosses in the foreground on its way to Sausalito from Meigg's Wharf at North Beach. This service began in 1868. (TBL)*

San Francisco artist Otis Oldfield painted this scene to hang in Coit Tower for the Public Works of Art Project in 1934. Oldfield, who studied and painted maritime subjects all his life, created in this painting a very accurate and realistic rendition of marine traffic on the bay and at the foot of Telegraph Hill. Vessels typical of the period can be easily recognized: a steam schooner and a steel freighter unloading lumber, a three-masted fishing schooner being assisted by a tug, sternwheel riverboats, and a motorized scow schooner with a load of hay. Courtesy, San Francisco Recreation and Park Department

Painted as a companion piece to the Otis Oldfield painting in Coit Tower, this oil on canvas by Jose Moya de Pino depicts the view from the top of Telegraph Hill looking northwest past Alcatraz to Richardson's Bay. Courtesy, San Francisco Recreation and Park Department

Facing page: *The Golden Gate is shown here from the top of the bridge, 750 feet above the water. Courtesy, Orville Andrews*

Completed in 1896, when the ferry business was the most lucrative one on the waterfront, the new Ferry Building replaced a smaller wooden structure. The new 275-foot tower withstood the great earthquake of 1906, although everything around it was reduced to rubble. Courtesy, Geoffrey Nelson

Above: *Somewhere along the beach named for Francis Drake the* Golden Hind *was careened, and the English party encountered the Coast Miwok Indians. Here also Sebastian Cermeño's Manila galleon was wrecked 16 years later. Shards of Chinese porcelain have been found in Miwok sites on the Point Reyes Peninsula. Both Drake and Cermeño are known to have been carrying porcelain, and differences in style and condition make it possible to distinguish which of these pieces came from which party. Those worn by sand and water are thought to be Cermeño's treasure. Courtesy, Geoffrey Nelson*

Facing page: *The construction by the U.S. Army of Fort Point was completed by 1857. A rectangular red brick structure, it is modeled after Fort Sumter in South Carolina. Fort Point's mission was to guard the entrance to San Francisco Bay from the ocean. The promontory on which it stands was also considered by the Mexicans to be a suitable site for fortification. In 1794 they constructed Castillo de San Joaquin here. Courtesy, Geoffrey Nelson*

Left: *This lighthouse at Pt. Reyes now watches over the rocky coastline explored by Drake and Cermeño. Courtesy, Geoffrey Nelson*

Below: *Fa'a Samoamoni (Spirit of Polynesia) performs Tongan and Samoan songs of the sea at the annual Festival of the Sea at the National Maritime Museum. They are performing in front of the enormous paddlewheel which was part of the bay ferry Petaluma at the turn of the century. Courtesy, Chris Giffen, Maritime Humanities Center*

Above: *Originally a lumber port, Redwood City port is now shared by fishing vessels, houseboats, and pleasure craft. Redwood from the coast range was put on sloops and schooners and sent to San Francisco in 1850. Courtesy, Geoffrey Nelson*

Left: *The branches of a cypress tree frame a northern San Francisco beach. Courtesy, Orville Andrews*

Facing page: *San Francisco encroached on the bay in the 1850s. Wharves became streets as the shallow cove was filled in. Today much of the city's financial district rises from what was once Yerba Buena Cove. Courtesy, Orville Andrews*

VI

Partners In Progress *by J.J. Lamb*

Historically, the maritime industry in the San Francisco Bay Region got off to a rather late start when compared to the East and Gulf coasts of the United States. In fact, the ocean shipping business was even thriving in Honolulu long before there was a need for merchant ships to call the West Coast of North America.

And when the first ships did start calling California, it was neither San Francisco nor Los Angeles that became the early center of commerce, but rather Monterey, the Mexican capital of the vast expanse of land that today comprises California, Nevada, Utah, and Colorado—inherited by Mexico in 1821 along with its independence from Spain.

There were, of course, several California coastal missions, including Yerba Buena (San Francisco) that had been established by the Spanish priests and continued to thrive under the Mexicans. Because of this, there was some commerce, but most of it moved overland rather than by sea.

In the San Francisco Bay area, it could be said that the maritime industry began with the local Indians, who hauled passengers, and later even mail, aboard tule rafts between the various shores of the bay.

Then, in 1835, Captain William A. Richardson introduced a more sophisticated for-hire service, using two schooners that shuttled produce and passengers between oceangoing ships in the bay and the Spanish missions at Yerba Buena and Santa Clara-San Jose. Richardson, for whom the northern area of the bay was named, also established the first tent-shack on the present site of downtown San Francisco.

Soon afterward, for-hire boating developed along a number of then-small East Bay settlements such as Oakland, San Antonio (now the Oakland Esturary), Clinton, and Alameda.

Just prior to the Gold Rush and the arrival of the forty-niners, the sloop *Pirouette* began sailing on a regular schedule between San Antonio and Yerba Buena. However, the discovery of gold at Sutter's Mill created a need for full-fledged ferryboat service on the bay, and the expansion of general ocean cargo services throughout the area.

It was this rapidly growing maritime traffic, generated by the gold-seeking argonauts, that spawned the Marine Exchange of the San Francisco Bay Region, which began operation in 1849.

Then in 1850, about the same time the forerunner to Tubbs Cordage Company was being founded, the sternwheeler *Kangaroo* began twice-weekly service, weather and tide permitting, between San Antonio and San Francisco. Typical fares were one dollar per person, hog, or sheep; three dollars per horse, wagon, or head of cattle; and 50 cents per hundredweight of freight. Within two years competition had reduced fares to 25 cents per passenger, while freight charges stayed at about five dollars per ton.

This also was the period when Pacific Mail Steamship, later to become American President Lines, began its operations on the West Coast, giving Oakland-based APL the distinction of today being the oldest continuously operating steamship company in the United States.

The early boom and bustle of the San Francisco Bay Region could not have been sustained without ocean shipping—the first transcontinental railroad was not completed until 20 years after the start of the Gold Rush. Initially, many more ships arrived than departed, bringing in a constant stream of immigrants, fortune hunters, merchants, and adventurers.

However, as the gold and silver moved out of the Sierra, two-way ship traffic also developed, resulting in the necessity to establish ancillary maritime businesses and services—ship building and repair, marine insurance, ship chandlery, importing and exporting, shipping agencies, stevedoring, tug and barge operators, and, of course, port facilities—all working together to create one of the most colorful, exciting, and close-knit port areas in the world.

The organizations whose stories are detailed on the following pages have chosen to support this important literary and civic project. They illustrate the variety of ways in which individuals and their businesses have contributed to the growth and development of San Francisco's maritime industry.

Facing page: *By the time this lithograph was produced, about 1856, the commerce of the city had changed to create a series of wharves and substantial brick warehouses for the discharging and storage of the goods required by the city. We are looking directly down Sansome Street to the North Point Dock and North Point Warehouse, last on the left, where the clipper* Great Republic *is discharging cargo. Directly to the right of this vessel are the Lombard Dock and the ship* Hurricane. *At right are the Greenwich Dock and the bark* Zenobia. *(TBL)*

MARINE EXCHANGE OF THE SAN FRANCISCO BAY REGION

Expanding upon a function initiated in 1849—to herald the arrival of ships at the Golden Gate—the Marine Exchange of the San Francisco Bay Region is today the nation's oldest maritime service and promotional organization.

Sometimes called the "eyes and ears of the Golden Gate" and the area's "Maritime Chamber of Commerce," the Exchange has had an almost revolutionary role in sparking innovations and improvements in not only the region's, but also in the nation's, ways of conducting maritime commerce and world trade.

Originally, in response to the needs of the gold rush, a lookout was set up on the San Mateo coastline to watch for ships approaching from the south. A rider, upon sighting a ship, would charge to Point Lobos at Land's End just south of the Golden Gate and advise the station of the impending arrival. A wooden semaphore then signaled the news to downtown San Francisco subscribers. Significantly, the relay point became known as Telegraph Hill, which preceded by several years the first western installation of Samuel F.B. Morse's electric telegraph.

Not surprisingly, the first use of the telegraph on the Pacific Coast, the year of its invention, was to replace the Exchange's wooden semaphore. Further, the first use of the telephone in San Francisco was by the Exchange, which later also pioneered a harbor radar and VHF radio vessel movement and location reporting system.

From Wylie.
Mar. 24, 1906.
I am on Mt. Tamalpais to-day. It is cloudy.

Today the Marine Exchange continues as the information center for harbor traffic and shipping activities—dispatching, recording, and relaying reports and advice, in addition to its many other roles.

As a membership organization, operations are financed in part by nearly 500 members. However, the principal source of income comes from services—shipping information, traffic reports, telephone answering, media relations, promotional activities, publications sales, and acting as secretariat or manager for several other maritime and port-related organizations.

The Marine Exchange currently answers about 80 telephone lines for many of the major steamship agencies and operators, pilot organizations, tugboat companies, and other maritime interests in the San Francisco Bay Region, from its operations station at Fort Mason. The facility is staffed around the clock, seven days per week, continuing a tradition that will be a century-and-a-half old before long.

Acting in its leadership role, the Exchange established a regional task force in 1956 to coordinate requests for federal funding of navigational studies, construction, and maintenance projects. Ultimately, this became the statewide California Marine Affairs and Navigation Conference (C-MANC), which is considered one of the nation's most effective specialized organizations of its kind, and is still served and staffed by the Exchange.

With a latter-day "shot heard around the world," the Exchange spearheaded 1959 publication in San Francisco of *Merchant Shipping on a Sea of Red Tape*. This analysis of excessive paperwork and cumbersome procedures affecting waterborne commerce soon resulted in the creation of an industry-U.S. government partnership to find solutions. Literally billions of dollars annually are now saved through reduction, simplification, and standardization of regulations and documents. Cargoes, vessels, crews, and passengers are now expedited, and international programs

increasingly assure uniformity in such facilitation. The Exchange continues to play a major role in such progress.

In 1967 the Exchange developed and initiated use of the first voluntary harbor safety vessel advisory service in the United States. Members agreed to adopt common radio-telephone frequencies, codes, procedures, and protocols for all ships within the Bay Region, with the Exchange acting as the relay point for information on vessel traffic.

The Exchange's system was so successful that the Coast Guard used it as a prototype to develop its own vessel traffic service (VTS). In 1981 the U.S. Maritime Administration selected the San Francisco Exchange to develop, test, and evaluate a new computerized, fully automated Vessel In-Port Locator system (VIPLOC). The resulting system went operational in early 1983 and became the agreed-upon standard for similar Exchanges on all three coasts.

One of the goals of the VIPLOC system is to create a national data base—an amalgamation of standardized information on ship locations and traffic to and from, and in, all American harbors. It will then be possible, for instance, to determine the whereabouts of every vessel of a particular nationality in U.S. waters; or how many tankers arrived in U.S. ports during a certain month; or the location of a specific vessel in the event of an emergency.

According to longtime Marine Exchange Executive Director Robert H. Langner, the future of the San Francisco association will be as it has been in the past—to continue to pioneer the use of modern technology to improve and expand its original, basic functions and services.

At the turn of the century, this was one of the Marine Exchange's stations for sighting vessels far out at sea. It was located atop Mt. Tamalpais in Marin County, north of the Golden Gate. From a 1906 postcard.

BLUE & GOLD FLEET, INC.

The steel bridge spans linking San Francisco with Oakland, and Marin County with Richmond, along with the Blue & Gold boats that currently cruise the San Francisco Bay waters, are the inspiration of a Bay Area family whose roots began with a tough-minded Irish immigrant who had planned to be married on April 18, 1906—the date of the San Francisco earthquake and fire.

It took Daniel Murphy two weeks after the earthquake to find his bride-to-be, an example of single-mindedness that later led him to become the first San Francisco sheriff to refuse to carry a gun. Daniel went on to father five children, one of whom began the maritime tradition that continues today in the form of the Blue & Gold Fleet.

As enterprising as his father was independent, son John Philip became a steel manufacturer and supervised placement of reinforcing steel in the Golden Gate Bridge roadway. He later formed Judson-Pacific-Murphy Corporation and built the Richmond-San Rafael, San Mateo-Hayward, Martinez-Benecia, and several other bridges throughout the western United States.

While primarily a construction feat, bridge building also required considerable maritime involvement since most of the steel had to be barged from the manufacturing site to the bridge-building locale. Despite the opinion of skeptics who claimed such a volume of heavy equipment could never be moved by water, John Philip Murphy obstinately tailored several tugboats to suit his purposes. The existing bridges attest to the wisdom of his determination.

Today Roger Murphy, son of John Philip and founder/vice-president/manager of the passenger-carrying Blue & Gold Fleet, is this

generation's standard-bearer for the family's nautical legacy.

With a background in sailing, hydroplane racing, and handling his father's workboat fleet, Roger formed Murphy Tugboats in 1971. The firm also operated a water taxi business on San Francisco Bay. This business was sold in 1978 in order to form the Blue & Gold Fleet, which presently operates three 400-passenger boats that offer both daily and charter Bay cruises.

While interested in the Bay cruise business for several years, it wasn't until the development of San Francisco's Pier 39 that a pier opening became available from which to operate. Starting with just himself and the backing of Pier 39 developer Warren Simmons, Murphy added two people from his former tug operation and brought in two captains. In its first four years the Blue & Gold Fleet progressed from a zero market share to a position where it has 50

The Oski is one of three identical 400-passenger Blue & Gold Fleet cruise boats that carry, in concert, up to a half-million sightseers per year. The boats, built in 1979, offer 75-minute cruises on San Francisco Bay, in addition to being available for private charters.

percent or more of the Bay cruise business, carrying up to 500,000 passengers per year.

Following the family tradition of innovation, Murphy's son, Skip, was the youngest person ever to win a captain's license from the U.S. Coast Guard for the operation of vessels up to 100 gross tons. Daughter Kelly is one of three female deckhands sailing aboard the Blue & Gold Fleet, and more recently, son Stephen has joined the deckhand ranks.

Pierside, there are two more Murphy sons waiting to take up the maritime tradition of their grandfather, father, sister, and brothers.

INTEROCEAN STEAMSHIP CORPORATION

It was 1929 when Erik Krag, not long from Denmark, formed Interocean Steamship Corporation in San Francisco. It was his desire to establish and operate an independent ship-husbanding operation on the West Coast that would maintain standards second to none.

Krag met his goal for ISC, which he continued to operate until the mid-1950s. About that time he became involved in growing papayas in Hawaii and allowed ISC to become little more than a shell corporation. However, despite numerous offers to purchase the agency, Krag preferred to allow it to stand idle rather than sell it to someone who might not maintain his standards.

In 1965 the principals of Marine Chartering Company impressed Krag sufficiently to gain his approval to buy into Interocean Steamship Corporation and reestablish it as a San Francisco-based ship agency. Krag's influence, however, continued: He was named honorary chairman, a position he held until his death in 1983.

The new owners, all working executives within the corporate structure, established their own philosophy: "Trade is the best chance we have to link ourselves permanently as nations and as peoples so that we all become members of one family, worldwide. That is the goal that goes beyond our mere business—providing the finest ships' agency services on the North American continent."

Initially, the *new* ISC was involved in agency services, ship chartering, and ship operating. However, five years after its revival, the business split into two corporate entities—Interocean Steamship Corporation and Marine Chartering Company, Inc.—with Jorgen With-Seidelin, one of the principals, heading ISC as president.

Operating on the principle that independence was central to its whole makeup, ISC concentrated only on husbanding services. The firm did not follow the trend to also become involved in stevedoring and

Represented by Interocean Steamship Corporation, this *Stolt* chemical tanker is part of a fleet of 42 vessels making regular calls in the Pacific Coast ports.

terminal operations.

ISC's growth was predicated primarily on acquiring clients that previously had not operated on the West Coast. But even that policy had unforeseen repercussions—when one of the carriers it represented expanded to serve the Gulf in addition to the West Coast, ISC also expanded to open new offices in New Orleans, Houston, and Dallas.

Today Interocean Steamship Corporation, a member of the Multiport Ship Agencies Network, continues as a completely independent organization, with eight fully staffed regional offices on the West and Gulf coasts. The staff currently numbers more than 200, an almost sixfold increase over the past two years.

Looking to the future, ISC expects its growth to continue and to remain one of the few independent ship agencies on the West Coast, while continuing to operate under the premise that "trade is the lifeblood of our world, linking nations in harmony, providing the means whereby men can share with one another and not war."

AMERICAN PRESIDENT LINES

American President Lines, with its headquarters in Oakland, is the oldest continuously operated steamship company in the United States. Today the firm is approaching a century and a half of service in the Pacific Basin.

APL's roots date to the establishment of the Pacific Mail Steamship Co. in 1848. Although PMSC was incorporated for the purpose of carrying mail between the Isthmus of Panama and the Oregon Territory, in 1867 the company expanded to inaugurate the first regular transpacific steamship service to Japan and China. Its fleet consisted of large, wooden side-wheel steamers to carry passengers, cargo, and mail.

Prior to the conclusion of World War I, PMSC began regular service to Manila, Singapore, Calcutta, and Colombo. In the interim, though, another ocean carrier integral to the development of APL—Dollar Steamship Lines—had been formed, first to operate along the California coast, then between the West Coast and the Orient, and finally in 1924 around the world with a regular, fortnightly service for passengers and cargo.

Regular transpacific service to Japan and China began in 1867 with a fleet of wooden side-wheel steamships such as the China, *belonging to American President Lines' predecessor company, Pacific Mail Steamship Co.*

By 1926 Dollar had acquired Pacific Mail Steamship Co. and a majority interest in the Pacific Northwest-based Pacific Steamship Company, which sailed transpacific under the name of Admiral Oriental Mail Line. The two acquisitions each operated five "535" passenger cargo ships, so named because of their length, under appointment from the U.S. Shipping Board. In 1922 the Shipping Board renamed all 10 ships in honor of U.S. Presidents.

Dollar Steamship Lines, affected by the Depression, was acquired by the United States government in 1938 and renamed American President Lines Ltd. During World War II, APL's ships became active units of the U.S. Army Transport Service and the U.S. Navy. During that period the company became responsible for the operation of more than 100 ships under the War Shipping Administration.

Following the war the fleet was rebuilt, cargo liners were added, and the around-the-world and transpacific sailings were complemented with a new service between the Atlantic Coast and Singapore. In addition, the passenger ships *President Cleveland* and *President Wilson* became part of the line's transpacific operations, offering luxury service for 26 years.

Management and ownership of APL changed hands in 1952 with its acquisition by a group headed by Ralph K. Davies and The Signal

Company.

A year earlier APL had begun its involvement with containerization by purchasing more than 1,000 relatively small eight-foot containers for use in its transpacific service. These were the forerunners of today's containers, which have revolutionized ocean and intermodal shipping. Not long afterward, APL began taking delivery of eight Mariner class cargo liners.

A final corporate acquisition took place in 1954 when APL became the majority owner of the Seattle-based American Mail Line, a cargo/passenger carrier that had been providing transpacific service to the Orient since 1917, as the successor of Admiral Oriental Line.

APL made its firm commitment to modern containerization in 1961 with the purchase of two combination container/break-bulk cargo ships. Similar ships were added and by 1968 the line had placed an order for four fully containerized ships, set for delivery in 1972-1973.

Later in the 1970s APL ended its Atlantic/Straits and around-the-world services, deciding to concentrate its containerships and multipurpose vessels in the Pacific and Indian Ocean trade lanes, while at the same time developing an intermodal network to serve all North America. The highlight of this intermodal system was the introduction of the "Linertrain" in 1979—an entire train of flatcars carrying only APL containers between Seattle and New York, and returning to Seattle by way of Oakland.

Also in 1979, two particularly significant events occurred. APL ordered, from Avondale Shipyards in New Orleans, three C9 class containerships—the largest ever to be built in the United States, and the first domestically owned and built containerships to be diesel-powered. Delivery of these

Special lightweight, five-segment articulated rail cars have been developed by APL to carry 10 containers (including 45-foot units), stacked two high. The cars, owned by APL, are used on the company's exclusive cross-country Linertrains.

The firm's new 115-acre container terminal at San Pedro, California, has storage space for 4,000 containers, two 1,000-foot ship berths with four gantry cranes, and a 122,000-square-foot container freight station.

three ships, which can each carry the equivalent of 2,750 twenty-foot containers, took place in 1982-1983. In 1979 the firm also became a wholly owned subsidiary of San Francisco's Natomas Company.

The Linertrain concept was expanded to offer express cross-country service between Los Angeles and the East Coast. APL's Linertrains make it possible for cargo to move from Japan to New York in just 15 days—seven days faster than conventional all-water carriage between the two points.

In mid-1980 APL started regularly scheduled service to the People's Republic of China, reestablishing historic ties that date back more than 110 years.

In 1981 APL introduced 45-foot containers for selective use in the U.S./Asia trade. These provided a 27-percent increase in interior capacity over standard 40-foot units, at approximately the same handling costs, and meant greater efficiency for APL and its customers.

Also in 1984, APL integrated into its fleet two additional diesel-powered containerships of comparable size to the C9s. This enabled the firm to

upgrade the efficiency and capacity of the entire fleet.

To further enhance the efficiency of intermodal transportation, APL subsequently participated in the design and development of a new generation of rail cars—lightweight, low-profile, articulated units capable of carrying containers stacked two high, and thereby doubling the capacity of each Linertrain. In 1984, with its initial order for the new

cars, APL became the first ocean transportation company to own its own railroad equipment.

Perhaps the greatest corporate development came in September 1983, when APL became an independent venture, spun off as part of a merger deal between Natomas Company and Diamond Shamrock Corporation of Dallas. APL is now the principal subsidiary of American President Companies Ltd. That corporation is headed by Bruce Seaton, who has served as president of APL since 1977.

From a pioneering steamship company established in 1848 to carry the U.S. mail, American President Lines has grown with the transpacific trade to become a multifaceted transportation firm. Today APL operates 16 containerships and five break-bulk vessels. The company maintains modern container-handling facilities at Los Angeles (San Pedro), Oakland, and Seattle and elsewhere throughout the Pacific Basin, and extends its transpacific cargo service to literally hundreds of key markets throughout North America by means of its intermodal (ocean-rail-trucking) network.

American President Line's containership President Lincoln, *one of three recently built diesel-powered vessels with a capacity of 2,750 twenty-foot containers, is shown entering the Port of Hong Kong harbor.*

LILLY SHIPPING AGENCIES

October 1, 1984, marked the 20th anniversary of Lilly Shipping Agencies, a San Francisco company that came into being as a result of an economic decision by the Japanese government to merge the former, and separate, Yamashita and Shinnihon steamship lines into Y.S. Line.

The decision by the Japanese created a conflict of interest within the existing agency of one of the lines, Norton, Lilly & Co. As a result, two of the agency's executives, Harry Lilly and Norman Handy, set up their own operation to serve Y.S. Line, opening offices in San Francisco, Los Angeles, and Long Beach with a staff of 14 people.

Less than two years after the formation of Lilly Shipping Agencies, another decision by the Japanese government affected the future of LSA. This time, the Japanese Council on Rationalization of Marine Transport and Shipbuilding recommended that container service be initiated

Norman L. Handy, president of Lilly Shipping Agencies.

between Japan and the U.S. Pacific Coast. The result was the formation of a consortium that included Y.S., Japan Line, "K" Line, and Mitsui O.S.K. Line.

In the United States the four lines, along with their agents (including LSA), founded the Oakland Container Terminal and the Los Angeles Container Terminal in the fall of 1968 to provide container facilities for the original four 800 TEU ships in the new

service. Initially there was only an eight-acre site with three yard areas and a small administration building.

The rapid growth of the container business (the three-year tonnage projection for the OTC was reached in only six months) proved a boon for both Y.S. and LSA. Currently the consortium operates eight 1,600 TEU containerships, quadrupling its original capacity. As a result, the OTC now covers 32 acres and operates from two berths.

While LSA has served other steamship lines since its founding, its primary client has continued to be Y.S. Line. It has been a good relationship, allowing LSA to grow into an operation of some 70 employees in its three offices.

In addition, LSA has entered into a partnership with Williams, Dimond & Co. to form CFS Corporation in Oakland, which is involved in the stuffing and stripping of containers. Another relatively new venture for LSA (1982) is its Consolidated Shippers subsidiary, which provides consolidation services for rail shipments.

According to Norman Handy, who took over as president of LSA when Harry Lilly retired in the early 1970s, the firm is constantly looking for new opportunities to serve the maritime industry in areas other than as agents.

Of particular interest to LSA has been the field of electronic data processing. For some time the agency's San Francisco office has been providing all computer services for Y.S. throughout the United States and Canada.

From its experience in the field of EDP, Lilly Shipping Agencies is now involved in establishing a new company that will specialize in developing computer programs and software specifically designed for the maritime industry.

The Kobe Port-Island No. 2 container wharf and the Tohbei-Maru, *a New York containership owned by Y.S. Line.*

OVERSEAS SHIPPING COMPANY

Christian Blom, Overseas Shipping Company's chairman of the board, at the firm's container terminal facility in Los Angeles.

Overseas Shipping Company was founded in 1950 by Christian L. Blom to represent the general ship agency activities of Barber and Barber Wilhelmsen Lines, Fernville Lines, and Klaveness Lines on the West Coast.

It was a rather auspicious beginning for a fledgling enterprise with offices in San Francisco, Los Angeles, Portland, and Seattle that started with 50 employees.

Since that time, though, the firm has branched out into other activities—container terminal cargo handling in Los Angeles, ship chartering in San Francisco, and general ship husbandry work along the West Coast for various European and Far Eastern principals.

In addition, Overseas Shipping has become involved in non-shipping projects of various kinds: in the leisure field, in the Silicon Valley, and in real estate.

While initially the company's main activity was in the general ship agency field, today—with the growing trend toward principal-owned general ship agencies—Overseas Shipping's primary emphasis is in the container terminal and chartering fields.

In Los Angeles, Overseas Terminal Company, a wholly owned affiliate, operates a container facility with close to 50 acres and 2,500 feet of main channel ship berthing. The facility has extensive reefer pad and wash rack facilities, in addition to a full complement of container terminal handling equipment, including its own dockside container cranes and four Paceco Transtainers for moving cargo containers around the storage yard.

While the terminal is primarily a container facility, it also caters to the roll-on/roll-off ship operations of Barber Blue Sea's super-carriers, and other lines that handle both container and break-bulk cargo.

Overseas Chartering Corporation, another affiliate, maintains a worldwide reputation for its capabilities in the ship brokerage and project fields. While the Pacific Rim is its specialty, Overseas Chartering is also well connected in the South American market, and highly regarded for its expertise in parcel trading, both dry bulk and tanker.

The parent organization, Overseas Shipping Company, harbors the firm's entrepreneurial activities. In this respect, the concern works very closely with its principal clients—Barber Blue Sea, Blue Star Line, Johnson ScanStar, East Asiatic Company, A. Johnson, Royal Viking Line, and Wlh. Wilhelmsen. A good example of that working relationship is Overseas Shipping's involvement in the development phase of Royal Viking Line 10 years ago. In fact, Christian Blom has been a director of Royal Viking Line since its inception in 1970.

Looking back, Christian Blom, Overseas Shipping's chairman of the board, came to the Pacific Coast from Norway in 1928. He was a partner of A.F. Klaveness & Co. A/S until retiring from that firm in 1971. During World War II he was deputy director of the Norwegian Merchant Marine in the United States and Canada and has been decorated twice for his services to Norway. He continues to remain active in local Norwegian affairs, and in the ocean shipping community.

Today Overseas Shipping Company is operated by the founder and his two sons, John C. and Carl F. Blom.

CROWLEY MARITIME CORPORATION

Not long after the turn of the century, Thomas B. Crowley, Sr., established the office of "Crowley's" on the San Francisco waterfront at the foot of Vallejo Street.

Through two generations, covering 90-plus years, there has been a Tom Crowley operating on the San Francisco waterfront.

Initially, it was 15-year-old Tom Sr., who started out in 1890 with an 18-foot Whitehall sail/rowboat transporting sailors and supplies to and from the ships anchored in San Francisco Bay. By the turn of the century he had acquired a gasoline-powered launch to replace the Whitehaller, enabling him to diversify his services. For a long time it was a one-man operation, with business strictly on the basis of "cash on the barrel head."

The operation went through a transition from "Crowley's," with an office on the waterfront at the foot of Vallejo Street, to Crowley Launch and Tugboat, which Tom Jr. joined after attending Stanford University.

By the mid-1950s the son had become president of Crowley Launch and Tugboat and embarked on a course that would expand and transform the privately held business into Crowley Maritime Corporation, with six divisions, some 500 vessels, more than 5,000 employees, and operations extending virtually worldwide.

Probably most familiar to San Franciscans and visitors to the Bay Area is Crowley's Red and White Fleet of ferry and cruise boats, which sail the Bay year-round, offering a considerably expanded service from that started by Tom Sr. in 1890. Operating from Piers 41 and 43, the seven-boat fleet offers Bay

A barge loaded with modules destined for Prudhoe Bay, Alaska, departs San Francisco Bay as part of Crowley's annual Arctic Sea-lift.

cruises, summer barbeques, private charters, and ferry service between Tiburon/Angel Island, Alcatraz, Sausalito, and San Francisco.

Crowley's strength comes from tug and barge work, common carrier transportation, oil industry support services, environmental services, vessel repair, and marine construction and salvage.

The six operations units are the California Division, headquartered in Long Beach; the Caribbean Division, headquartered in Jacksonville, Florida; the Northwest & Alaska Division, headquartered in Seattle; the International Division, and the Merlin Petroleum Division, headquartered in San Francisco; and the Latin American Division, headquartered in Teaneck, New Jersey.

A primary impetus for Crowley's growth was the Alaska Pipeline, which allowed the company to capitalize on its experience in supplying the Distant Early Warning (DEW Line) installations on the Arctic coast of Alaska and throughout the Aleutians. With this background, Crowley was able in 1970 to put together the largest-ever peacetime convoy—more than 80 tugs and barges loaded with 200,000 tons of cargo for Alaska's North Slope, including 170 miles of 48-inch pipe that became the northernmost leg of the Trans-Alaska Pipeline. These Arctic Sea-lifts have been performed annually since 1968.

In the past 15 years Crowley Maritime Corporation has expanded into other areas with the development of Trailer Marine Transport of Jacksonville, a pioneer of the ro/ro concept of moving cargo in truck trailers; establishment of the Alaska Hydro-Train, a ro/ro rail car barge operation; and the purchase of Delta Steamship Lines, a long-established company serving the Latin American trade.

TED L. RAUSCH COMPANY

In the tradition of numerous Bay Area maritime service businesses, the Ted L. Rausch Company began as a sole proprietorship, with the firm's namesake as the only employee.

Organized in 1958 as strictly a customhouse broker, Ted Rausch set up business in the historic San Francisco Ferry Building and adapted the structure's stylized world symbol as his own logo. The business remained there through its first four years, moving to other locations as it became necessary until settling at its present Townsend Street location.

The primary goal from the beginning was to provide a highly personalized, professional, and quality service. While expansion and growth were not high priorities, additional services and locations became not only desirable, but virtually a necessity.

Within a short time after incorporating in 1967, Rausch opened its first branch office in Southern California, initially in San Pedro but later moving to the historic Ocean Center Building in Long Beach, where it remains today.

In response to business demands, Rausch added other services and opened more branch offices—in Burlingame, Fresno, Portland, Sacramento, and Los Angeles. The Portland branch was separately incorporated in 1974 as the Ted L. Rausch Company of Oregon, adding a branch office of its own in Seattle in 1980. This second Rausch venture grew from a partnership between Ted Rausch and David C. Buttam, a longtime Pacific Northwest freight forwarder.

At the same time, the company, which had been exclusively a customhouse brokerage, began moving into other related service areas in order to better serve its customers.

With the organization of an

Vice-president and director Helmut K. Boeck (left) and founder and president Ted L. Rausch discuss business matters from the World Trade Club, which is located in the historic Ferry Building and overlooks San Francisco Bay.

export department, Rausch became a licensed international independent ocean freight forwarder, and added insurance services. This was followed by an appointment from the International Air Transport Association (IATA) to handle air cargo, and licensure as an Interstate Commerce Commission property broker.

Despite the expansion, Rausch has managed to preserve its original goal of providing personalized service while at the same time incorporating the use of modern business tools, including computerization.

Contributing to this achievement has been a loyal, carefully trained staff, headed by vice-president and director Helmut K. Boeck, who joined Rausch as an associate soon after the formation of the firm.

To preserve its professional stature, Rausch maintains memberships in the National Customs Brokers' & Freight Forwarders' Association of America and the local associations of Washington, the Columbia River, San Francisco, and Los Angeles. Ted Rausch also has served as an officer of the San Francisco and national organizations, in addition to being twice president of the Marine Exchange and a director of the World Trade Club and the British-American Chamber of Commerce.

TUBBS CORDAGE COMPANY

While the cordage business is one of the oldest industries in the United States—antedating the nation's independence from English rule by at least 100 years—it wasn't until the mid-1800s that the West Coast had a ropewalk of its own.

The idea for that first cordage factory evolved when 22-year-old Alfred L. Tubbs, representing the Boston wholesale house of Pecker, Dodge & Co., arrived in San Francisco in 1850 to dispose of two shiploads of general merchandise and, in so doing, test the market in the rapidly growing gold rush city.

In a very short time Tubbs was convinced that San Francisco was well on its way to prominence and affluence. As a result, he stayed on and entered into a partnership with Captain William Folger (patriarch of the Folger's Coffee clan) to form a ship chandlery firm in late 1850. The venture became so successful that Alfred convinced his older brother, Hiram, to also leave New England and settle in San Francisco.

Alfred and Hiram formed their own ship chandlery business, Tubbs & Company. Then, on the first day of 1854, Folger & Tubbs was dissolved, and the brothers bought out the interests of Captain Folger, who was in ill health and wanted to retire.

Before two more years had passed, Tubbs & Company was ready to open its own ropewalk. However, before the factory could become operational, Hiram had to scour New England in search of machines. Due to a shortage of the required equipment, it became necessary to build much of the machinery by hand. Hiram also persuaded a group of experienced eastern ropemakers to leave their homes and jobs and come west to work for the new company.

The first rope was produced at the Potrero Hill factory on July 23,

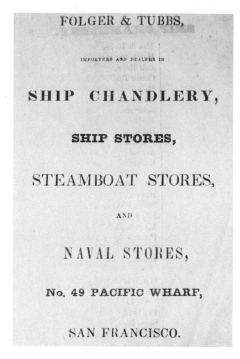

FOLGER & TUBBS,

IMPORTERS AND DEALERS IN

SHIP CHANDLERY,

SHIP STORES,

STEAMBOAT STORES,

AND

NAVAL STORES,

No. 49 PACIFIC WHARF,

SAN FRANCISCO.

This was the cover of the first catalog of Folger & Tubbs, forerunner of Tubbs Cordage Company, issued about 1851 in San Francisco.

1856. It was also the first rope to be manufactured in the United States west of New England. In 1862 the San Francisco ropewalk was incorporated as the San Francisco Cordage Manufactory. The mill remained operational for almost 100 years. In the interim, however, the name was changed to Tubbs Cordage Company.

During this same period Tubbs & Company, as did Folger & Tubbs previously, became involved in whaling out of San Francisco. In taking over the Folger interests, the Tubbs brothers acquired the ships *Leonore* and *Tuskina*. They then added the *Mary Ellen,* the *Ocean Bird,* and the brig *Boston.* And between 1853 and 1860 they outfitted and sent several of them on whaling voyages. However, by the end of the 1850s, the number of whalers operating in Pacific waters had increased considerably, and the price of whale oil declined to the point where Tubbs & Company felt it did not justify either the outlay or the risk involved.

In order to expand and solidify their West Coast cordage business, the Tubbs brothers purchased the Portland (Oregon) Cordage Company in 1892. Later, in 1904, a branch mill was established in Seattle. These two mills supplied agricultural, fishing, and marine ropes to the Pacific Northwest, and served to discourage the establishment of rival mills in the area.

The noon whistle blows at "The Ropewalk at the Potrero" in 1856. This is the earliest known photo of Tubbs' San Francisco cordage mill.

When the brothers died within five months of each other, in 1896 and 1897, Tubbs Cordage Company continued on as a family business, with Alfred's son, Alfred S., becoming president, and Hiram's son, Herman, becoming vice-president. Today the organization is still run by descendants of the two founders.

The great earthquake and fire of 1906 had a far lesser affect on Tubbs Cordage Company than on most of the rest of the city. The towering smokestack tumbled and many of the small buildings had minor damage. While none of the buildings fell, one of the main structures had walls so badly cracked that it was feared they would not be able to support the heavy French tile roof. However, within one day a contractor had been engaged to effect repairs, and three months later the plant was operating at full capacity.

In 1923 Tubbs Cordage Company purchased the Capstan Rope and Twine Works in Manila, making it the first and only American rope

manufacturer to own and operate a mill in the land that traditionally has had a virtual monopoly on abaca—the basic natural fiber used in ropes. Tubbs continues to hold an interest in the renamed Manila Cordage Company.

During the 1930s and 1940s Tubbs products helped build the Hoover and Grand Coulee dams, and many other notable construction projects. The firm also provided all of the rope to create the famous life-saving

This was the ropewalk (manufacturing area) at Tubbs Cordage Company in San Francisco in the late 19th century.

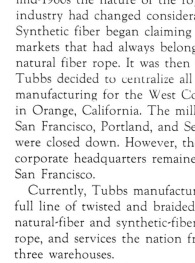

About the time of World War I, Tubbs Cordage Company was delivering its rope products in this hard-rubber-tired truck.

net that was suspended beneath the ongoing construction work for the Golden Gate Bridge.

In 1947 Tubbs merged with Great Western Cordage Company of Orange, California, and by the mid-1960s the nature of the rope industry had changed considerably. Synthetic fiber began claiming markets that had always belonged to natural fiber rope. It was then that Tubbs decided to centralize all rope manufacturing for the West Coast in Orange, California. The mills in San Francisco, Portland, and Seattle were closed down. However, the corporate headquarters remained in San Francisco.

Currently, Tubbs manufactures a full line of twisted and braided natural-fiber and synthetic-fiber rope, and services the nation from three warehouses.

Tubbs Cordage Company has grown from first supplying, and then manufacturing, only ship hawsers, to servicing fields as diverse as the utility, petroleum, workboat, fishing, and heavy marine industries. Rope manufacturing facilities are still located in Orange, California, and the Philippines, with one synthetic carpet yarn plant in California's San Joaquin Valley. Also, there are rope distribution centers in San Francisco, and in Seattle, Washington.

GRAHAM & JAMES

The legal firm of Graham & James was organized as an admiralty practice in San Francisco in 1934 by Chalmers G. Graham, who opened his offices in the Robert Dollar Building at 311 California Street.

Graham's legal career in San Francisco, however, began shortly after World War I when he became an employee of attorney Ira Lillick. Primarily an admiralty lawyer, Lillick practiced as an individual attorney for more than 20 years before deciding to form a partnership, which included Chalmers Graham.

On his own Graham also practiced as an individual attorney before forming a partnership in 1941 with Henry Rolph, who later became a judge. A year later Clarence Morse became a partner and went on to become first general counsel and later chairman of the Federal Maritime Commission. Then, in 1947, Leonard James became a partner in the firm.

Having just celebrated its 50th anniversary, Graham & James has grown considerably since Chalmers Graham went out on his own. While the firm began as an admiralty practice, it quickly expanded into a general practice, with a focus on international business.

Today Graham & James maintains 12 offices and has about 140 attorneys worldwide, plus some 160 non-lawyers. In the United States, the firm's offices are in San Francisco, Los Angeles, Long Beach, Newport Beach, and Palo Alto, California; New York; and Washington, D.C. Overseas, there are offices in Milan, Singapore, Hong Kong, and Kuwait, in addition to a representative "presence" in Beijing.

More specifically, Graham & James specializes in the representation of business and financial activities of foreign and domestic commercial,

This carved granite walrus (above) which greets visitors to Graham & James' San Francisco office, adorned the Alaska Commercial Building (right) at 310 Sansome Street from 1908, when the facility was constructed, until its demolition in 1975. When a conservation movement failed, it was presented to the law firm in honor of its 40 years of practice there. The walrus has been adopted as Graham & James' symbol.

banking, and corporate clients in the United States. From its foreign offices, the firm represents U.S. and foreign corporations and financial institutions in their investment and commercial interests in Europe, Asia, and the Middle East.

Graham & James continues its 50-year relationship with the maritime industry, primarily through its San Francisco, Long Beach, and Washington, D.C., offices, which maintain very active practices in this area. These offices represent many of the major steamship lines, shipping conferences, cruise lines, and international maritime insurance associations.

The firm's maritime work also

involves admiralty litigation in the federal and state courts; representation before the Federal Maritime Commission and Maritime Administration; and a number of specialized matters such as charter parties, ship acquisitions and financing, bills of lading, stevedore and terminal contracts, passenger cruise matters, maritime taxes, fisheries regulation, policy and joint ventures, and offshore operations.

Other clients of Graham & James' general practice include major banks, airlines, trading companies, and manufacturers in the United States and overseas. And to serve this diverse clientele, many of the firm's attorneys have actual overseas experience and speak one or more foreign languages, including Japanese, Korean, various Chinese dialects, Arabic, Persian, and those of Europe.

While the size and scope of Graham & James have increased considerably during the past 50 years, one thing has remained constant—San Francisco continues as the firm's largest office.

STAR SHIPPING A/S

Star Shipping's Star Eagle *represents the carrier's fifth generation of open-hatch ships, which are designed to carry bulk, unitized, and container cargo.*

The Star Shipping name is only 15 years old in the San Francisco Bay Area, but the shipping activities of its parent companies date back to the mid-1800s.

Norway-based, Star Shipping was started in 1962 by Per F. Waaler when his business, A/S Billabong, joined forces with another Norwegian firm, Westfal-Larsen & Co., and with San Francisco's own Crown Zellerbach Corporation. At the very early stages, Waaler, Per Grieg, and Bjørn Østervøld from Norway and Clyde Jacobs from San Francisco formulated many of the concepts and innovations that allowed this young enterprise to become one of the foremost forestry-products carriers in the world.

In 1970 Crown Zellerbach sold its interest in the concern to Fred. Olsen & Co., resulting in total Norwegian ownership. While the original name was Star Bulk Shipping Company, it was changed to Star Shipping A/S in 1971. However, by that time, vice-president and general manager Howard W. Harrington had already established a U.S. West Coast office in San Francisco under the name of Star Shipping (U.S.W.C.) Inc. (the initials standing for United States West Coast).

The Fred. Olsen organization commenced shipping in 1848 and started its North Pacific service in 1915 with the S.S. *Bravo,* the first Norwegian ship to pass through the Panama Canal. Service was interrupted by two world wars, but each time resumed and continued until 1966.

Westfal-Larsen was founded in Norway in 1905. A North American West Coast service—called "Westfal-Larsen Line"—was started in 1926 and was renamed Interocean Line in 1930.

In 1966 the Fred. Olsen and Westfal-Larsen companies established a joint liner cargo service between the Pacific Coast and Europe under the name Fred. Olsen Interocean Line (FOIL). By 1970 shipping had changed to the point where the firm decided to terminate the 55-year-old Pacific service and put its resources into Star Shipping.

Today the Star fleet consists of 34 vessels ranging in size from 27,000 to 44,000 dwt and a total dead weight of about 1.4 million tons. Some 22 vessels are specialized open-hatch vessels used to carry unitized forestry products and/or containers. The remaining 12 vessels are conventional geared bulk carriers used for handling bulk and neo-bulk cargoes such as ore, fertilizers, coal, grain, and lumber.

Star operates the geared bulk carriers virtually on a worldwide basis. The open-hatch fleet combines forestry products and containers outbound and primarily containers inbound. The main areas served from the United States and Canada are North Europe, the Mediterranean, and the Far East.

In addition to the San Francisco headquarters of Star Shipping (U.S.W.C.), there are district offices in Seattle, Portland, and Long Beach, with a representative in Eureka, California. Other major North American entities are Star Shipping (New York) in Stamford, Connecticut; and Star Shipping (Canada) in Vancouver, British Columbia.

The Star Hong Kong *is capable of carrying 1,344 twenty-foot containers. This type of ship operates between the Far East, the Mediterranean, Continental Europe, the United Kingdom, and the West Coast of North America.*

NORTON, LILLY & CO., INC.

Founded in 1841 as John Norton & Company in New York City, Norton, Lilly & Co., Inc, is currently the oldest shipping company in the United States. While the original business was that of merchants, charterers, and owners of sailing packets in the South American trade, the firm has since become involved in virtually every aspect of international ocean transportation.

During the 1890s, together with three British owners, Norton & Sons established the first direct steamship service from New York to India, South America, Australia, and New Zealand. Later, services were started to China, Japan, and Southeast Asia.

Earlier, the advent of steam had brought about rapid expansion in the company's activities. Under its own Norton Line flag, the firm operated the first scheduled steamship service to the East Coast of South America. This service continued without interruption until the early 1970s.

During world wars I and II, Norton, Lilly's management of ships for the U.S. War Shipping Administration and its performance as agents for the British Ministry of War Transport and the Norwegian Government Shipping Agency earned the venture recognition for outstanding achievement. During this period Norton, Lilly also owned and operated two of its own ships.

Today the company is engaged in agency work throughout the United States, representing all types of vessels, including both conventional liners and containerships, tramp vessels, tankers, ore carriers, heavy-lift ships, and fishing vessels.

On January 1, 1983, a holding company was formed—Norton, Lilly International Inc.—which is now the parent of Norton, Lilly & Co., Inc., and a number of subsidiaries. In the

10 preceding years, Norton, Lilly had expanded into or acquired a number of subsidiary operations including stevedoring, terminal operations, container storage and repair facilities, and travel, and computer services.

In the interests of providing national marketing services and local logistical support, Norton, Lilly established regional offices on all four U.S. seaboards, with San Francisco serving as the control center for clients whose main sphere of operation is on or through the Pacific Coast.

The agency currently provides customer services on the West Coast for several major foreign and domestic shipowners. The West Coast office represents such lines as The Shipping Corporation of India,

Cia.; Chilena de Navegacion Interoceanica, S.A.; China Ocean Shipping Corporation; Westwood Shipping Lines; and Inter-Pacific Shipping Corporation.

Norton, Lilly's five West Coast regional offices are under San Francisco's direct supervision and management; all other company offices outside the six western states and British Columbia provide necessary support and service to facilitate total coverage of North America.

All told, Norton, Lilly & Co., Inc., has more than 100 staff people in its West Coast offices.

An old Norton, Lilly & Company advertisement that appeared in Pacific Shipper *on October 3, 1927.*

UNITED STATES LINES, INC.

United States Lines had gone through many owners and owned many ships during its more than a century of existence. Its origins go back to 1871, when the American Line was formed with the financial support of the Pennsylvania Railroad to operate between Philadelphia and Liverpool, England.

New owners—International Navigation Co. of New Jersey—took over in 1893 and, at the turn of the century, merged with Atlantic Transport Company to form the nucleus of J. Pierpont Morgan's International Mercantile Marine Company.

Under Morgan, International Mercantile Marine acquired the British fleets of White Star Line, Leyland Line, Dominion Line, Oceanic Steam Navigation, and Shaw, Savill & Albion Ltd. At its peak, the company controlled more than 120 major passenger and freight vessels and virtually dominated Atlantic shipping.

In the interim, the U.S. government found itself with a fleet of ex-German transport and supply vessels at the end of World War I. European service was inaugurated with eight of these ships by a new firm called U.S. Line Mail Steamship Company. The operation failed in mid-1921 and the government reclaimed the ships. The U.S. Shipping Board sailed them until 1929 under the trade name U.S. Lines prior to selling the fleet to Paul W. Chapman & Co., which also defaulted after a short time.

In 1931 International Mercantile Marine merged with the Roosevelt Steamship Company, and together they purchased the U.S. Lines name and fleet. At the same time, the company bought the American Merchant Line vessels to operate in London service and discontinued the American Line name.

Records show that during its half-century of operation, American Line never lost a ship, a passenger, or a bag of mail. It did not do quite so well financially.

After gradually disposing of its foreign-flag tonnage, the corporation in 1943 discarded its international designation and assumed the name of its principal subsidiary, United States Lines.

Following World War II, USL focused most of its attention on its cargo business, acquiring seven C-2 freighters for its North Atlantic service in 1945. Eighteen more of these ships were added over the next two years.

During the following decade USL introduced a Far East service from New York, and in the 1960s the carrier became involved in the containerization revolution. By 1970 the line had introduced a tri-continent, fully containerized

---

United States Lines' new containership, American New York, *departs Hong Kong Harbor on her maiden voyage. Calls were also made at Busan, Korea; Kaohsiung, Taiwan; and Kobe and Yokohama, Japan, directly to Savannah and New York. The vessel has a container capacity of 2,241 forty-foot equivalent units and a cruising range of 30,000 nautical miles at 18 knots. The* American New York *is the first of 12 being built for U.S. Lines by Daewoo Shipbuilding & Heavy Machinery Ltd., in South Korea.*

service covering a 15,000-mile trade route.

As part of its Far East service, USL began calling the West Coast ports of Oakland and Long Beach, and in the process provided the only intercoastal general cargo service available to shippers. At the beginning of 1983 USL bought Moore McCormack Lines and its 13 ships as part of its continuing expansion program. Service routes now include Africa; Europe; South America; and the East, including Southeast Asia.

United States Lines was purchased in 1978 by McLean Securities, Inc., wholly owned by Malcom P. McLean, the pioneer of containerization, and founder of Sea-Land Service, which he sold in 1969. In mid-1983 McLean took his company public.

In May 1984 the first four of 12 new containerships were christened. These vessels are the largest containerships ever built, with a capacity of 2,241 forty-foot equivalent units. Plans are to use these vessels in an around-the-world service calling every week at 13 ports. The complete around-the-world cycle for each ship will take 84 days. With the addition of these 12, U.S. Lines will be operating a fleet of 36 container vessels, all registered under the United States flag.

JOHNSON & HIGGINS OF CALIFORNIA

As the Bay gave birth to San Francisco's maritime industry, so it was that this blossoming industry gave birth to Johnson & Higgins, which today is the nation's oldest and largest independent insurance brokerage firm.

The company was founded in New York in 1845 by two enterprising young men, Henry W. Johnson and Andrew F. Higgins. The two, known for their expertise in average adjusting, soon became trusted by shipowners to purchase marine insurance for them. Thus, by 1846, they had become insurance brokers—serving the buyers of insurance rather than the sellers.

By the 1880s New York had become the undisputed center of United States commerce. Yet, San Francisco also had emerged as a metropolis with a rivaling maritime industry.

While the gold rush had passed, San Francisco's port still bustled with activity. However, the Panama Canal would not become a reality for another three decades and ships traveling from east to west still faced the long and dangerous trip around Cape Horn. Also, while marine insurance was an established business in Europe and on the East Coast of the United States, it was still in its infancy in San Francisco—as many a troubled shipowner learned to his regret.

It was just this kind of trouble that brought Johnson & Higgins to San Francisco and the West Coast.

September 2, 1883, was a particularly festive day at the city's Spear Street Wharf. A sleek new steamer, *Queen of the Pacific,* insured through Johnson & Higgins, set sail for the Pacific Northwest. Among the dignitaries traveling on the ship were a former governor of California and the presidents of the San Francisco Board of Trade and the Chamber of Commerce—all

invited to celebrate the completion of the Northern Pacific Railroad and the driving of the golden spike in honor of the first transcontinental railroad to reach the Pacific Northwest.

Two days later the *Queen of the Pacific* arrived at the mouth of the Columbia River and, at approximately 2:00 p.m., she unceremoniously ran aground on Clatsop Spit. The passengers were safe, but in order to free the ship from the sandy bottom, 700 tons of valuable cargo had to be jettisoned.

Johnson & Higgins received word in New York of the unfortunate incident a few days later. They promptly sent James B. Dickson to the West Coast, where he was to stay until all matters concerning the loss had been settled. However, when Dickson arrived in San Francisco and saw its burgeoning maritime business, he soon convinced New York to open the company's second office—at 315 California Street. Throughout the firm's 100 years in San Francisco, Johnson & Higgins has remained on California Street.

By the turn of the century the new office had a staff of seven and was headed by W.H. LaBoyteaux, who was later to become president of the parent organization—a position he held for 30 years. In the meantime, though, in 1905 Johnson & Higgins created a new department, fire insurance, which proved to be somewhat prophetic.

During this same period, San Francisco had grown so rapidly that wooden construction was the rule, with masonry the exception—a condition that proved devastating on April 18, 1906, when the great earthquake struck and precipitated fires throughout the city.

Alfred Yates, Johnson & Higgins' senior fire insurance executive, was dispatched from New York to ensure that all client claims were satisfied. The task took six months and contributed greatly to the company's reputation in the West for credibility, integrity, and

San Francisco Bay from Telegraph Hill, circa 1882. Courtesy of the California Historical Society.

perseverance.

The period between the earthquake and 1945 was tumultuous —two world wars, a stock market crash, and the Great Depression made economic tidal waves throughout the land, although San Francisco fared better than most cities.

Discovery of great new oil fields in the 1920s provided an economical fuel for industrial use, and soon major industries were establishing operations in California. Development of the state's other natural resources spurred further growth, which soon was reflected in the insurance marketplace, and the subsequent growth of the Johnson & Higgins organization in California.

However, the Depression of the 1930s brought the company's expansion to a virtual standstill in California, and throughout the rest of the United States. But with careful planning, Johnson & Higgins managed to survive, and did so without having to terminate a single employee.

While World War II brought a boom to the maritime insurance business, it was the postwar growth era that brought significant sociological changes. Widespread concern about individual welfare gave impetus to the creation of employee benefit programs, including group health and life insurance and pension plans, an area in which Johnson & Higgins quickly gained a position of strength.

In the '60s and '70s commerce and technology flourished in California, which was reflected in Johnson & Higgins' list of clients. In addition to its traditional services, the firm began establishing a record for serving companies associated with agriculture, food processing, forest products, banking and finance, and the professions—medical, dental,

The grounding of the steamer, Queen of the Pacific, *on a Columbia River sandbar gave birth to Johnson & Higgins' San Francisco office. Courtesy of the San Francisco Maritime Museum.*

and legal. Then, with the development and growth of high-technology companies throughout the Bay Area, Johnson & Higgins added many of these to its expanding client list.

The opportunity that James B. Dickson saw in San Francisco 101 years earlier has proved to be well founded. Johnson & Higgins of California has grown to five offices, with more than 700 employees. Not only is the company the oldest insurance broker operating in San Francisco, it is also the oldest in the country, having established its first office in New York in 1845.

On both coasts, Johnson &

Higgins was born out of the maritime industry, helping shipowners manage the risks of lost ships and cargo, whether at sea or ashore. Today the firm has expanded into all areas of commercial insurance, risk management, and employee benefit planning. From its two offices of 100 years ago, Johnson & Higgins has grown to 38 U.S. and 48 international offices, plus a worldwide network of exclusive correspondents.

The challenge of Johnson & Higgins' second 100 years in California will be the challenge of change. It is a challenge that will be met with the help of computerization and other technologies, along with the experience and expertise of some 5,500 employees throughout the entire organization.

OAKLAND INTERNATIONAL TRADE CENTER

Within three years of opening its doors the Oakland International Trade Center, which operates Oakland's Foreign Trade Zone, had already established itself as an innovator and created a prototype for the promotion of U.S. exports.

This auspicious beginning came as a result of the first Asian/Pacific Med/Ex, held at the OITC in 1983. The three-day exhibition of American medical technology and hospital equipment by 70 participants was organized by the OITC in cooperation with the U.S. Department of Commerce. It attracted some 300 buyers from 11 Pacific Rim nations and resulted in about $15 million in export sales.

The exhibition was unique in that it was the first major export promotion to be conducted by a U.S. Foreign Trade Zone. Previously, FTZ activities throughout the United States had been only import-oriented.

Considering that the OITC was only a concept six years prior to the Med/Ex, the latter's success is even more significant. According to OITC president and chairman Captain Nelson Tsui, the 13-acre site and its 130,000-square-foot facility might never have come into existence if it had not been for the prodding of his wife, Julia, who felt strongly about the need for such an operation in the East Bay to help bridge the gap between importers and exporters and their markets.

Tsui, who is also general manager of the Oakland Container Terminal, arranged to purchase the OITC property next to the Oakland Coliseum in 1977. The application for an FTZ was started the following year and the City, Port of Oakland, and the Chamber of Commerce became co-sponsors. The U.S. Department of Commerce granted the license in 1980. The OITC opened its doors as operator of the

Julia Tsui

FTZ, a trading company, and a Select Foreign Buyer Program in 1981.

Currently, more than 50 companies have been attracted to the site. In 1982 the inventory within the FTZ was valued at $900,000. By 1983 it had grown to more than $76 million.

Tsui is convinced that part of the key to the success of the OITC has been a reliance on thorough study and research, even though an initial $15,000 feasibility study on such a

facility produced negative results. The OITC, a private corporation, has worked closely with the University of California in researching the potential of trade with China. Tsui was recently able to arrange a meeting with the leading trade people within the People's Republic of China.

In its pioneering effort to promote the export of U.S. goods and services, the OITC offers potential exporters help with tax problems, contracts, domestic and foreign government regulations, protocol, procedures, and interpreters.

The Pacific Rim countries, Tsui notes, currently represent the fastest-growing and potentially the largest market in the world, a market the Oakland International Trade Center intends to continue to open up to both exporters and importers in the United States.

At the Asian Pacific MED-EX are (left to right) Julia Tsui; Captain Nelson Tsui; Wong Lei, vice-minister of the State Economic Commission (SEC); and Zhao Yinghua, vice-president of the China Enterprise Management Association (CEMA).

OAKLAND CONTAINER TERMINAL

The story of the Oakland Container Terminal actually begins in 1966 in Japan. At that time, the Japanese Council on Rationalization of Marine Transport and Shipbuilding recommended to the government that containership services should be initiated between Japan and the West Coast of the United States.

Two years later the Oakland Container Terminal was founded by four major Japanese shipping companies, and their San Francisco-based agents—Mitsui O.S.K. Line/Williams, Dimond & Co.; "K" Line/Kerr Steamship Co.; Japan Line/Transpacific Transportation Co.; and Yamashita-Shinnihon Line/Lilly Shipping Agencies.

The first step was to lease two rooms in the former Matson Navigation Company building in San Francisco. Then, from June through October 1968, the owner representatives and their agents discussed the details and made the arrangements to create a container terminal in Oakland. By November the Oakland Container Terminal had become a reality and the first of the original four ships that were used in the trade, the *American Maru,* arrived at the new facility at the Port of Oakland's Outer Harbor.

The Oakland Container Terminal has expanded rapidly since that time. Starting with only an eight-acre site, with three storage areas for full containers and a small administration building, the facility now encompasses 32 acres, consisting of eight storage areas, a large yard for empty containers, a 12,560-square-foot maintenance building, a third-generation container crane, and an administration building with almost four times the original space at Berths 2 and 3 of Oakland's Outer Harbor.

As did many others who foresaw the potential of containerization, the OCT benefited from the rapid growth of this ocean shipping innovation, reaching its three-year tonnage projection in only six months. During 1983 the terminal handled more than 60,000 twenty-foot-equivalent units (TEU).

Currently, 11 vessels from the four-carrier consortium call at the OCT, each with a capacity of approximately 1,600 TEU. Described by vice-president and general manager Captain Nelson Tsui as second-generation containerships, 20-foot containers average about 7.8 tons per container inbound from Japan and about 13.5 tons outbound from the United States.

The variety of cargo through the OCT is extensive, says Captain Tsui, who notes that the fully cellularized ships using the facility can be adapted to carry almost anything. Many shippers, he says, do not think of containerships having the capability of carrying heavy equipment. However, he explains, because of the larger open spaces on the decks of the containerships, they can handle heavy and outsize cargoes that could not be accommodated on general cargo vessels.

As for the future, Captain Tsui claims the current capacity of the OCT is sufficient to handle anticipated growth over the next two years.

Loading trucks and tires on a container vessel as deck cargo.

CHANCELLOR HOTEL

Only five years after the 1906 San Francisco earthquake and fire, Congress selected the city as the site for the planned 1915 Panama-Pacific Exposition, which was to celebrate both the opening of the Panama Canal and the quarter-centenary of Balboa's discovery of the Pacific Ocean.

This honor prompted an even greater effort on the part of San Franciscans to rebuild the destroyed portions of the city, and to add numerous structures, including a new city hall, a civic auditorium, and facilities to house the millions of visitors expected to attend the sea-oriented exposition.

Among the hotels constructed primarily for the Pan-Pacific was the 16-story Chancellor, purportedly the first fire- and earthquake-proof hotel to be built after the 1906 disaster. While it was one of several hotels of a similar size to be built during that era, it later achieved its own status.

Fronting on the colorful Powell Street cable-car line, the 140-room Chancellor offered a location just a few steps away from the green hedges and palm trees of Union Square. The centrally located hotel also was within easy walking distance of the city's finest shops, its theaters, Nob Hill, Chinatown, and the financial district.

In 1920 the original owners sold the hotel to Isador Rosenberg, who moved from Woodland, California. His purpose in relocating was to educate his family in the better institutions of higher learning. Rosenberg previously had owned a general merchandise store. His oldest son, Edgar, came into the industry after college to learn the hotel

business. He eventually became manager of the Chancellor Hotel and operated it until his death in 1944.

Significantly, ownership has remained within the family, although the owners now number seven, including two of the originals, plus four offspring and the late Edgar Rosenberg's second wife, Alice Post. Today the Chancellor is one of the last hotels in San Francisco, and probably the oldest, to be family-owned.

Also, the Chancellor was one of only two hotels in the city that

continued to operate, and make a profit, during the Great Depression.

The Chancellor was Isador Rosenberg's first venture into the hostelry business. He later took over management of an under-construction hotel, the William Taylor, which the Methodist Church had started but had insufficient funds to finish. Rosenberg completed the structure and renamed it the Hotel Empire (the building is currently owned by the University of California and is used for student housing).

At the Empire, which had no

The Chancellor Hotel in 1915, shortly after its completion. Union Square is in the foreground.

facilities for an off-the-lobby cocktail lounge—both because of the Methodists' planning and the existence of Prohibition—Rosenberg later solved the problem by opening the city's first rooftop facility. For a long time after its introduction, the lounge attracted long lines of people that extended around the block at ground level.

Possibly Edgar Rosenberg's favorite venture was the Paso Robles Inn. Recognizing that automobile travel was becoming more and more popular, he purchased land about halfway between San Francisco and Los Angeles to build the inn, which became a famous overnight stop for travelers.

Neither the Hotel Empire nor the Paso Robles Inn remain in the Rosenberg holdings: Edgar sold the Empire and the family sold the inn when he died in 1944.

The success of the Chancellor is attributed primarily to the close supervision given it by the owners, who have devoted considerable attention over the years to establishing a repeat clientele. For instance, the hotel began many years ago catering to the jewelery sales trade by creating a special closet room where the salesmen could keep their large display cases. One of the jewelry people has been returning regularly to the Chancellor since 1927.

Because of its convenient location, the Chancellor also has been a favorite of people who come into the city from the suburbs and want to stay overnight after a day of shopping or an evening of entertainment. In some instances, the children—and now even the grandchildren—of early-day guests continue this tradition.

It should be noted that it's not only the guest and the owners who have established a tradition of longevity at the Chancellor. For instance, the present manager is only the third since 1920; the second one served for 49 years.

Perhaps not surprisingly, the Chancellor does very little advertising. It enjoys a good reputation that is passed along among travelers by word-of-mouth.

The management proudly notes that the hotel has "always offered extremely reasonable rates," but according to regular guests, it's not just the rates that cause people to come back time after time. Inside, the atmosphere is one of quiet understatement. While the decor of rooms, lobby, and other facilities are refurbished on a regular basis, a special effort has been made to preserve the original feeling of the structure. And finally, because the original builders were more than generous in their use of materials, the Chancellor claims to be one of the most solid, sound-proof hotels in the city today.

The Chancellor Hotel as it appears today.

MATSON NAVIGATION COMPANY

Matson Navigation Company was launched when a 33-year-old Swedish-born skipper named William Matson sailed a small three-masted schooner—the *Emma Claudina*—out of the Golden Gate on April 10, 1882, bound for Hilo, Hawaii.

Within three years the shipping business to Hawaii had outgrown that initial ship. Captain Matson sold the *Emma Claudina* and replaced her with a larger brigantine, *Lurline*, the first of several ships to bear that name. This move also established a trend that has never ended—increasing capacity to serve the needs of what was first a territory and is now the United States' 50th state.

On February 9, 1901, Matson Navigation Company was incorporated in San Francisco, with the ceremony held in Captain Matson's small office, only about one block from the firm's present headquarters at 333 Market Street.

The second *Lurline* joined the

Sailing from San Francisco is the combination container and trailer vessel Lurline, the fifth vessel to carry the name. The ship has a capacity for nearly 1,200 containers (24-foot equivalents) and 225 automobiles in garage stowage.

fleet in 1908, with accommodations for 51 passengers. Modern tourism to Hawaii was born two years later with the introduction of the 146-passenger S.S. *Wilhelmina*, which offered appointments to rival the finest cruise ships then transiting the Atlantic Ocean.

Matson added newer and larger freighters to its fleet in the years following World War I, and in 1927 introduced the 690-passenger liner *Malolo* to California-Hawaii service. To accommodate the growing volume of Hawaii visitors, Matson acquired the Moana Hotel and built the Royal Hawaiian Hotel at Waikiki Beach.

In the early '30s the passenger liners *Mariposa, Monterey,* and the

third *Lurline* joined the *Malolo* in West Coast-Hawaii service and became world renowned as the "white ships" in the Pacific. Matson also added two more Waikiki hotels in the mid-'50s—the Princess Kaiulani and Surfrider.

During World War II Matson's four passenger liners and 35 freighters carried troups and military cargoes throughout the world. After the war *Lurline* was reconverted for peacetime passenger service and the three other liners were laid up and sold. The new passenger liners *Mariposa* and *Monterey,* converted from Mariner freighters, entered South Pacific cruise service in 1956-1957 and the new *Matsonia,* reconverted from the prewar *Monterey,* joined *Lurline* in Hawaii service in 1957.

On August 31, 1958, Matson introduced the first cargo container service in the Pacific, with the inaugural sailing of the converted freighter *Hawaiian Merchant,* which carried a deckload of 20 containers. Containerization revolutionized ocean shipping worldwide.

Matson's container service initially utilized converted conventional cargo vessels, including the *Hawaiian Citizen,* the first all-container ship in the Pacific, which was converted in 1960. Those vessels were replaced by four big, fast 720-foot containerships—the *Manukai, Manulani, Maui,* and *Kauai*—and the fifth *Lurline,* a combination container-trailer carrier, "stretched out" to 826.5 feet by the addition of a 126.5-foot midbody section.

With this modern fleet and ocean terminals in West Coast ports and Hawaii, Matson Navigation Company, now a subsidiary of Hawaii-based Alexander and Baldwin, is able to provide the most efficient and dependable service in its history of more than 100 years in the Hawaii trade.

Captain William Matson set sail on the Emma Claudina, *a three-masted schooner, from San Francisco in 1882, headed for Hilo, Hawaii. It was the first voyage for what was to become Matson Navigation Company.*

SEA-LAND SERVICE, INC.

With the year 1972 a new chapter began in the history of Oakland: Sea-Land Service, Inc., inaugurated the city's first waterfront container terminal. Today the giant, unsubsidized, U.S.-flag carrier maintains the largest single facility in the port. The Sea-Land terminal has grown from 11 acres, one berth, and no cranes 22 years ago, to 70 acres, two berths, and three massive cranes today.

Along with expansion of the Sea-Land operation, Oakland has shown record container traffic growth over these two decades, making the harbor the top container port in the Bay Area and one of the busiest on the West Coast. Oakland today takes in Sea-Land microbridge business headed for 30 major inland cities, with outbound commerce to 10 Asian nations.

With the renewal of Sea-Land's Oakland lease in 1980, covering two more decades, the carrier reaffirmed support for its $60-million-plus investment in the port. Sea-Land currently shows a payroll of 375 in the Bay Area. This facility handles an inventory of approximately 2,500 company-owned boxes on individual chassis in the Oakland yard available to West Coast customers.

Sea-Land's Oakland ship visits involve more than half of the firm's transpacific D-9 diesel-powered container vessels, each with a capacity nearly double that of the first ship put into full container operation back in 1962. Sea-Land, which originated what is today the world's main mode of general cargo shipping, was originally known as the "sea-land service" of the Pan Atlantic Steamship division, Waterman Steamship Corporation. In 1960 Pan Atlantic changed its name to Sea-Land Service, Inc., and after another five years the remaining Waterman assets were sold by then-owner Malcolm McLean.

McLean sold Sea-Land to R.J. Reynolds Industries, Inc., in 1969. In 1984 Reynolds spun off the Sea-Land group of companies to its shareholders as the Sea-Land Corporation, an independent, publicly-owned company listed on the New York Stock Exchange.

Sea-Land today serves 58 countries and territories through more than 180 ports and cities, with a fleet of over 60 vessels. Sea-Land, Oakland, and containerization represent inseparable parts of a common history. The story began, ultimately, in 1956, with shipping of truck-trailers on the decks of vessels. Full trailership and, then, cellular containership operations soon followed.

Sea-Land has set itself the goal of demonstrating that the main asset of a major organization is its ability to better serve the public and the customer. The Sea-Land partnership with Oakland proves the point: As Sea-Land has benefited, the community has profited. That's how it should be. That's what Sea-Land is here for, in Oakland and around the world.

The Sea-Land containership Elizabethport *inaugurated intercoastal service between Elizabeth, New Jersey, and Oakland in 1962, arriving at the Port of Oakland with a capacity load of 476 thirty-five-foot containers.*

The Sea-Land Patriot, *first of twelve 897-container-capacity, diesel-powered containerships, is shown arriving on its maiden voyage from Asia to the Bay Area in 1980.*

PORT OF OAKLAND

The Port of Oakland currently claims title to being the largest container port on the West Coast, and among the top 10 in the world.

While the port today is a thriving, independent agency of the City of Oakland, running its affairs through a seven-member board of commissioners nominated by the mayor and approved by the city council, its origins were somewhat less distinguished.

Looking back to 1852 and the founding of the city, one of the three major sponsors, Horace W. Carpentier, managed to gain exclusive rights to the Oakland waterfront in return for five dollars, two percent of all wharfage fees,

Up until World War II, the port's outer harbor area was mostly empty land and waterside warehouses for the handling of general break-bulk cargo.

construction of three wharves, and the building of a public school—a fight that involved not only Carpentier, but also the virtually all-powerful railroads.

By 1897 the city won a signal victory when the California Supreme Court ruled that the shoreline boundaries of the original waterfront granted to Carpentier had been greatly extended as a result of enormous landfill over the years and that the *new* waterfront had since become publicly owned.

With new facilities and important railroad connections, large-scale improvement plans were launched

and shipping activity increased during the early 1900s.

Shipbuilding brought prosperity during World War I, but by 1925 there was still a great deal of public dissatisfaction with the pace of the port's growth.

A permanent, independent, and unpaid board of port commissioners was established in 1927. Harbor activity immediately began to accelerate. By comparison, in 1925 the port operated at a deficit of $400,000; one year after seating of the first port board, the port was in the black and has operated without benefit of city tax appropriations ever since.

Cargo tonnage doubled between 1926 and 1934, and port activity increased sharply during World War II. After the war cargo tonnages resumed their steady but unremarkable growth until the early 1960s, when the advent of the container age resulted in dramatic changes.

A measure of the resultant growth is evident in statistics that show that only 400,000 revenue tons of container cargo passed through the port in 1965, but by 1983 the figure had jumped to more than 11 million tons.

Currently, some 50 steamship companies use the Port of Oakland's facilities, and more than 1,300 ships call at the port annually.

Looking to the future, the port, which has had a 60/40 bias toward exports in the recent past, is working to achieve a balance in its export/import business. At the same time, the Port of Oakland wants to retain its position as having the highest value per ton of foreign trade of any port on the U.S. West Coast.

The port commission also has responsibility for the operation of Oakland's two airports and the commercial development of some 19 miles of shoreline.

The Port of Oakland's outer harbor facility today is fully developed and one of the most active container ports on the West Coast.

HOYT SHEPSTON, INC.

Thomas A. Hughes, a "Forty-niner," was but one of an estimated 25,000 people who arrived in San Francisco before 1850, virtually all of them drawn by the prospect of becoming rich as a result of the gold being mined in the Mother Lode.

Hughes, though, was not a mining prospector. Rather, he recognized, as did a few others, that there was money to be made from providing the goods and services required by Northern California's burgeoning population. Thus it was that Hughes became a customs appraiser, starting a firm in his own name that eventually became the customhouse brokerage and freight-forwarding firm that is today's Hoyt Shepston.

It was a valid decision on Hughes' part because almost the entire resident population of the Bay Area had headed east for the gold fields —merchants, farmers, clerks, lawyers, doctors, journalists, and laborers.

As a result, Californians were producing very little to supply their own needs. Almost everything had to be imported by sea. By 1851 San Francisco had become the fourth-largest port in the United States with respect to the value of its foreign trade. In the 12 months preceding the start of the gold rush in April 1848, 84 ships dropped anchor at San Francisco, bringing in a total of about 50,000 tons of goods. Seven years later the number of ship arrivals had increased to 1,250, carrying more than 550,000 tons of cargo.

However, even the captains and crews of the arriving ships were caught up in the gold mania. By 1851 some 775 abandoned and rotting vessels lay at anchor off the Embarcadero, and more ships were sailing into San Francisco Bay every day.

It was this bustling ocean commerce that had attracted Hughes, who later in 1854 took on a partner,

The Merchants Exchange, also known as the U.S. Court Block and Federal Building, was the home of Hoyt Shepston's predecessor firm, Hughes & Hunter, for 41 years from 1856 to 1897. The building was destroyed by the 1906 earthquake and fire. Courtesy of the California Historical Society, San Francisco. G.R. Farndon, photographer.

A.A. Hunter, to form Hughes & Hunter, Ship and Custom-House Brokers, and Australian Agency. In 1856 they set up business in the Merchants' Exchange on Battery Street, opposite the new U.S. Customhouse and Post Office; and there the business remained for the next 41 years, although not always under the same name.

Early on in the history of the predecessors of Hoyt Shepston, it was decided that rather than create a family business, employees would be allowed to buy in and succeed the active management. As a result, the firm changed names several times as new managing partners took over its operations. In 1919 the company became Hoyt, Shepston & Sciaroni, the name under which it was incorporated in 1960. Since then it has operated under the simplified name of Hoyt Shepston (dba).

Regardless of the various managing owners and various corporate names, the firm has continued intact for about 135 years, missing only a few days of business in that time, and that was during the 1906 earthquake and fire.

In the past the company used horse-and-buggy drayage, sail and steam ships, quill pens, and rudimentary communication systems. Today, under president Robert Mullins, Hoyt Shepston is involved in intermodal transportation (trucks, airplanes, and containerships), computer and satellite communications, and other state-of-the-art systems to expedite clients' cargoes into and out of the United States.

This ad for Hoyt Shepston's predecessor firm appeared in Le Count & Strong's 1854 San Francisco City Directory. Courtesy of the California Historical Society, San Francisco.

LILLICK McHOSE & CHARLES

The law firm of Lillick McHose & Charles traces its origins back to 1897 when Ira S. Lillick, a member of Stanford University's first law class, entered the legal profession in San Francisco.

A native Californian from Santa Clara County, Lillick at first contemplated becoming a teacher in Modesto. However, finding teaching jobs somewhat scarce, he went to San Francisco and offered his services to several lawyers and law firms, including T.C. Van Ness of the prominent firm of Van Ness & Redman.

Unfortunately, young lawyers, like young teachers, were not much in demand, despite excellent letters of recommendation. Disappointed and broke, Lillick returned home only to find the railroad stationmaster waiting for him with a telegram from Van Ness offering a job as "errand boy" at $15 per month. He took the job even though the best room-and-board arrangement he could find cost him a money-losing $16 a month.

To Lillick's credit, a promotion and a doubling of his salary came within a short time. However, T.C. Van Ness, Jr., was taken into the firm upon receiving his law degree and took over the work Lillick had been handling. On the suggestion of a friend, Lillick decided to concentrate on admiralty law and obtained a job with the leading admiralty lawyer of the period.

In 1905 Lillick opened his own one-room law office in the Mills Building on Montgomery Street and later took a larger room in the Kohl Building at the corner of Montgomery and California. In the following years he worked with several associates, including, ironically, T.C. Van Ness, Jr. Lillick, though, was hesitant to form a law partnership. He practiced as an individual attorney for more than

Ira S. Lillick, a graduate of Stanford University's first law class, began his legal career in San Francisco in 1897. In 1905 he started his own practice, which eventually became Lillick McHose & Charles.

20 years, with younger lawyers working for him. By 1928, however, increasing specialization developed a need for an association of lawyers who were adequately qualified in various legal areas. Thus the firm of Lillick, Olson & Graham came into being, with J. Arthur Olson, Chalmers G. Graham, and Theodore M. Levy—all former employees—as partners. Associate lawyers of the new firm were Joseph J. Geary, John C. McHose, and Allan E. Charles, all of whom later became partners.

Following World War I the firm moved into the Balfour Building at California and Sansome. The next relocation came after World War II, into the Dollar Building at Battery and California; and finally, in 1975, Lillick McHose & Charles moved into its present headquarters at Two Embarcadero Center.

Up until the 1950s the law firm

was primarily involved in maritime practice. To this end, a branch office was established in Los Angeles in 1930. Expansion in the '50s put the firm into banking, real estate, industrial, and general litigation law. In addition, it is the only law firm in the Western United States that also has specialists in public affairs and legislation.

The entire firm now comprises more than 200 lawyers, with paralegal assistants, investigators, managers, technicians, secretaries, and other support personnel working out of offices in San Francisco, Los Angeles, San Diego, Sacramento, and Washington, D.C.

EAGLE MARINE SERVICES, LTD.

Eagle Marine Services, Ltd., a wholly owned subsidiary of American President Lines, only began operations at the beginning of 1979 but already has become one of the largest stevedoring and terminal management firms on the West Coast.

As might be expected, Eagle Marine's primary reason for coming into being was to perform stevedoring and other terminal operations for APL ships, with a projected goal of effecting cost savings for the Oakland-based U.S.-flag carrier.

From the very beginning Eagle Marine managed to reduce APL's annual stevedoring costs. By 1984 projected savings in this one area alone were estimated at more than four million dollars. Equally impressive savings were achieved for container yard, gate, and container freight station services.

However, rather than limiting its scope to being just a captive provider of dockside marine services, Eagle Marine from the beginning solicited business from other carriers. This "history in the making," as it is described by Eagle Marine, provided additional income the first year and

has been growing steadily ever since. Overall, EMS expects to handle almost 290 vessel calls in 1984 and nearly 270,000 containers.

Current operations involve facilities at Oakland, Los Angeles, and Seattle. While specializing in intermodal container handling, EMS offers full terminal and stevedoring services for break-bulk, bulk, and passenger ships. With respect to the latter, EMS handles more sailings of passenger ships than any other stevedoring firm.

Eagle Marine attributes much of its early success to incorporating state-of-the-art procedures such as preplanned computerized vessel stowage; remote-controlled gate operations; sophisticated, high-speed computer programs for processing documentation; computer-controlled yard placement and location of containers; and precise intermodal interfacing between various modes of transportation—ocean, rail,

Eagle Marine Services, Ltd., a wholly owned subsidiary of American President Lines, has become one of the largest stevedoring and terminal management firms on the West Coast. Here APL's President Kennedy *avails itself of those services.*

road, and air.

The company is understandably proud that in such a short time it has become the operator of the largest container-handling facility on the West Coast and is the largest container freight station operator on the coast in terms of total tonnage. Much of its success is due to personalized, customized service.

The next big step for Oakland-based Eagle Marine will be the opening of a new 115-acre container terminal at San Pedro in Southern California, comprising two 1,000-foot deep-draft berths; a 154,000-square-foot container freight station; an administration building; a 39,000-square-foot, 22-bay container and chassis maintenance and repair facility; and dedicated space for close to 2,000 containers and 3,500 chassis. There are another 40 acres available for expansion, which would include an additional ship berth.

Some 50 acres of the new facility will be occupied by American President Lines. Eagle Marine Services, Ltd., is making the other 65 acres available for use by other shipping lines as well as all other terminal and marine facilities.

FRITZ COMPANIES, INC.

After more than 50 years in business, Fritz Companies, Inc., considers itself in its prime and as committed as it was in the beginning to providing dependable, total transportation services to importers and exporters on an international basis.

Fritz Companies began as a family enterprise in 1933 when Arthur J. Fritz, Sr., opened a three-person customhouse brokerage office in San Francisco with the assistance of his wife and sister.

Despite early setbacks resulting from waterfront strikes and the Depression, the small venture managed to persevere. In 1937 Arthur J. Fritz & Co. was licensed by the Federal Maritime Commission as an international

The Fritz Building, at 142 Sansome Street in San Francisco, houses all of the maritime operations of the Fritz Companies, Inc. Photo courtesy of Richard Stone.

ocean freight forwarder and, later, as the firm completed its first 10 years, it was serving about 100 clients.

According to Arthur J. Fritz, Sr., the original intent was to organize a full-service, multinational transportation company. With this long-range goal in mind, the family worked steadily toward its achievement, increasing offices and services one by one, eschewing dividends, and reinvesting all profits back into the business.

Initial expansion into other cities, however, came about more as a result of unforeseen circumstance rather than from planning. During World War II San Francisco became a port of embarkation and was closed to regular commercial shipping. So Fritz opened an office in Los Angeles and became involved in the South American trade. However, Los Angeles soon was designated a port of embarkation, also. To maintain the new South American business, Fritz opened a third office in New Orleans.

From an original base of only three clients and a specialized product list of only liquor and Chinese-food products, Fritz operations have expanded to serve a roster of more than 15,000 companies involved in virtually every type of product, commodity, and raw material.

And from a single small office, barely large enough for the three family founders, the Fritz organization has grown into a worldwide network of 65 offices in 43 locations with nearly 2,000 employees in two dozen distinct divisions.

Essentially, the privately held corporation has fulfilled the original intent of Arthur J. Fritz, Sr., and in so doing has become the largest customhouse broker in the United States, the fourth-largest

Fritz Companies, Inc., started as a family business and continues as such today. Involved are (seated) daughter Sandra Fritz Davis, treasurer, and founder Arthur J. Fritz, Sr., chairman of the board. Standing are sons Lynn C. Fritz, executive vice-president, and Arthur J. Fritz, Jr., president. Photo courtesy of Richard Stone.

international ocean freight forwarder, the eighth-largest international air freight forwarder, and the largest national duty drawback organization. Current annual gross trading exceeds two billion dollars.

Helping maintain this status has been the development of a cost-effective data-processing system that provides computer-to-computer communications for all transportation documentation between Fritz' offices, clients' offices, and other Fritz physical locations throughout the world.

However, regardless of size or modern techniques, founder Arthur J. Fritz, Sr., still believes the basis for success is commitment. "We continue to do business the old-fashioned way," he says proudly.

CONTINENTAL MARITIME INDUSTRIES

Originally known as San Francisco Welding & Fabricating Inc., today's Continental Maritime Industries was started in 1946 by Albert Picchi and a handful of men. At that time, the company specialized in steel fabrication and technical welding consulting.

Not long after its founding, CMI expanded into marine repairs and has held Master Ship Repair contracts with the U.S. Military Sealift Command, Coast Guard, and Army since 1950. It wasn't long before marine work became the firm's primary marketing area.

Until 1979 CMI operated from 528 Folsom Street in San Francisco, where it maintained complete shop facilities for machining, plate, pipe, ship cleaning, and carpentry. Major ship-repair work, including hull repairs, boiler and engine work, voyage repairs, machinery repairs, and small conversions, was carried out both on-site and in the field.

In addition, the company performed specialty welding on submarines, manufactured test gimbels for rockets, did fabrication work for the Crescent City nuclear power plant, and built screening devices for the Stanford University laser laboratory.

Roger A. Picchi, son of the founder, became president of CMI in 1979, the same year principal operations were moved to Pier 54 in order to create a greatly expanded ship-repair facility with adjacent ship berths.

That same year CMI received its first large contract—conversion of the tanker USNS *Kawashiwi* to civilian manning. The $25-million project was, at that time, the largest Small Business Administration set-aside contract ever awarded.

During the next two years CMI won a national competition to perform a second similar tanker conversion on the USNS *Ponchatoula,* and was awarded back-to-back major Navy overhaul jobs.

For the past 10 years the company has enjoyed a steady and sustained

---

Continental Maritime Industries, which started in a small warehouse-type location on Folsom Street, today operates from Pier 54 (left) and a portion of Pier 50 (right), giving it a deep-water ship-repair facility and 4,436 feet of berthing space.

growth pattern, which it attributes to a willingness to commit the necessary capital and financial resources in order to compete for, and successfully perform, large-scale conversions and major overhauls.

In line with CMI's stated policy of continuing to invest in facilities, personnel, equipment, and management systems in order to pursue and win major ship-repair contracts, a lease was recently signed to take over a portion of nearby Pier 50, which can handle ships with drafts of up to 45 feet and has berthed such ships as the USS *Kitty Hawk* and the USS *New Jersey*. This now gives the firm a total of 4,200 feet of pier berthing.

The next major step is to have built a 682-foot by 172-foot floating dry dock that will be moored at the end of Pier 50.

As a company, CMI, with its 300 to 500 employees, is organized to take advantage of the "hands-on" attitude of a privately owned business. But at the same time, the firm has grown to a size where it has the capability to function as a major ship-repair facility, perhaps among the top three on the West Coast.

SANDERS TOWBOAT SERVICE

Occupying the 100-year-old Benicia slip of the long-abandoned Benicia-Martinez ferry on Carquinez Strait, Sanders Towboat Service currently performs about 60 percent of the ship-assistance business in the area, handling an average of 1,500 dockings per year.

While Sanders has been operating from Benicia only since 1976, that in no way represents the accumulated experience of the company. Don E. Sanders, its founder and president, began working on towboats in 1940. His initial experience came in waterborne construction.

After starting Sanders Towboat Service in 1958 with a single 45-foot tug, Sanders stayed on in San Francisco and continued to specialize in marine construction, subcontracting his services to various prime contractors. At the same time, he performed some ship-assisting work.

Sanders tugs carried the first materials for the Bay Area Rapid Transit underwater tube between Oakland and San Francisco, and barged away the first excavation materials. In 1970 the firm merged with Murphy Pacific Marine Salvage. However, two years later Murphy went out of business and Sanders decided to take a break for a couple of years.

It wasn't the first time, though, that the family-run enterprise had taken an extended leave of absence from the Bay Area. During 1962-1964 it headed south for Peru under contract with International Petroleum. But, in keeping with the tradition of tug operators, it wasn't possible to steam the entire distance unencumbered. Off Nicaragua, Sanders learned of a disabled U.S. tuna boat, which it picked up and towed to Panama for repairs.

Following the later 1974-1976 hiatus Sanders purchased two surplus Navy tugs, and in 1976 the

Typical of the ships assisted by Sanders Towboat Service tugs at the Port of Benicia is this large tanker, Exxon North Slope. Exxon operates a refinery at the Benicia Industrial Park.

operation was moved to Benicia to take advantage of the conversion of the former Benicia Army Arsenal into a vast industrial park and port. Since then the principal business of the firm has been ship assistance, although Sanders does some towing and owns three flat barges.

Ship-assistance work for Sanders at Benicia involves bulk carriers, tankers, and automotive carriers. Significantly, a recent survey showed Benicia to be the best port on the West Coast for the handling of imported automobiles.

Sanders' current tug fleet can not only handle ships of up to 170,000 dwt—virtually anything currently afloat—but also has fire-fighting capabilities comparable to the fireboats of the ports of San Francisco and Oakland and the Mare Island Navy Shipyard.

In keeping with the family tradition, the tugs are named *Gail L. Sanders* for Don Sanders' daughter, *Mary Dee Sanders* for his late wife, and *Donald D. Sanders* for a son who died several years ago at the age of 22.

Further, the principals of the operation, in addition to Sanders, are daughter Gail, who runs the office, and son-in-law Bill Skarich, who is port engineer and general manager.

One of the three tugboats operated by Sanders Towboat Service demonstrates its fire-fighting capability off the Port of Benicia.

HANJIN CONTAINER LINES LTD.

While Hanjin Container Lines Ltd. is a relative newcomer to ocean shipping, having been established only in 1977, its roots go back to the end of World War II when Choong Hoon Cho, the present chairman, formed the Hanjin Transportation Company.

Since 1945 the Hanjin Group has expanded to include 12 companies that are involved in land, sea, and air transportation; financial services; terminal operations; insurance; real estate; construction; travel; mining; agriculture; and two educational foundations. Total company revenues exceed $2.1 billion.

Significantly, Korean shipping did not become seriously involved in the ocean containerization revolution until about the mid-1970s. Hanjin, recognizing a need to containerize the nation's shipping industry if it were to expand, compete internationally, and not have to rely almost totally on foreign-flag carriers, formed Hanjin Container Lines.

Hanjin Container Lines began operations in 1978 by opening the first container transportation service between Korea and the Middle East, using a single containership. Then, in 1979, the carrier inaugurated its independent transpacific service with four new containerships built under the Korean government's shipbuilding program.

Today Hanjin operates six fully containerized vessels. Four have a capacity of 575 and two have a capacity of 595 forty-foot-equivalent containers. Hanjin operates between Korea, Japan, and Taiwan in the Far East, and the U.S. ports of Seattle, Oakland, and Long Beach, providing weekly service at each port. Hanjin also provides intermodal service between these West Coast ports and destinations throughout the United States and Canada. Both full-container-load (FCL) and

less-than-container-load (LCL) service is available. The carrier currently has an inventory of 6,700 forty-foot containers and 200 twenty-foot containers.

Hanjin is one of only a few transpacific carriers that provides its own chassis for each container at point of origin and port of discharge. Hanjin owns and operates its own container handling piers and terminals in both Incheon and Pusan.

Hanjin maintains its North American headquarters in Oakland, and in addition has nine other offices throughout the United States, employing a total staff of approximately 130 people. In Canada, Hanjin utilizes the services of its agent, Protos Shipping Ltd. Unlike some carriers operating in the United States, Hanjin is a Korean corporation and represents no other line in this country other than itself. Also, the Oakland office serves as a training ground for home office staff members, who come to the Bay Area for three-year

One of Hanjin Container Lines' six containerships offloads at the Port of Oakland's outer harbor facility, bringing goods from Korea, Japan, and Taiwan to the West Coast.

tours of duty.

Since opening its transpacific service, Hanjin Container Lines has established itself as the leading carrier of containerized cargo between Korea and North America, and in its first seven years has become the fourth-largest contributor of revenue within the Hanjin Group.

Hanjin Container Lines' Hanjin Seoul, *loaded with containers in San Francisco Bay.*

TUG 'N TOW CORPORATION

Purchase of the pilot boat *Golden Gate* in 1975 provided the impetus for Dick McKnight to form his own maritime service company, Tug 'N Tow Corporation, and thus fulfill a longtime ambition to be directly involved in the maritime tradition of the San Francisco Bay.

A year later came the purchase of two fiberglass boats for charter as Bay party vessels, resulting in an even stronger desire to become an integral part of the area's day in, day out commercial maritime activities.

In working to fulfill that aspiration, McKnight purchased his first workboat, the tug *Brant,* in 1977. He soon bought another tugboat, the *Mudhen,* plus two supply barges—the *Vincent F* for water service and the *Harbor Barge No. 1* for bulk lubrication oils.

These vessels became the nucleus of Tug 'N Tow, a division of McKnight's RCM International, which had been established in San Francisco in 1963 as an import/export company.

The *Brant,* built by Crier Boat Yard of Alameda in 1930, is one of the last working wooden tugboats on the Bay. She also is symbolic of McKnight's predilection to purchase, use, and maintain older, sometimes almost antique, equipment, for both his businesses and his personal use.

McKnight later added two more vessels to his fleet, the *Sea Hawk,* a former U.S. Coast Guard auxiliary boat used for towing pleasure craft, and the tug *Casey Lee.* In addition, three cranes of 10-, 15-, and 25-ton capacity became part of the inventory of shoreside support equipment.

From that point, business began to grow for Tug 'N Tow, which found a comfortable niche as a marine services contractor, operating under the premise that dependability is more important

The Golden Gate, *after serving in World War II, was a pilot boat for the San Francisco Bar Pilots until it was sold to the Tug 'N Tow Division of RCM International.*

than size. Initial contracts were with the U.S. Navy for hauling fuel barges, and with the Port of San Francisco to primarily move pile drivers and accessory equipment.

Operating only on the Bay, with occasional assignments in Stockton and Sacramento, Tug 'N Tow provides the only water service for the area, and lube service for small ships and boats. Other services involve towing of both commercial and pleasure craft, ships' stores, oil and garbage removal, tank cleaning, dry warehouse storage, paint floats, sandblasting, portable power equipment, forklift service, and

barge rentals.

Today RCM International operates from Pier 46 of the San Francisco waterfront and occupies 18,000 square feet of warehouse space and leases 30,000 square feet of open space for its operations, which include being the world's largest birthday candle importer—about 1.5 million dozen candles per year.

Early in 1984 Tug 'N Tow signed a lease for Pier 56, the former Intrepid Building, as the new base for its tugboat operations, which will provide more room for the expanding import business on Pier 46.

Two of Tug 'N Tow's tugboats, Mudhen *and* Brant *(left to right) at rest. The* Brant, *built in 1930, is one of the last working wooden tugboats on the Bay.*

ORIENT OVERSEAS CONTAINER LINE

Orient Overseas Container Line, part of the extensive C.Y. Tung Group which is headquartered in Hong Kong, began operations in 1961 under the name of Orient Overseas Line, serving the West Coast of North America as a breakbulk carrier.

By 1969 OOCL had fully containerized its U.S. West Coast/Far East service, and within three years it became one of the first carriers to offer fully containerized service from both the West and East coasts of North America to the Far East.

Historically, the C.Y. Tung Group has been operating its shipping business and gaining a worldwide reputation for about 40 years. It presently is considered one of the largest independent ship owners and operators in the world, handling a mixed fleet of more than 160 merchant vessels, including dry-cargo ships, bulk carriers, tankers, and passenger ships. The latter includes the American Hawaii Cruise Line, which operates two passenger ships inter-island in Hawaii and has its headquarters in San Francisco.

In addition to pursuing merchant shipping, OOCL's parent organization is dedicated to conducting international education on the high seas aboard the S.S. *Universe,* which offers the popular "Semester at Sea" in collaboration with the University of Pittsburgh.

From the beginning, OOCL has attempted to offer a comprehensive and dependable service between the Far East and North America. To achieve this end, the C.Y. Tung Group acquired an interest in Dart Containerline in 1973. This was followed by the acquisition of Furness, Withy & Company, a major British shipping company, in 1980, which included Manchester Liners, an operator in the North Atlantic trade. The next year the organization took over Seapac Container Service, a one-time subsidiary of Seatrain Lines in the United States, which operated between the U.S. West Coast and the Far East and had an extensive intermodal system.

The Seapac operation eventually became the marketing arm for OOCL, acting as the line's general agent in North America under the name of Seapac Services, with headquarters in Oakland.

The Dart, Furness, Withy, and Seapac acquisitions gave OOCL a globe-encircling network of ocean-going ships. Since then, OOCL has expanded its North American intermodal service to cover 100 key points. Further, the carrier's 65 offices in North America and the Far East provide an integrated service for shippers in both directions. In the United States alone, Seapac has about 25 offices and some 400 employees.

Today OOCL claims to be the fastest-growing international shipping line, while at the same time offering the widest selection of direct service and the greatest frequency of service between North American and Far Eastern ports. In addition to its service between the Far East and the West and East coasts of North America, OOCL operates in several other trades: Far East/Europe, Far East/Australia, Far East/Middle East, Far East/West Africa, Far East/Mediterranean, and interport within the Far East.

Orient Overseas Container Line's containership Oriental Executive *follows a pilot boat under the Oakland Bay Bridge as it leaves the San Francisco Bay area for the Far East. Photo by Ken Altshuler, Berkeley.*

BANK OF AMERICA

From its beginnings in 1904 as the Bank of Italy in a converted North Beach tavern, to its present position as one of the world's leading financial institutions, the Bank of America has had close ties with the maritime community throughout the San Francisco Bay Area. This involvement is even evident in the portrayal of the U.S. Navy sloop-of-war *Portsmouth* in the bank's original seal.

A.P. Giannini was 34 years old when he started his bank with $150,000 in capital, offering the then-revolutionary idea of providing wage earners and small businesses with the banking services traditionally reserved for wealthy individuals and large companies. At the end of 1904 the one-office bank had deposits of $703,024 and resources in excess of one million dollars after just two and one-half months in operation.

Today the bank, which became Bank of America in 1930, operates under its own name and through various subsidiaries of the bank and its holding company, BankAmerica Corporation, in 76 countries from more than 2,000 offices with approximately 80,000 employees. Deposits amount to about $95 billion and assets exceed $121 billion.

A 1920 newspaper advertisement noted: "The Bank of Italy is keenly interested in shipbuilding, and in the financing of foreign trade." In general, the bank's maritime policy at that time was to provide selective short-term working capital lines of credit to shipping companies and specialized trade finance lines to companies engaged in export and import activities. However, late in 1969, Bank of America's London office began to seriously tap into the shipping market. Gradually, important relationships were established with major ship brokers, admiralty firms, insurance

The Bank of Italy, predecessor of the Bank of America, opened for business on October 17, 1904, in a converted tavern at the corner of Washington Street and Columbus Avenue.

underwriters, shipping institutions, and a wide cross-section of shipping companies and individual ship owners.

Today, of the more than 10,000 commercial ocean-going vessels now afloat, Bank of America has financed about 475, representing approximately four percent of its total loan portfolio. The vessels range from mammoth oil tankers and highly specialized natural gas carriers, through conventional cargo ships and containerships, to tugs, dredges, oil rigs, and canal barges. In addition to London, the bank has offices in Hong Kong and New York that specialize in ship financing, and a branch in Piraeus, Greece, devoted exclusively to ships and shipping.

A more recent development—passage of the Export Trading Company Act of 1982—has provided the impetus for BankAmerica Corporation to become even more integrally involved in ocean shipping. Under this act, BankAmerica World Trade Corporation has formed a San Francisco-based export trading company to offer a wide range of trade-related services, including shipping, freight forwarding, insurance, trade financing, and countertrade. The company can also take title to goods for resale in international trade.

Aware that more than 95 percent

In 1941 Bank of America employees presented founder A.P. Giannini with the helm of the former sloop-of-war USS Portsmouth, *which had brought the first American flag to California in 1846. The ship had anchored at a spot that in 1908 became the site of the then-Bank of Italy's first headquarters building at Clay and Montgomery streets.*

of the world's trade—calculated by weight—is transported by water, Bank of America's long-term outlook is that the prospects for ocean shipping will be excellent for many years to come.

FRANK P. DOW
DIVISION OF F.W. MYERS & CO., INC.

Just before the turn of the century, Frank P. Dow opened a customhouse business in Seattle for the purpose of clearing imported cargoes of Chinese silk destined for Midwest manufacturers. The exclusivity of the business was prompted by the value of the cargo, which was considered so important that trains carrying the silk were given priority over all other rail traffic, even passenger trains.

Such cargoes were valuable not only to the shippers and consignees, but particularly to the U.S. government. Into the mid-1800s, customs duties were the sole source of federal income. In fact, in 1852 President Franklin Pierce requested a reduction in tariff rates because the $59-million income exceeded the $55-million U.S. annual budget. Even as late as 1910 customs fees accounted for 60 percent of federal income; today the percentage is less than one percent.

Dow soon expanded both the scope of his business and the area covered by opening partnership offices in San Francisco and Portland. In the Bay Area the Dow office obtained its original license as a customhouse broker on December 12, 1918.

Somewhat earlier, on the East Coast of the United States, John Myers became the first agent of the Champlain and St. Lawrence Railway Company at Rouses Point, New York, at the intersection of the New York, Vermont, and Quebec borders. It became quite natural in 1852 for him to perform customs brokerage as a sideline.

In 1860 Myers formed a partnership with his two sons to become the customhouse brokerage firm of F.W. Myers & Co., Inc. Thirty years later the firm also entered the insurance business, but still confined its operations to upstate New York and Vermont. It wasn't until 1960 that Myers began to expand its operations into other areas, primarily Michigan and other parts of New England.

Back on the West Coast, William D. White bought out Dow, including the partnerships in San Francisco and Portland, just after World War II. White also opened a Los Angeles office, where he eventually moved the headquarters of the Frank P. Dow Company from Seattle.

By the mid-1960s Myers decided to divest its insurance business and concentrate on expanding to provide a total transportation system throughout the United States and parts of Canada. As part of this expansion, Myers acquired the Frank P. Dow Company operations in 1971.

Today within the seven divisions of The Myers Group are customs brokers, ocean freight forwarders, marine insurance, break-bulk agents, air freight forwarders, ocean and air charters, warehousing, distribution, import/export financing, and Far East consolidation services.

Serving the San Francisco Bay Area is the Frank P. Dow Division in South San Francisco. Services include customhouse brokerage, ocean freight forwarding, marine insurance, air freight forwarding via Myers Airspeed, ocean freight consolidation through Myers Maritime, and trucking via Myers Express.

The Frank P. Dow Division of The Myers Group operates from this headquarters and warehouse (center) at 165 Mitchell Avenue in South San Francisco. Prior to moving here in 1981, Dow was at 500 Sansome Street in San Francisco for many years.

DORR, COOPER & HAYS

Retired partner John Hays (left) and senior partner George Waddell.

As the Civil War was drawing to a close, Milton Andros left his home and law practice in New Bedford, Massachusetts. Traveling west, he sailed first to the Isthmus of Panama, made the land crossing, and sailed to San Francisco aboard the steamer *Colorado,* arriving in December 1865.

Upon admission to the California Bar, Andros opened a law office that eventually became today's Dorr, Cooper & Hays. Having become familiar with maritime law in Massachusetts, he quickly gained a reputation as one of San Francisco's foremost maritime attorneys.

As Andros' practice grew, he served as counsel in virtually every maritime case. To handle the increased volume of work, he formed an association with attorney Charles Page. Eventually, Andros and Page agreed to end their legal relationship since they were frequently requested to represent both sides in the major maritime cases they handled. However, they continued to maintain a close friendship, despite being frequent adversaries, and walked to work together almost every day until Andros' death in 1908. During the intervening years, Andros formed a partnership with Nathan Frank and just before Andros' death, he made his son-in-law, Louis Hengstler, a partner. Hengstler was a mathematician as well as a lawyer and served as assistant professor of mathematics at the University of California.

The firm continued as Andros & Hengstler until 1926, when Frederick W. Dorr became a partner. Dorr, who had previously worked for his father's law firm in Seattle, settled in California after serving in the Navy in World War I. He worked for Pillsbury, Madison & Sutro before joining Andros & Hengstler in 1919. Dorr continued to practice as a member of the firm through various changes in its name until his retirement in 1950.

Archie Stevenson joined the firm in 1929 and became a partner in 1936, creating Hengstler, Dorr & Stevenson, which was shortened to Dorr & Stevenson upon Hengstler's death in 1940. During World War II Stevenson served with the War Shipping Administration as an assistant general counsel. Jay T Cooper became a partner and in 1946 California native John Hays, who had been insurance counsel for the War Shipping Administration, joined the firm. When Stevenson left in 1947 to join a New York firm, the name became the present Dorr, Cooper & Hays.

Significantly, until the late 1940s, Dorr, Cooper & Hays was never more than a four- or five-man practice. Until about 1950 the firm was involved almost exclusively in admiralty law, although it did handle some probate and corporate work. However, after World War II, Dorr, Cooper & Hays began to expand into other areas of law. John Hays, who retired in 1975, continues to act as a consultant.

Today Dorr, Cooper & Hays is active in insurance, commercial litigation, security, bankruptcy, and insolvency law. However, it continues to maintain its long involvement with maritime law and several partners are active in the Maritime Law Association including the senior partner, George Waddell, who currently chairs the Subcommittee on P&I Insurance. Symbolic of Dorr, Cooper & Hays' continuing maritime activity is the fact that its oldest continuing client, dating back to the late 1800s, is steamship agent Williams, Dimond & Co.

DERBY, COOK, QUINBY & TWEEDT

THE STREET AND THE SEA

There are dwellers in houses of steel and stone
    Who list to the voice of the street.
There are seekers of ocean trails dim and lone,
    Where the far horizons meet.
They are sundered apart, these two, by the space
    That lies from star to star—
The toiler who walks in the market-place
    And the spirit who roves afar.

I have prayed to the God of the canyon'd land
    And the God of the off-shore breeze,
For I yearn in the fullness of time to gain
    A little from each of these,
An echoing thrill from the cruising fleet—
    A boon that my place shall be,
Where the smell of the sea comes up to the street
    And the street goes down to the sea.

© 1971 by James A. Quinby

Secure with a law degree from the University of Virginia, Edmund B. McClanahan traveled west in the 1890s, farther west than any of his family had probably imagined, and settled in Hawaii to open a law office in Honolulu in 1892.

Ten years later McClanahan was joined by S. Hasket Derby, a Harvard Law School graduate and descendant of one of the oldest ocean shipping families on the East Coast. In addition to its shipping activities, the Derby family also operated privateers during the formative years of the United States. Young Nathaniel Bowditch first sailed as a cadet on a Derby ship. Bowditch later became famous as the author of *American Practical Navigator,* a standard that is still in use today.

McClanahan and Derby, who specialized in admiralty law, decided in 1905 to move their practice to San Francisco and made arrangements for space in the Merchants Exchange Building, then under construction. The uncompleted facility was damaged by the earthquake and fire of April 1906. However, by late summer of that same year McClanahan and Derby were able to move into the new building and the firm remained in that location until 1969.

After McClanahan's retirement in 1922, the name of the firm became Derby, Single & Sharp. When James A. Quinby and Lloyd M. Tweedt became partners in 1928, the name was changed to Derby, Sharp, Quinby & Tweedt. The partnership adopted its present name in 1953.

Today there are 19 attorneys in the firm, including the present eight partners, all practicing from San Francisco offices at 333 Market Street, only the third location for the firm in the city since McClanahan and Derby arrived from Honolulu in 1906.

The firm's present practice reflects two fundamental decisions by its past and present management. First, it decided not to expand into a full-service law firm, choosing instead to concentrate in the fields of admiralty, marine insurance, and commercial law. Second, management chose not to establish any offices outside of San Francisco, believing that its clients could be better served if all its lawyers and staff were in one central location. Notwithstanding these self-imposed limitations on growth, Derby, Cook, Quinby & Tweedt has continued to expand and looks forward to further expansion in the years ahead, serving clients who range from North Beach fishermen to multinational corporations.

In a unique tribute to the firm's then senior partner James A. Quinby (now of counsel), a group of Pacific Coast admiralty lawyers combined in 1971 to publish a collection of poems he had written as a hobby. This book, now something of a collector's item, offers a rare insight into the challenge and appeal of the waterfront in general, and of maritime law in particular. The title verse is reproduced (above left).

PORT OF SAN FRANCISCO

About a year prior to the Colonists on the East Coast declaring their independence from England, Lieutenant Juan Manuel de Ayala sailed the Spanish naval supply ship *San Carlos* into San Francisco Bay, becoming the first known European to navigate the narrow tide-whipped channel and drop anchor in the magnificent natural landlocked harbor.

However, even though Jose Ortega had found San Francisco Bay via land in 1769, and de Ayala had arrived by sea in 1775, it still took another 75 years for the settlement of Yerba Buena to become something more than a Spanish mission and military outpost. During those intervening years the area, which was a favorite of raucous wintering mountain men, was visited only infrequently by supply ships, Yankee traders, and warships.

Thus it was that when James Marshall discovered gold in the foothills of the Sierra in 1848, the resulting floodtide of ships that inundated San Francisco Bay found one of the world's finest harbors, but some of the world's worst berthing.

Anchorage and docks silted up with tidal mud almost overnight, rendering many wharves useless. Cargo-loaded vessels were forced to stand in the Bay for weeks while their owners bid against each other for berthing space. Many of those ships never made it to a pier and were abandoned where they lay by captains and crews eager to get to the gold fields.

Eventually, the Board of State Harbor Commissioners, established in 1863, adopted as its prime objective the construction of a seawall to control the mud, stabilize the waterfront line, and allow the filling of tidal flats at the Port of San Francisco.

The more than two-and-one-half miles of seawall was completed in 1887, creating at the same time some 800 acres of prime filled land, which today includes the city's financial district and much of the downtown commercial area.

In 1898 the city celebrated the opening of the new Ferry Building, which immediately became one of San Francisco's most famous landmarks. The structure was also the center of one of the world's largest ferry systems. By 1930 there were as many as 60 ferry boats on the Bay, with one leaving every few minutes from the Ferry Building for virtually every area surrounding the Bay.

Earlier, 23 piers had been completed by 1908, extending from Hyde Street to India Basin. However, construction and reconstruction to meet the needs of maritime and commercial interests has never stopped.

Significantly, after more than 100 years as a state-run operation, the Port of San Francisco was transferred in trust to the City and County of San Francisco in 1969.

Today the Port is engaged in a major capital improvement and maritime expansion program that includes greatly enhanced container-handling facilities and an extensive rail transfer facility to meet the intermodal shipping requirements of the 25 ocean carriers that regularly call the Port of San Francisco.

The San Francisco Container Terminal-South (formerly Pier 94-96) currently offers 64 acres of terminal area. The three berths are served by four container cranes, immediate freeway access, and a direct rail link, giving the port true intermodal capability.

Port facilities at San Francisco developed rapidly after the discovery of gold in the mid-1800s. By the end of the decade an ever-increasing number of new piers were filled with sailing and steam ships from all over the world, in addition to fleets of ferry boats serving communities throughout the Bay Area.

Patrons

The following individuals, companies, and organizations have made a valuable commitment to the quality of this publication. Windsor Publications and the Marine Exchange of the San Francisco Bay Region gratefully acknowledge their participation in *International Port of Call: An Illustrated Maritime History of the Golden Gate.*

Acret & Perrochet
American President Lines*
Bank of America*
Beaver Insurance Company
Blue & Gold Fleet, Inc.*
John Bonner and Associates, Marine Surveyors
Burt & Dulay Real Estate Services, Inc.
George F. Butler Co. Inc.
Thomas W. Callinan
Chancellor Hotel*
Chevron Shipping Company
Continental Maritime Industries*
Crowley Maritime Corporation*
Derby, Cook, Quinby, & Tweedt*
Design Marketing International Corp.
Dorr, Cooper & Hays*
Frank P. Dow, Division of F.W. Myers & Co., Inc.*
EAC Steamship Agencies
Eagle Marine Services, Ltd.*
Eagleson Engineers Inc.
Fritz Companies, Inc.*
Graham & James*
Hanford Freund & Co.
Hanjin Container Lines Ltd.*
Hornblower Yachts, Inc.
Henry W. Hotchkiss
Hoyt Shepston, Inc.*
Interocean Steamship Corporation*
Johnson & Higgins of California*
Kerr Steamship Company, Inc.
Lillick McHose & Charles*
Lilly Shipping Agencies*
Lloyds Bank International Limited
Marin Tug & Barge, Inc.
Matson Navigation Company*
Matson Terminals, Inc.
Morris Guralnick Associates, Inc.

Norton, Lilly & Co., Inc.*
Oakland Container Terminal*
Oakland International Trade Center*
Orient Overseas Container Line*
E.D. Osgood/Foreign Trade Services FTZ #3
Overseas Shipping Company*
Pacific Shipper, Inc.
Pasha Maritime Services. Inc.
Polynesia Line. Ltd.
Port of Oakland*
Port of San Francisco*
Rathbone, King & Seeley, Inc.
Ted L. Rausch Company*
Richard Lloyd Shaw-Chancellor Hotel
Sanders Towboat Service*
Sea-Land Service, Inc.*
Showa Maritime USA, Inc.
Star Shipping A/S*
Stevedoring Services of America
F. & C. Tomsick
Tubbs Cordage Company*
Tug 'N Tow Corporation*
United States Lines, Inc.*
Captain Gregg Waugh, S.F. Bar Pilot
Western Steamship Services, Inc.
Westward Dental Products Company

*Partners in Progress of *International Port of Call: An Illustrated Maritime History of the Golden Gate.* The histories of these companies and organizations appear in Chapter 6, beginning on page 128.

Bibliography

Ammen, Daniel. *The Navy in the Civil War: The Atlantic Coast* (New York, 1883) p. 42.

Anderson, Roy. *White Star* (Prescot, Lancashire, England, 1964) p. 68.

Armentrout-Ma, Eve L. "Chinese in California's Fishing Industry, 1850-1941," *California History* (Summer, 1981).

Bancroft, H.H. *History of California*, 7 volumes, (San Francisco, 1885-97).

——————. *The New Pacific* (San Francisco, 1899).

Berthold, Victor M. *The Pioneer Steamer California: 1848-1849* (Boston, 1932) pp. 39-50.

Bostoce, J.R. *Steam Whaling in the Western Arctic* (Dartmouth, 1977).

Branch, L.L. *History of Stanislaus County, California* (San Francisco, 1881).

Browne, J. Ross. *Etchings of a Whaling Cruise* (Cambridge, 1968) pp. 513, 519, 135, 536, 496.

Burns, Walter N. *A Year with a Whaler* (New York, 1913) pp. 11, 18-19, 14.

Chamberlain, W.H. et al. *History of Sutter County, California* (Oakland, 1879).

——————. *History of Yuba County, California* (Oakland, 1979).

Chapelle, Howard I. *American Small Sailing Craft: Their Design, Development, and Construction* (New York, 1951).

——————. *The Search for Speed Under Sail: 1700-1855* (New York, 1957).

Chinn, T.W., Mark Lai, H. Choy, *A History of the Chinese in California: A Syllabus* (San Francisco, 1969).

Clark, A.H. *The Clipper Ship Era* (7c's Ed.: Connecticut, 1970).

Cleland, R.G. *A History of California: The American Period* (New York, 1922).

Coman, E.T. and Gibbs, H.M. *Tide and Timber: A Century of Pope and Talbot* (Stanford, 1949).

Cook, Sherburn. *The Conflict Between the California Indian and White Civilization* (Berkeley, 1976).

Coolidge, Mary R. *Chinese Immigration* (New York, 1909).

Cutler, C.C. *Greyhounds of the Sea: The Story of the American Clipper Ships* (New York, 1930).

Dana, R.H. *Two Years Before the Mast* (Modern Library Ed.: New York, 1936).

——————. *To Cuba and Back* (Reprint: Urbana, 1966).

Dillon, Richard H. *Shanghaiing Days* (New York, 1961).

——————. *Embarcadero* (New York, 1959).

Dyke, D.J. *Transportation in the Sacramento Valley* (Thesis: University of California, 1933).

Elliott, G.H. "The Presidio of San Francisco," *Overland Monthly* (April, 1870).

Fairburn, W.A. *Merchant Sail* Vols. III, IV (Maine, 1945-55).

Gavin, John, ed. *The First Spanish Entry into San Francisco Bay* (San Francisco, 1971) p. 91.

Gilbert, F. *History of San Joaquin County, California* (Oakland, 1879).

Green, W. *Colusa County, California* (San Francisco, 1880).

Gumina, Deanna P. *Italians of San Francisco* (New York, 1978).

——————. "The Fishermen of San Francisco Bay: The Men of 'Italy Harbor,' " *Pacific Historian* (Spring, 1976).

Gundelfinger, E.R. *The Pacific Mail Steamship Company: 1847-1917* (Thesis: University of California, 1917).

Hare, C.M. Lloyd. *Salted Tories: The Story of the Whaling Fleets of San Francisco* (Mystic, 1960).

Heizer, R.F. *Handbook of North American Indians* (Washington, 1978).

——————. *Destruction of the California Indians* (Salt Lake City, 1974).

Hittell, J.S. *A History of the City of San Francisco* (San Francisco , 1878) pp. 131-32.

——————. *The Commerce and Industries of North America* (San Francisco, 1882).

Howard, A.D. *Evolution of the Landscape of the San Francisco Bay Region* (Berkeley, 1962).

Hugill, Stan. *Shanties from the Seven Seas* (London, 1961).

Jackson, W.A. *The Doghole Schooners* (Republished: Mendocino, 1977).

Jobson, W.J. and Hildebrandt, W.R. "The Distribution of Oceangoing Canoes on the North Coast of California," *Journal of California and Great Basin Anthropology* (Winter, 1980).

Jordan, David Starr. "The Fisheries of California," *Overland Monthly* (November, 1882).

Kemble, John Haskell. *The Panama Route: 1848-1869* (Berkeley, 1943).

——————. "A Hundred Years of Pacific Mail," *The American Neptune* (April, 1950).

——————. "The Big Four At Sea: The History of the Occidental and Oriental and Steamship Company," *Huntington Library Quarterly* (April, 1940).

——————. *Sidewheelers Across the Pacific* (San Francisco, 1942).

Kroeber, A.L. *Handbook of the California Indians* (Washington, 1925).

Langley, H.D. *Social Reform in the United States Navy* (Illinois, 1967).

Leet, R.R. *American Whalers in the Western Arctic: 1879-1914* (Thesis: University of San Francisco, 1974).

Lemisch, Jesse. *Jack Tar vs. John Bull: The Role of New York's Seamen in Precipitating the Revolution* (PhD. dissertation: Yale, 1962).

——————. "Jack Tar in the Streets: Merchant Seamen in the Politics of Revolutionary America," *William and Mary Quarterly* (July, 1968).

Lewis, E. *Tehama County, California* (San Francisco, 1880).

Lubbock, Basil. *The China Clippers* (Glasgow, 1919) pp. 45-46.

——————. *The Downeasters.* (Glasgow, 1929).

——————. *The Last of the Windjammers* Vols. I, II (Glasgow, 1927).

Lydon, Sandy. "The Chinese," *A Day On the Bay* (Santa Cruz, 1980).

MacArthur, Walter. *The Seaman's Contract* (San Francisco, 1919).

——————. *Last Days of Sail on the West Coast* (Reprint: Seattle, 1968).

McGowen, J.A. *San Francisco-Sacramento Shipping, 1839-1854* (MA thesis: University of California, 1939).

MacMullen, Jerry. *Paddle-Wheel Days in California* (Stanford, 1944).

——————and McNairn, J. *Ships of the Redwood Coast* (Stanford, 1945).

Marryat, F. *Mountains and Molehills, Or Recollections of a Burnt Journal* (New York, 1855).

Melville, Herman. *Moby Dick* (Norton Critical Ed.: New York, 1967), pp. 261, 486.

——————*Omoo* (Massachusetts, 1951), p. 42.

——————*White Jacket or The World in a Man-of-War* (Grove Press Ed.: New York, 1956), pp. 279, 146

——————*Redburn: His First Voyage* (Anchor Book Ed.: New York, 1957), p. 31.

Monaghan, J. *Australians and the Gold Rush* (Berkeley, 1966).

——————*Chile, Peru, and the California Gold Rush of 1849* (Berkeley, 1973), p. 44.

Morison, Samuel Eliot. *The Oxford History of the American People* (New York, 1965), p. 584.

——————*The Maritime History of Massachusetts* (Sentry Ed.: Massachusetts, 1961).

Morphy, Edward. *The Port of San Francisco* (Sacramento, 1878) p. 9, 42.

Nash, Robert. *The Chinese Shrimp Fishery of California* (PhD. dissertation: University of California, 1973).

Nordhoff, C. and Hall, J. *Botany Bay* (New York, 1941) p. 62.

Ogden, Adele. *The California Sea Otter Trade* (Berkeley, 1941).

Osio, Antonio María. "Historia de California," Bancroft Library, pp. 14-15, 24-25.

Palmer, Roy. *The Valient Sailor* (Cambridge, England, 1973).

Richie, C.F. Hager, R.A. *The Chumash Canoe*

(San Diego, 1973).

Ringgold, C. *A Series of Charts with Sailing Directions, State of California* (Washington, 1852).

Saxton, Alexander. *The Indispensable Enemy: Labor and the Anti-Chinese Movement in California* (Berkeley, 1971).

Scammon, Charles M. "The Pacific Coast Codfishery," *Overland Monthly* (May 1870), pp. 436-37.

_____. *The Marine Mammals of the Northwestern Coast of North America* (Dover: New York, 1968) p. 213, 263.

_____. "The California Gray," *Overland Monthly* (July 1869), p.38.

Scanland, J.M. ed. "Evolution of Shipping and Ship-Building in California," *Overland Monthly* (February, March 1895) p. 12.

Scheffer, V.B. "The Status of Whales," *Pacific Discovery* (January, 1976).

Schwendinger, Robert J. "Investigating Chinese Immigrants and Sailors," *The Chinese American Experience: Papers from the Second National Conference on Chinese American Studies* (San Francisco, 1984).

_____. "Fearful Summer of '88: Shipwreck and Exclusion," *Ports in the West* (Kansas, 1982).

_____. "Coolie Trade: The American Connection," *Oceans* (January, 1980).

_____. "Thirty-five Million Voyagers: The Atlantic Migration," *Oceans* (July, 1979).

_____. "Chinese Sailors: America's Invisible Merchant Marine," *California History* (Spring, 1978).

_____. "Bibles and Opium: China's Early Trade," *Oceans* (May, 1978).

_____. "Flights of Spirit Before the Mast," *The American West* (May, 1977).

_____. "The Temperate Mutiny," *The American West* (May, 1975).

Shaler, William. *Journal of a Voyage Between China and the Northwestern Coast of America Made in 1804* (Claremont, CA, 1935).

Shinn, Charles H. *Mining Camps: A Study in American Frontier Government* (New York, 1948) pp. 234-35.

Soule, F. et al. *The Annals of San Francisco* (Palo Alto, 1966).

Stackpole, E.A. *The Sea Hunters* (Philadelphia, 1953).

Stillman, Jacob D. "Seeking the Golden Fleece," *Overland Monthly* (September, 1873). p. 226, 227, 228.

Takaki, Ronald. *Pau Hana: Plantation Life and Labor in Hawaii* 1835-1920 (Honolulu, 1983).

Taylor, Bayard. *El Dorado: Or Adventures in the Path of Empire* (New York, 1882) pp. 160, 162.

Taylor, Paul S. "Spanish Seamen in the New World During the Colonial Period," *The Hispanic American Historical Review* (November, 1922), p. 649.

_____. *The Sailor's Union of the Pacific* (New York, 1923).

Tooker, Richard. *Notes on Doghole Schooners*, at J. Porter Shaw Library, National Maritime Museum, San Francisco.

Tower, W.S. *A History of the American Whale Fishery* (Philadelphia, 1907).

Twiss, Sir Travis, ed. *The Black Book of the Admiralty* Vol. III. (London, 1871-76) pp. 219, 233.

Weaver, J.L., Jr. "Salt Water Fisheries of the Pacific Coast," *Overland Monthly* (August, 1892).

Willis, W. *History of Sacramento County, California* (Los Angeles, 1913).

Wiltsee, W.A. *Gold Rush Steamers* (San Francisco, 1938).

G.R.G. Worcester. *Sail and Sampan in China* (London, 1966), pp. 26-27.

Page numbers for the quoted source material in the text are included in this bibliography.

Richard Henry Dana's handbook for sailors, A Seaman's Friend, includes this chart showing distinctive sail and rigging patterns of different vessels. (NMMSF)

Index

The Pacific Mail steamer Japan was built in
New York and entered the San
Francisco-Hong Kong-Yokohama service. Its
hull was made of a variety of woods, and
its first class accommodations were
luxuriously appointed. Steerage class was
made up of Chinese immigrants to the
United States, crowded into the hold.
Shown here circa 1870 in Hong Kong, the
Japan later burned at sea. (TBL)

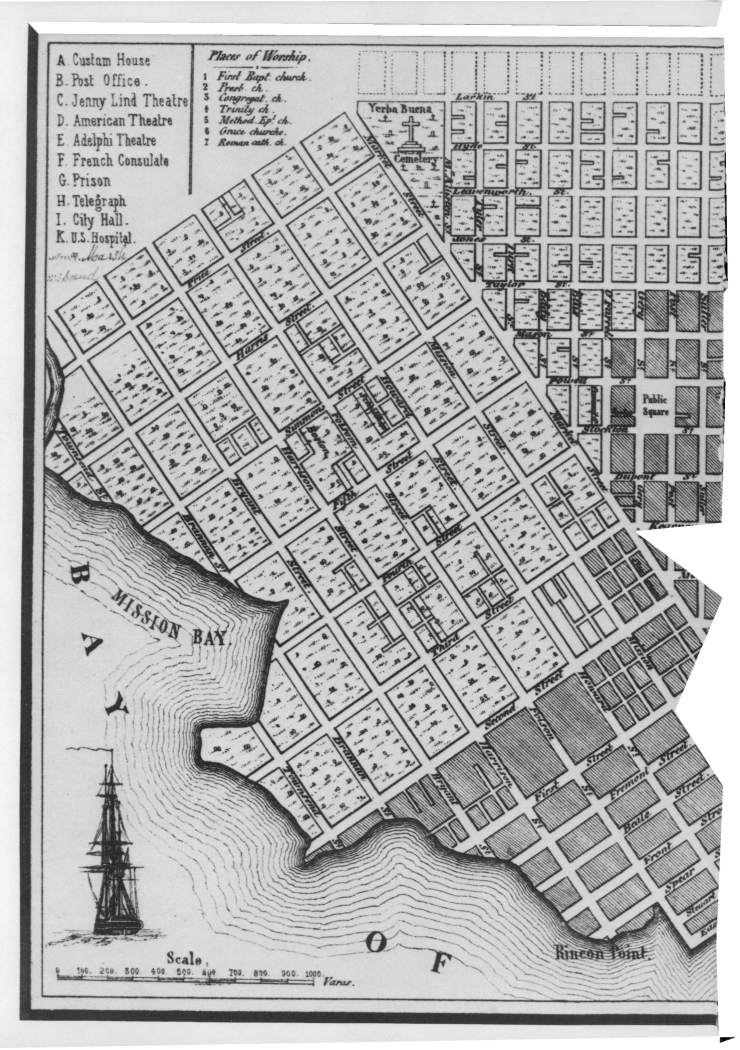